WORDSEARCH PUZZLES

1. FISHY TAILS

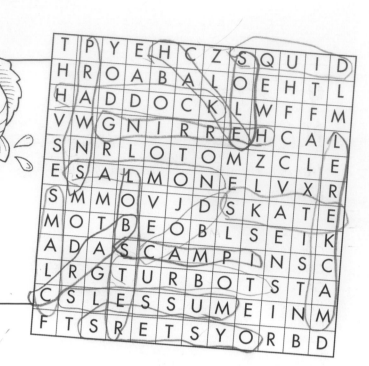

Go fishing! How many can you catch?

- CLAMS
- COD
- CRAB
- HADDOCK
- HAKE
- HERRING
- LOBSTER
- MACKEREL
- MUSSELS
- OYSTERS
- PRAWNS
- SALMON
- SCAMPI
- SKATE
- SOLE
- SQUID
- TURBOT

T	P	Y	E	H	C	Z	S	Q	U	I	D
H	R	O	A	B	A	L	O	E	H	T	L
H	A	D	D	O	C	K	L	W	F	F	M
V	W	G	N	I	R	R	E	H	C	A	L
S	N	R	L	O	T	O	M	Z	C	L	E
E	S	A	L	M	O	N	E	L	V	X	R
S	M	M	O	V	J	D	S	K	A	T	E
M	O	T	B	E	O	B	L	S	E	I	K
A	D	A	S	C	A	M	P	I	N	S	C
L	R	G	T	U	R	B	O	T	S	T	A
C	S	L	E	S	S	U	M	E	I	N	M
F	T	S	R	E	T	S	Y	O	R	B	D

2. DESSERT DELIGHT

There are plenty of desserts and pastries for you here!

- CHEESECAKE
- CUSTARD
- FLAN
- GATEAU
- JELLO
- MERINGUE
- MOUSSE
- PIE
- SEMOLINA
- SORBET
- SUNDAE

C	H	E	E	S	E	C	A	K	E	J	A
U	N	L	S	O	T	N	G	H	P	K	C
S	E	M	O	L	I	N	A	G	I	I	J
T	A	O	B	F	T	G	H	O	R	O	O
A	C	U	A	E	T	A	G	I	K	F	S
R	S	S	C	W	C	T	S	F	L	A	N
D	U	S	X	O	Z	P	O	L	A	O	L
E	N	E	I	E	C	E	R	E	E	G	O
D	D	P	C	P	K	E	B	A	V	E	L
Z	A	P	P	Y	P	I	E	W	L	P	L
T	E	E	A	G	E	J	T	V	M	N	E
F	R	M	E	R	I	N	G	U	E	W	J

3. SUPERSTARS

Find the ten superstars hidden in the puzzle.

- STARBURST
- STARDOM
- STARDUST
- STARFISH
- STARFLOWER
- STARGAZE
- STARLIGHT
- STARRY
- STARSHINE
- STARSHIP

S	T	A	R	L	I	G	H	T	A	S	C
T	C	G	C	K	N	V	V	A	T	T	E
A	E	T	H	A	M	A	S	A	S	A	H
R	N	P	S	T	A	R	R	Y	T	R	A
B	I	A	T	O	T	F	Y	O	A	F	W
U	H	R	Z	I	I	P	Y	O	R	L	T
R	S	T	T	T	S	S	T	A	R	D	O	M
S	R	Y	H	A	R	V	E	S	U	W	O
T	A	P	R	O	V	I	S	T	S	E	R
P	T	O	P	L	A	N	S	G	T	R	N
C	S	T	A	R	S	H	I	P	E	D	E
D	A	T	E	E	Z	A	G	R	A	T	S

4. SPACE MISSION

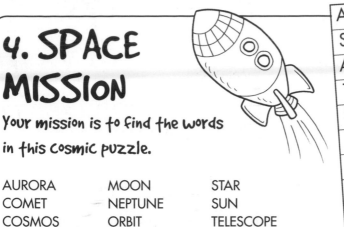

Your mission is to find the words in this cosmic puzzle.

AURORA	MOON	STAR
COMET	NEPTUNE	SUN
COSMOS	ORBIT	TELESCOPE
GALAXY	PLANET	UNIVERSE
JUPITER	ROCKET	URANUS
MARS	SATURN	VENUS

```
A J A M P O T C O M E T
S U N A U R T I N O M E
A P E R O C K E T O D L
T I S S R P U C K N E E
S T A R B L A U T G H S
R E T B I A S O M S O C
G R U M T N H U S B N O
A B R K E E N M A R V P
L U N E P T U N E R E E
A U R O R A S E V Y N M
X S A T U S U N A R U E
Y T U R U N I V E R S E
```

5. MAGIC WORDSEARCH

These words are linked to Halloween and magic!

ABRACADABRA	HALLOWEEN	VANISH
BROOM	MAGIC	WAND
CAULDRON	POTION	WARLOCK
CHARM	PUMPKIN	WISH
CLOAK	SPELLS	WITCH
DISAPPEAR	TRICK	WIZARD

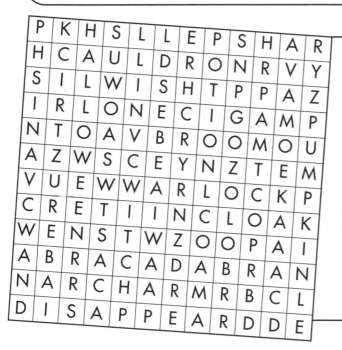

```
P K H S L L E P S H A R
H C A U L D R O N R V Y
S I L W I S H T P P A Z
I R L O N E C I G A M P
N T O A V B R O O M O U
A Z W S C E Y N Z T E M
V U E W W A R L O C K P
C R E T I I N C L O A K
W E N S T W Z O O P A I
A B R A C A D A B R A N
N A R C H A R M R B C L
D I S A P P E A R D D E
```

6. SCHOOL IS COOL!

Have fun playing this school word puzzle.

ART	CRAYONS	PLAYGROUND
ASSEMBLY	DESK	READING
BLACKBOARD	GRADES	TEACHER
BOOKS	HOMEWORK	
CALCULATOR	MATH	
CHALK	PENCILS	
CLASS		
COMPUTER		

```
O X C C U H T A M A R W
L C A L C U L A T O R I
D O E A R A O S S R E B
E M M S A C C S V A H L
K P A S Y K S E D R C A
R U S K O O B M N E A C
O T L L N A S B N A E K
W E I A S U E L B D T B
E R C H U N D Y P I O O
M A N C T R A R T N O A
O L E Y U I R A T G I R
H C P L A Y G R O U N D
```

7. WHAT'S THE BUZZ?

Find the noises animals and creatures make.

BARK	GROWL	QUACK
BELLOW	GRUNT	SNARL
BLEAT	HISS	SNIFF
BUZZ	HOOT	SNORT
CACKLE	HOWL	SQUEAK
CHIRP	MOO	WARBLE
COO	PURR	WOOF

```
P U Z I W O E L B R A W
B U Z Z E O F F R E D O
E T R G T K C A U Q A O
L C J R A A C R L T A F
L A I E E M O O W F E V
O C P W L S K S O F L E
W K R A B A W G R U N T
P L A P E S U N G H B T
Z E T U S N A R L E B R
Q U Q I P Y T O W A J O
A S N I F F T O O H O N
C H I R P F Y Q H I S S
```

8. HAUNTED HOUSE

Who is in the haunted house?

GARGOYLES	PHANTOMS	VAMPIRES
GHOSTS	SKELETONS	WEREWOLF
GHOULS	SPECTERS	ZOMBIES
MONSTERS	SPOOKS	

```
G A R G O Y L E S P I E
H A P P A M S P O O K S
S O N E Y L I H P T O N
P S E R I P M A V S S M
E A Y R N T W N O S C O
C A L G H O S T S S A N
T I H L Q W O E E R S
E C K O R O E M E I V T
R C E U O Q A S H B E E
S K M L W U L L K M C R
F T U S K E L E T O N S
F L O W E R E W A Z H P
```

9. TREASURE CHEST

What gems and jewels are hidden in the treasure chest?

AMBER	EMERALD	SAPPHIRE
AMETHYST	JADE	TOPAZ
BANGLE	NECKLACE	TURQUOISE
BRACELET	PENDANT	ZIRCON
CORAL	RING	
DIAMOND	RUBY	

```
D A Z Z A M E T H Y S T
R R Z A E K E G A N D U
U D I A M O N D S T O R
B R R P E L O N S N T Q
Y W C K R E B M A A O U
B C O C A S C O P D P O
A H N Z L G T L P N A I
N L O G D J N C H E Z S
G A V V S H E I I P A E
L R T E L E C A R B A T
E O A J M I N T E D A J
E C A L K C E N A C G O
```

10. FAB FRUIT

Gather as many of these pieces of fruit as you can.

APRICOT
BANANA
CHERRY
DATES
GOOSEBERRY
GRAPES

KIWI
LEMON
MELON
ORANGE
PEACH
PEAR

PINEAPPLE
PLUM
RASPBERRY
STRAWBERRY

```
C R O O R A N G E Y E S
H A B A N A N A A T L T
E S N O O R Y P N Q P R
R E J O V A R B W Q P A
R S T P L U M O T T A W
Y R R E B E S O O G E B
S H R A N O M E L D N E
C A G R A P E S O F I R
I W I K I R I W I R P R
F A T R A S P B E R R Y
T O C I R P A A R H A Y
D P E A C H S E T A D O
```

11. COLOR CRAZY

All these words are brightly colored!

BALLOONS
CARNIVAL
CLOWN
CRAYONS
FIREWORKS

FRUIT
GEMS
MARBLES
NEON
PAINTS

PARROT
RAINBOW
SUNRISE
SUNSET

```
F R O L L A V I N R A C
I J E E S W O B N I A R
R A M C S C R F T E D A
E B A Q D G E M S S E Y
W M R U C A T H U H H O
O T B A L L O O N S T N
R O L E O J R G R O O S
K M E R W T R C I T H O
S A S E N H A H S U O M
R S T N I A P I E P O C
I F W H H F W L N E O N
T E S N U S F R U I T S
```

12. CANDY STORE

Seek the treats inside the candy store.

CANDY
CARAMELS
CHEWS
CHOCOLATE
FUDGE

GUMDROPS
LICORICE
LOLLIPOPS
MARSHMALLOW
MINTS

SHERBET
TOFFEE

```
C A N D Y B R L Y T L S
A E T T E B R E H S O L
R I U Q C E K I T S L I
A S G U M D R O P S L C
M X R T I A R T W O I O
E F T F N S E H N C P R
L G O S T H C C S S O I
S V F I S M M S S V P C
I X F R S N B B W O S E
E J E G D U F O S E Z E
G U E E T A L O C O H C
M A R S H M A L L O W C
```

13. FLOWER GARDEN

Find the flowers hidden in the garden.

BLUEBELL
BUTTERCUP
CROCUS
DAISY
HOLLYHOCK

LILAC
LILY
MARIGOLD
PANSY
POPPY

ROSE
SNOWDROP
SWEET PEA

M	A	R	I	G	O	L	D	B	O	R	O
D	C	A	L	B	A	E	D	L	R	O	J
V	B	U	T	T	E	R	C	U	P	S	K
A	R	V	T	H	A	S	T	E	T	E	S
E	O	Q	D	S	T	W	E	B	I	V	U
P	O	C	A	L	I	L	V	E	M	T	C
T	G	W	I	A	R	R	E	L	B	S	O
E	F	Y	S	N	A	P	U	L	E	E	R
E	R	P	Y	G	O	O	O	E	I	C	C
W	O	P	Z	O	I	N	M	A	V	L	E
S	N	O	W	D	R	O	P	M	I	L	Y
T	M	P	K	C	O	H	Y	L	L	O	H

14. TREEHOUSE

What are the kids' treehouses made of?

APPLE
BIRCH
CEDAR
CHERRY
CHESTNUT

FIR
OAK
PALM
PEAR
PLUM

POPLAR
ROWAN
SYCAMORE
WALNUT
WILLOW

T	R	H	C	R	I	B	I	S	C	K	S
E	E	C	H	E	S	T	N	U	T	A	T
H	U	H	W	C	D	C	A	P	U	R	S
B	O	E	T	G	P	A	L	M	K	T	E
T	S	R	S	R	A	T	R	W	M	E	R
U	E	R	R	A	L	P	O	P	O	O	O
N	B	Y	L	U	H	I	W	I	H	K	M
L	E	Q	U	K	R	S	A	S	T	E	A
A	F	I	Z	A	A	E	N	H	M	I	C
W	I	L	L	O	W	C	R	H	U	I	Y
A	R	L	A	R	O	Z	O	O	L	A	S
A	P	P	L	E	B	R	A	E	P	I	E

15. SEASHORE SEARCH

Search the seashore for the hidden words.

BOAT
CRAB
JELLYFISH
ROCKPOOL
SANDCASTLE

SEAWEED
SHELLS
STARFISH
SURF
SWIMMERS

TIDES
WAVES

O	S	E	L	T	S	A	C	D	N	A	S
S	T	T	S	W	I	U	G	A	V	E	E
C	A	H	U	C	R	D	A	V	D	W	A
W	R	E	R	W	A	V	E	S	R	S	W
O	F	S	F	C	R	E	P	S	U	P	E
T	I	R	O	C	K	P	O	O	L	P	E
V	S	H	O	L	I	D	O	S	C	I	D
I	H	I	S	H	D	T	A	O	B	S	X
K	F	P	S	L	K	S	K	Y	A	I	U
O	S	W	I	M	M	E	R	S	R	E	T
S	H	E	L	L	S	F	I	V	C	S	P
M	A	J	H	S	I	F	Y	L	L	E	J

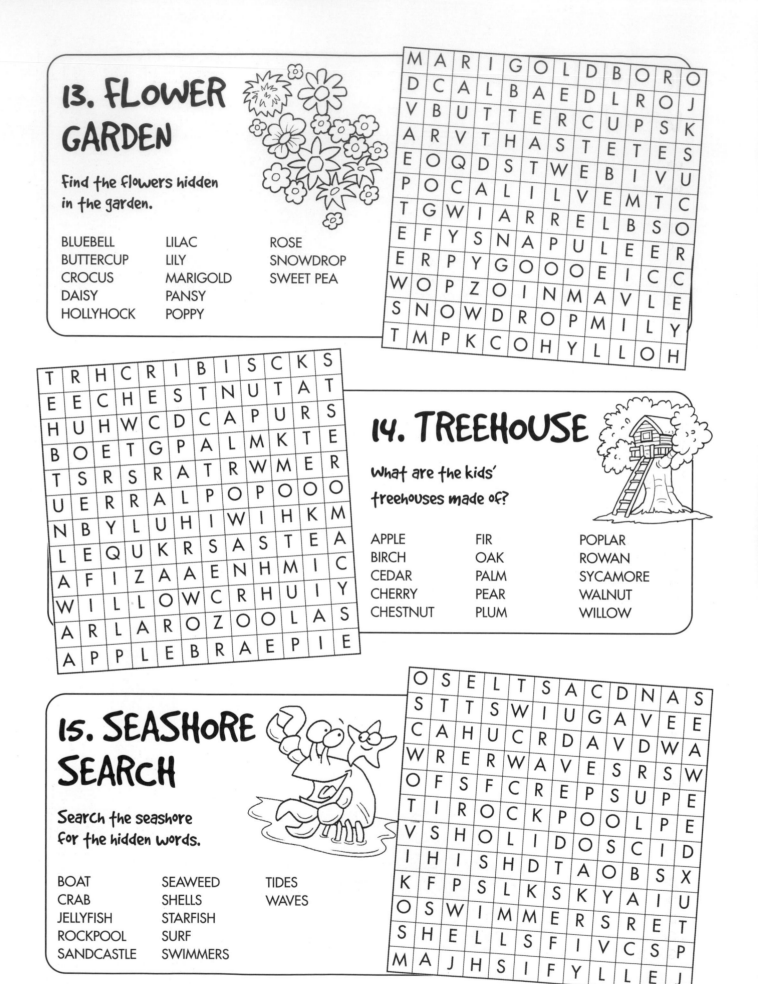

16. WILD WEATHER

What's hidden in the weather chart?

CLOUDY
COOL
CYCLONE
FREEZING
FOG
FROST
HAILSTORM

HAZY
HOT
HURRICANE
ICY
LIGHTNING
MIST
RAIN

SNOW
THUNDER
TORNADO
WET
WINDY

H	U	R	R	I	C	A	N	E	R	R	F
A	C	Y	C	L	O	N	E	R	D	T	R
I	S	O	W	O	R	D	C	A	S	S	E
L	T	R	O	R	I	B	C	I	V	E	E
S	N	O	W	L	Y	B	M	N	W	R	Z
T	O	R	N	A	D	O	B	C	E	E	I
O	S	D	E	J	N	U	H	O	T	D	N
R	D	B	R	O	I	H	A	P	E	N	G
M	B	C	V	F	W	P	Z	I	O	U	Z
M	Y	D	U	O	L	C	Y	W	I	H	S
I	C	A	C	G	L	F	R	O	S	T	S
L	I	G	H	T	N	I	N	G	O	G	G

17. FUNNY WORDS

Enjoy searching for these humorous words.

CARTOON
COMEDY
FUNNY
GAG
GIGGLE

HILARIOUS
HOWL
HUMOROUS
JEST
JOKE

LAUGH
PUN
SNIGGER
WIT

S	N	I	G	G	E	R	H	G	A	G	C
W	A	V	E	R	C	C	A	Y	K	I	T
E	W	K	A	L	A	J	O	K	E	S	E
L	A	U	G	H	T	E	P	T	U	U	M
T	I	W	I	V	B	S	Z	L	W	O	H
R	C	W	G	B	O	T	Q	M	K	R	Y
A	L	Y	G	I	C	A	R	T	O	O	N
H	E	N	L	J	X	D	O	Y	R	M	U
C	O	M	E	D	Y	J	J	E	A	U	P
A	V	L	O	Z	Y	N	N	U	F	H	M
B	R	I	D	A	Y	L	R	O	R	F	N
Y	S	U	O	I	R	A	L	I	H	J	O

18. ANIMALS

Can you find these hidden animals?

CAT
CHICKENS
COW
DOG
DONKEY
DUCKS
GEESE
GOATS

HAMSTER
HORSE
LAMBS
MICE
PIG
RABBITS
RATS
SHEEP

S	T	S	C	C	G	H	E	O	O	P	V
T	A	H	D	O	G	S	Y	T	T	L	A
I	R	E	I	W	R	A	E	S	R	O	H
B	V	E	T	H	D	E	K	O	P	C	A
B	E	P	I	G	I	R	N	U	I	N	M
A	V	C	A	M	O	T	O	A	R	V	S
R	R	E	A	X	S	T	D	F	C	A	T
E	Y	S	N	E	K	C	I	H	C	S	E
S	S	K	C	U	D	H	S	R	O	U	R
O	Z	E	H	F	S	B	M	A	L	A	M
M	I	C	E	I	L	A	T	T	E	Y	P
P	R	O	G	G	O	A	T	S	N	Q	M

19. TOYS!

See how many toys you can find.

BALL
BAT
BICYCLE
BOAT
CRAYONS

DOLL
GAMES
KITE
PAINTS
RATTLE

SKATES
TRAIN
YOYO

O	T	A	O	B	O	O	C	K	I	B	E
O	R	R	I	K	N	B	F	E	E	B	T
R	A	T	T	L	E	H	O	U	Z	I	T
Q	I	U	V	S	N	O	Y	A	R	C	M
S	N	O	W	B	R	I	O	X	X	Y	O
R	I	A	D	O	L	L	Y	M	K	C	O
S	O	W	O	N	L	H	O	P	C	O	N
K	H	E	I	M	A	U	W	A	A	E	B
A	I	O	T	A	B	S	B	I	L	B	O
T	M	C	G	B	A	I	T	N	T	H	N
E	B	O	A	P	R	V	E	T	I	K	N
S	E	M	A	G	A	Z	Y	S	K	N	E

20. GROCERY STORE

Can you find the items hidden in the store?

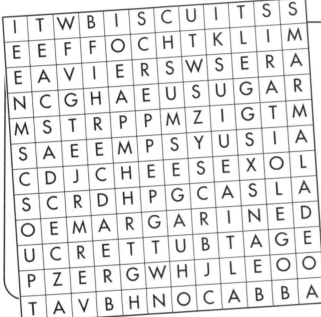

BACON
BEANS
BISCUITS
BREAD
BUTTER
CHEESE
COFFEE

EGGS
JAM
MARGARINE
MARMALADE
MILK
PEPPER
SOUP

SUGAR
TEA

I	T	W	B	I	S	C	U	I	T	S	S
E	E	F	F	O	C	H	T	K	L	I	M
E	A	V	I	E	R	S	W	S	E	R	A
N	C	G	H	A	E	U	S	U	G	A	R
M	S	T	R	P	P	M	Z	I	G	T	M
S	A	E	E	M	P	S	Y	U	S	I	A
C	D	J	C	H	E	E	S	E	X	O	L
S	C	R	D	H	P	G	C	A	S	L	A
O	E	M	A	R	G	A	R	I	N	E	D
U	C	R	E	T	T	U	B	T	A	G	E
P	Z	E	R	G	W	H	J	L	E	O	O
T	A	V	B	H	N	O	C	A	B	B	A

21. VEGETABLE PATCH

Find the selection of vegetables here.

ARTICHOKE
BEET
BROCCOLI
CABBAGE
CARROT

CAULIFLOWER
KALE
LEEKS
ONION
POTATOES

SPINACH
SPROUTS
SQUASH
ZUCCHINI

J	E	Z	U	C	C	H	I	N	I	V	E
O	E	R	T	S	Q	U	A	S	H	I	R
F	S	S	K	A	L	E	F	R	E	D	E
E	I	L	O	C	C	O	R	B	O	E	W
S	S	E	D	E	A	U	O	A	L	N	O
E	P	G	A	A	R	W	N	O	D	J	L
O	I	A	B	U	R	N	I	P	C	E	F
T	N	B	E	L	O	Z	O	O	E	Q	I
A	A	B	E	T	T	K	N	K	B	X	L
T	C	A	T	F	F	J	S	F	B	S	U
O	H	C	E	K	O	H	C	I	T	R	A
P	A	S	T	U	O	R	P	S	Z	X	C

22. OCEANS AND SEAS

Go sailing! Find the oceans and seas in the grid.

ADRIATIC	BALTIC	DEAD	RED
ARCTIC	BLACK	INDIAN	
ATLANTIC	CARIBBEAN	NORTH	
ANTARCTIC	CASPIAN	PACIFIC	

D	E	R	A	H	O	U	B	L	A	C	K
R	E	F	B	I	A	T	E	R	R	T	G
E	C	A	S	P	I	A	N	O	C	H	P
F	I	T	C	P	P	U	F	W	T	I	A
C	T	L	D	J	I	V	G	L	I	P	C
I	L	A	E	K	E	W	A	K	C	N	I
T	A	N	T	A	R	C	T	I	C	A	F
A	B	T	F	L	Q	X	G	D	M	I	I
I	D	I	K	M	R	Y	I	A	A	D	C
R	E	C	A	R	I	B	B	E	A	N	L
D	V	U	G	N	S	Z	J	D	W	I	N
A	T	H	T	R	O	N	K	T	I	M	O

23. WHAT'S IN THE BATHROOM?

How many things can you find in the bathroom?

BUBBLE BATH	SHOWER	TOILET
FAUCET	SINK	TOOTHBRUSH
MAT	SOAP	TOOTHPASTE
MIRROR	SPONGE	TOWEL
SHAMPOO	TILES	

T	H	I	M	B	L	V	K	N	I	S	U
O	S	E	L	I	T	E	W	S	T	P	Q
P	U	R	R	S	H	A	M	P	O	O	H
H	R	Q	U	H	S	A	U	R	I	N	T
O	B	W	S	O	A	P	T	S	L	G	A
R	H	W	R	W	A	N	T	I	E	E	B
D	T	O	W	E	L	C	H	I	T	G	E
E	O	E	D	R	L	H	A	F	U	O	L
N	O	F	A	U	C	E	T	G	H	I	B
T	T	O	O	T	H	P	A	S	T	E	B
A	C	A	T	Y	H	O	T	F	A	U	U
M	I	R	R	O	R	F	A	T	B	O	B

24. WHAT'S IN THE KITCHEN?

How many things can you find in the kitchen?

BLENDER	OVEN	STOVE
FREEZER	PANS	TOASTER
GRILL	POTS	
KETTLE	REFRIGERATOR	
MICROWAVE	SINK	

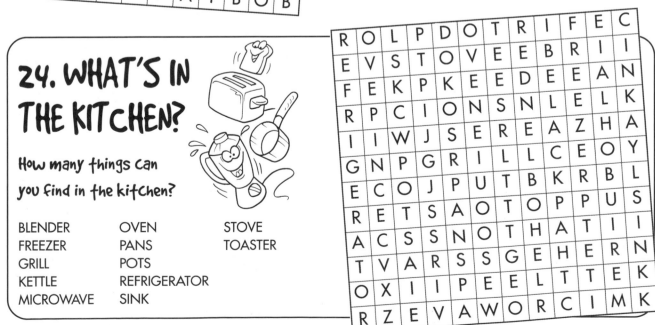

R	O	L	P	D	O	T	R	I	F	E	C
E	V	S	T	O	V	E	E	B	R	I	I
F	E	K	P	K	E	E	D	E	E	A	N
R	P	C	I	O	N	S	N	L	E	L	K
I	I	W	J	S	E	R	E	A	Z	H	A
G	N	P	G	R	I	L	L	C	E	O	Y
E	C	O	J	P	U	T	B	K	R	B	L
R	E	T	S	A	O	T	O	P	P	U	S
A	C	S	S	N	O	T	H	A	T	I	I
T	V	A	R	S	S	G	E	H	E	R	N
O	X	I	I	P	E	E	L	T	T	E	K
R	Z	E	V	A	W	O	R	C	I	M	K

25. BIRDS

How many birds can you spot?

BLACKBIRD
BUDGIE
CANARY
DOVE
HAWK

LAPWING
LARK
LINNET
MAGPIE
NIGHTINGALE

PARROT
PIGEON

A	C	T	I	C	B	U	N	S	X	Z	N
P	A	R	R	O	T	Q	R	E	N	V	I
R	N	A	T	W	L	A	P	W	I	N	G
D	A	R	E	I	B	E	E	F	O	G	H
R	R	C	N	B	N	T	X	W	I	N	T
I	Y	H	N	C	O	E	W	D	I	R	I
B	A	A	I	R	M	P	I	G	E	O	N
K	R	A	L	J	A	N	T	A	R	T	G
C	W	O	P	S	G	O	G	H	R	S	A
A	C	A	T	X	P	W	B	L	O	R	L
L	A	T	H	W	I	N	A	D	O	V	E
B	U	D	G	I	E	E	W	N	W	F	R

26. GO NUTS!

This puzzle will drive you nuts!

ACORN
ALMOND
BRAZIL
CASHEW
CHESTNUT
COCONUT

FILBERT
GROUNDNUT
HAZEL
MACADAMIA
PEANUT
PECAN

PISTACHIO
WALNUT

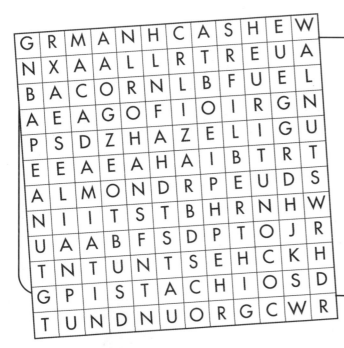

G	R	M	A	N	H	C	A	S	H	E	W
N	X	A	A	L	L	R	T	R	E	U	A
B	A	C	O	R	N	L	B	F	U	E	L
A	E	A	G	O	F	I	O	I	R	G	N
P	S	D	Z	H	A	Z	E	L	I	G	U
E	E	A	E	A	H	A	I	B	T	R	T
A	L	M	O	N	D	R	P	E	U	D	S
N	I	I	T	S	T	B	H	R	N	H	W
U	A	A	B	F	S	D	P	T	O	J	R
T	N	T	U	N	T	S	E	H	C	K	H
G	P	I	S	T	A	C	H	I	O	S	D
T	U	N	D	N	U	O	R	G	C	W	R

27. PRIVATE DETECTIVE

Become a private detective and track down these words.

CASE
CLUES
CRIME
DATA
FACTS
FINGERPRINTS
FORENSIC
GUMSHOE

HUNT
IDENTITY
PROOF
SEARCH

SLEUTH
SOLVE

T	R	F	A	C	T	S	E	E	V	J	K
O	T	C	R	I	M	E	E	S	T	V	M
Y	S	L	E	U	T	H	N	A	V	A	U
I	L	U	J	E	V	J	K	M	R	I	T
C	E	E	V	E	J	I	G	Y	T	C	Y
I	M	S	E	O	N	E	U	T	N	U	H
S	J	F	O	O	R	P	O	I	Z	A	C
N	A	O	H	L	Q	A	R	T	R	A	I
E	C	I	S	K	V	T	E	N	S	O	R
R	C	G	M	D	D	E	T	E	T	Y	I
O	A	R	U	Y	A	T	A	D	J	A	C
F	I	N	G	E	R	P	R	I	N	T	S

28. ROBOTS

Find the words linked to robots.

ANDROID
COMPUTER
CONTROLS
CYBORG
FUTURISTIC

HUMANOID
INTELLIGENCE
MACHINE
MEMORY
PROCESS

PROGRAM
ROBOT
TECHNOLOGY

```
S H I S L O R T N O C S
P T E C H N O L O G Y S
D V N O U F B H E R B E
V N I M H G O H O R O C
K H P S D T M A X R O R
W C U E C E B A R G R P
S A T D M A R G O R P
A X M E C I T E R E U E
N I D R B J U N E I E J
O E C I T S I R U T U F
I N T E L L I G E N C E
D I O R D N A S T E R Z
```

---

29. AROUND THE WORLD

Find the continents and countries in the puzzle.

AFRICA
AMERICA
AUSTRALIA
BELGIUM
BRITAIN
CHINA

EGYPT
FRANCE
GERMANY
ICELAND
ITALY
JAPAN

NORWAY
RUSSIA
SPAIN
SWEDEN

```
S P A I N Y I N A P A J
W K I C O M M M J F M R
E E S E S O U S X E E D
D C S L P N I A T I R B
E D U A L O G H P W I U
N S R N A R L O Y A C Z
E C M D V W E U G C A E
C H O A C A B S E I S S
N I T A L Y Y E E V R R C
A N D R H I T R E F R I
R A U S T R A L I A I C
F R O I L Y N A M R E G
```

---

30. GLOBE TROTTERS

Can you find these countries?

AUSTRIA
BRAZIL
CANADA
DENMARK
FINLAND
GREECE

GREENLAND
HOLLAND
HUNGARY
INDIA
MEXICO
PERU

PORTUGAL
SWITZERLAND
THAILAND
TURKEY

```
I A V A L L C A N A D A
N H M E X I C O F I N U
D U Y O R Z N R O B A S
I N E K R A M N E D L T
A G K G R R E A T N R R
X A R E X B W D H A E I
E R U T D F E Z A L Z A
C Y T R U E T E I N T R
E P O R T U G A L I I V
E Q E R C V G H A F W A
R P C H O L L A N D S L
G R E E N L A N D J R O
```

31. CREEPY-CRAWLY

This puzzle is full of creepy-crawly creatures.

BEETLE
BUG
CATERPILLAR
CENTIPEDE
COCKROACH
EARWIG

LADYBUG
NIT
PARASITE
SCORPION
SLUG
SPIDER

TARANTULA
WEEVIL
WORM

B	I	R	F	S	L	U	G	A	L	O	R
C	E	G	R	E	A	C	U	T	Y	O	A
O	K	E	X	D	G	U	B	Y	D	A	L
C	A	A	T	I	Q	I	O	T	R	S	L
K	K	R	R	L	M	R	O	W	I	C	I
R	D	W	A	E	E	W	L	E	F	G	P
O	O	I	J	S	P	I	D	E	R	B	R
A	K	G	A	P	T	O	V	V	W	X	E
C	A	Y	P	A	R	A	S	I	T	E	T
H	T	A	R	A	N	T	U	L	A	R	A
A	I	H	E	D	E	P	I	T	N	E	C
J	N	O	I	P	R	O	C	S	Z	O	I

32. INCREDIBLE INSECTS!

Can you find the insects?

ANT
BLUEBOTTLE
BUTTERFLY
FIREFLY
FLEA

GNAT
GREENFLY
HORNET
LOCUST
MIDGE

MOSQUITO
MOTH
TICK
WASP

F	I	R	E	F	L	Y	T	H	O	C	E
L	P	R	I	B	C	Z	W	T	A	N	G
E	S	H	O	R	N	E	T	R	E	P	D
A	S	T	I	R	S	H	I	J	L	O	I
I	G	M	O	O	C	W	C	I	T	N	M
T	R	D	O	P	A	R	K	V	T	M	A
P	E	D	O	T	I	U	Q	S	O	M	R
T	E	P	Z	O	H	I	V	S	B	V	T
P	N	S	S	I	G	M	T	O	E	T	O
T	F	A	H	A	R	L	O	C	U	S	T
X	L	W	A	F	R	E	R	S	L	U	S
I	Y	L	F	R	E	T	T	U	B	U	H

33. GOBBLEDYGOOK

All these words mean utter nonsense!

BLAH
BLETHER
DAFT
DRIVEL
FABLE
FLAPDOODLE
FLIMFLAM

GOBBLEDYGOOK
NONSENSE
PRATTLE
ROT
SILLY
STUPID

Z	A	H	P	P	Y	L	L	I	S	Y	O
A	N	S	A	B	R	B	B	U	H	R	O
G	O	B	B	L	E	D	Y	G	O	O	K
M	N	O	W	T	B	L	A	G	H	T	F
M	S	C	A	R	T	E	B	F	S	L	B
A	E	H	F	A	B	L	E	M	T	A	L
L	N	A	F	L	E	T	B	I	U	N	E
F	S	F	L	E	S	T	E	T	P	C	T
M	E	Q	I	V	A	A	L	U	I	E	H
I	A	U	N	I	N	R	G	L	D	T	E
L	Z	I	B	R	R	P	I	B	D	U	R
F	L	A	P	D	O	O	D	L	E	I	R

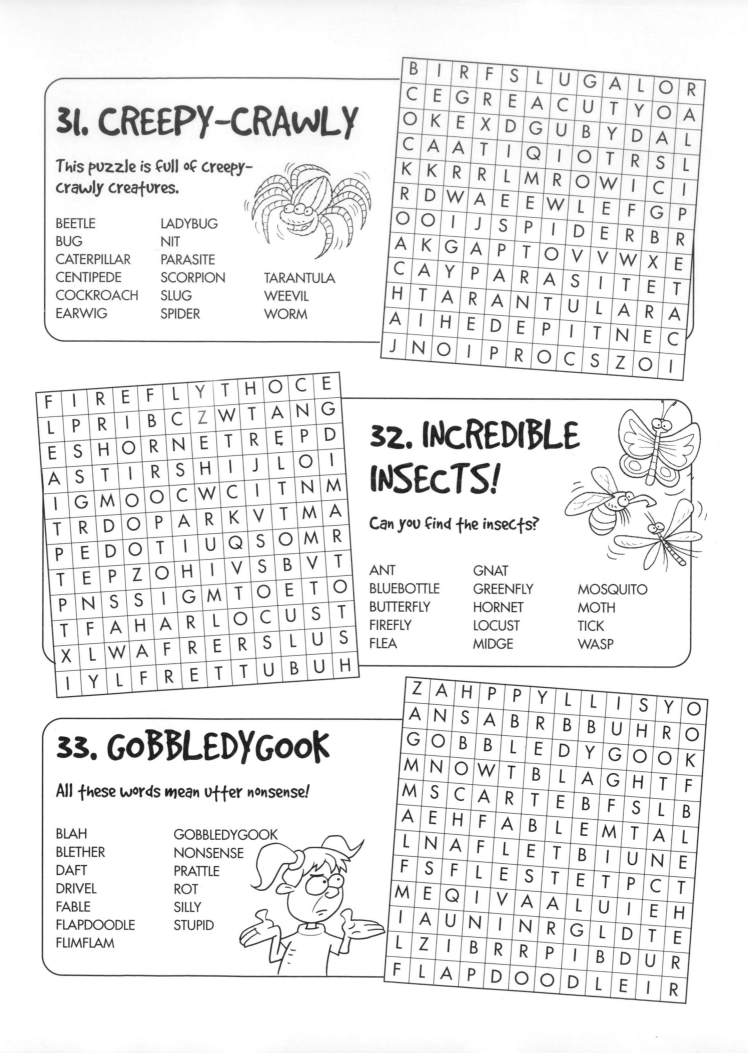

34. MUSICAL INSTRUMENTS

Can you fnd the instruments?

BAGPIPES
BANJO
BELLS
FLUTE
GUITAR

HARMONICA
KAZOO
KEYBOARD
OBOE
PIANO

RECORDER
TAMBOURINE
VIOLA
VIOLIN

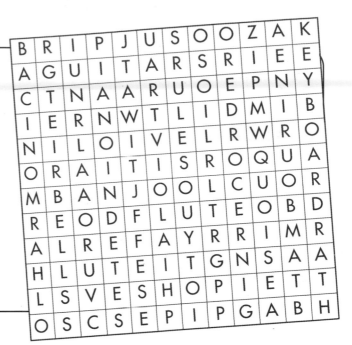

B	R	I	P	J	U	S	O	O	Z	A	K
A	G	U	I	T	A	R	S	R	I	E	E
C	T	N	A	A	R	U	O	E	P	N	Y
I	E	R	N	W	T	L	I	D	M	I	B
N	I	L	O	I	V	E	L	R	W	R	O
O	R	A	I	T	I	S	R	O	Q	U	A
M	B	A	N	J	O	O	L	C	U	O	R
R	E	O	D	F	L	U	T	E	O	B	D
A	L	R	E	F	A	Y	R	R	I	M	R
H	L	U	T	E	I	T	G	N	S	A	A
L	S	V	E	S	H	O	P	I	E	T	T
O	S	C	S	E	P	I	P	G	A	B	H

35. "A" WORDS

All these words start
with the letter A.

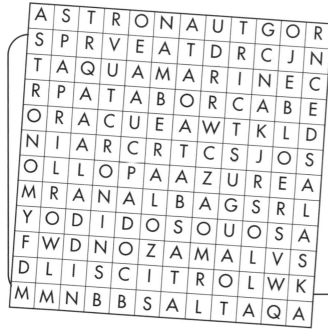

A	S	T	R	O	N	A	U	T	G	O	R
S	P	R	V	E	A	T	D	R	C	J	N
T	A	Q	U	A	M	A	R	I	N	E	C
R	P	A	T	A	B	O	R	C	A	B	E
O	R	A	C	U	E	A	W	T	K	L	D
N	I	A	R	C	R	T	C	S	J	O	S
O	L	L	O	P	A	A	Z	U	R	E	A
M	R	A	N	A	L	B	A	G	S	R	L
Y	O	D	I	D	O	S	O	U	O	S	A
F	W	D	N	O	Z	A	M	A	L	V	S
D	L	I	S	C	I	T	R	O	L	W	K
M	M	N	B	B	S	A	L	T	A	Q	A

ABACUS
ACROBAT
ALADDIN
ALASKA
AMAZON
AMBER

APOLLO
APRIL
AQUAMARINE
ART
ASTRONAUT
ASTRONOMY

ATLAS
AUGUST
AZURE

36. MORE "A" WORDS

Again, every word begins with the letter A.

ACTION
ADVENTURE
ALMOND
ALPHABET
APPLE
APRICOT
APRON
ARCADE

ARCTIC
ARENA
ARITHMETIC
ASTEROID
ATMOSPHERE
ATTIC
AUBURN

H	E	R	E	H	P	S	O	M	T	A	U
A	M	I	L	K	I	R	O	S	E	R	H
D	N	O	M	L	A	A	R	C	T	I	C
V	B	E	W	A	A	P	P	L	E	T	O
E	U	A	S	T	E	R	O	I	D	H	U
N	Z	N	T	M	C	I	T	T	A	M	S
T	Z	E	I	A	R	C	A	D	E	E	R
U	R	S	T	P	K	O	H	A	W	T	C
R	A	N	E	R	A	T	K	I	T	I	Z
E	S	E	I	O	N	N	O	I	T	C	A
A	T	O	M	N	R	U	B	U	A	S	Q
A	L	P	H	A	B	E	T	K	A	J	U

37. BIRTHDAYS!

All these words are associated with birthdays.

CAKE
CANDLES
CELEBRATE
DANCING
DECORATIONS
FRIENDS
FUN
GAMES
GIFTS
HAPPY
HATS
ICING
MUSIC
PARTY
PRESENTS
SINGING
WISH

S	R	I	B	O	G	I	F	T	S	N	S
I	C	I	N	G	O	R	D	E	N	U	F
N	W	H	I	T	E	B	L	A	O	C	K
G	N	I	C	N	A	D	T	R	I	P	S
I	S	C	E	L	E	B	R	A	T	E	H
N	H	A	P	P	Y	C	H	D	A	R	O
G	E	K	S	T	N	E	S	E	R	P	R
M	E	E	R	Y	A	W	O	R	O	L	P
U	S	T	A	H	D	R	A	S	C	L	A
S	L	A	R	T	S	G	A	M	E	S	R
I	C	R	O	F	R	I	E	N	D	S	T
C	A	N	D	L	E	S	W	F	G	H	Y

R	E	L	G	A	E	B	D	B	P	W	Y
O	G	J	A	L	S	A	T	I	O	N	O
T	O	N	S	O	S	S	X	H	M	W	A
T	E	A	M	V	H	S	C	T	E	O	B
W	E	M	H	H	E	E	A	M	R	L	E
E	R	R	I	E	E	T	S	I	A	F	S
I	S	E	S	R	P	O	J	H	N	H	E
L	A	B	R	A	D	O	R	T	I	O	N
E	Z	O	L	G	O	R	M	T	A	U	I
R	D	D	R	I	G	R	O	C	N	N	K
A	R	D	N	U	H	S	H	C	A	D	E
A	S	E	T	T	E	R	H	A	P	I	P

38. DOGS

Find the dogs in the word puzzle.

BASSET
BEAGLE
CHOW
CORGI
DACHSHUND
DOBERMAN
LABRADOR
PEKINESE
POMERANIAN
ROTTWEILER
SETTER
SHEEPDOG
WOLFHOUND

39. MORE DOGS

Discover the dogs hidden here.

AIREDALE
BLOODHOUND
BOXER
BULLDOG
CHIHUAHUA
COLLIE
DALMATIAN
GREYHOUND
HUSKY
NEWFOUNDLAND
POODLE
PUG
SPANIEL
WHIPPET

A	D	O	G	I	L	E	I	N	A	P	S
C	A	I	R	E	D	A	L	E	I	O	T
D	L	E	E	A	D	E	R	S	T	O	B
N	M	A	V	C	R	O	I	L	C	D	L
U	A	U	B	O	X	E	R	A	H	L	O
O	T	B	U	L	L	D	O	G	I	E	O
H	I	I	K	L	S	C	U	E	H	I	D
Y	A	W	H	I	P	P	E	T	U	U	H
E	N	C	O	E	T	E	A	C	A	L	O
R	M	P	U	T	Y	K	S	U	H	A	U
G	E	R	B	I	E	F	O	P	U	C	N
N	E	W	F	O	U	N	D	L	A	N	D

40. TRAIN STATION

Find the words associated with train stations.

BUFFERS
CARRIAGES
DRIVER
GUARD
PASSENGERS

PLATFORM
RAILS
SHUNTER
SIGNALS
SLEEPER

TICKETS
TIMETABLE
WHISTLE

```
B S E G A I R R A C H W
R R E A D S T E K C I T H
S D R I V E R I V A I L S
R E E A W I F E A L M S
E A P S I G N A L S E T T
F V E E I L D R O J T L
F I E S T B S D E P A E
U P L A T F O R M D B P
B D S U N N E A W S L P
A S U R E T N U H S E A
W O R G H O R G S Q U I
T A S R E G N E S S A P
```

41. FOOTBALL CRAZY

Search for the football words.

BALL
COACH
DEFENSE
END ZONE
FIELD
FLAG

HUDDLE
KICK
PASS
PENALTY
POINTS
REFEREE

TACKLE
TEAM
TOUCHDOWN

```
R S T B S L P A S S E E
I M A E T U H U E D S N
T L C W E V E O F O U D
L M K I N E L F E R B Z
I R L H T M D I R D S O
K R E I I A D E E B E N
S E F K N N U L E O S E
T F T O U C H D O W N I
N E F L A G C I K A E O
I R A R E E R O C S F N
O E C O A C H K I N E A
P E N A L T Y E K E D F
```

42. COWBOY RANCH

Find the ranching words.

BRONCO
CATTLE
CHAPS
COWBOY
HORSE
LARIAT
LASSO
PRAIRIE

RANCH
RANGER
SADDLE
SHEEP
SPURS
STETSON
TROUGH

```
R E G N A R D R H A W R
A S C A R F B R O N C O
R T R U E B E X R I O U
S E I R I A R P S E V J
T R O U G H V E E A C B
E E C A T T L E L G F E
T W O D B A V H O U S A
S E W I S O B S R E S H
O I B S V P L S P A H C
N E O A E V U P A R K N
S D Y D S L A R I A T A
J O J E L D D A S W O R
```

43. CIRCUS

Find the words linked to the circus.

ACROBAT   JUGGLE   SHOWS
ACTS   LIONS   TIGERS
CLOWNS   MAGIC   TRAINER
ELEPHANTS   RIGGING   TRAPEZE
HORSES   RING   TENT

E	L	G	G	U	J	I	G	Z	I	P	Z
L	W	I	P	T	R	A	P	E	Z	E	B
E	C	M	A	G	I	C	R	T	D	Y	I
P	J	R	F	E	N	P	J	A	C	T	S
H	G	N	I	G	G	I	R	B	L	E	H
A	S	D	F	N	E	O	F	O	O	S	O
N	E	O	R	D	S	B	K	R	W	U	W
T	S	E	S	R	O	H	Z	C	N	J	S
S	A	R	E	S	D	S	T	A	S	G	K
R	O	G	W	J	A	E	W	E	B	E	E
L	I	O	N	S	R	T	Q	V	N	F	N
T	R	A	I	N	E	R	R	A	R	T	O

44. COMPUTERS

Use your skills to find the computer words.

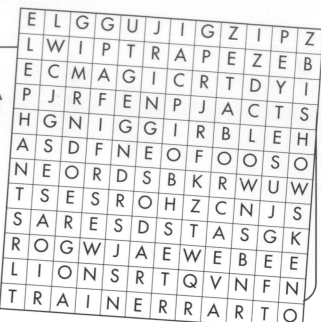

COMPUTER   KEYBOARD
DESKTOP   INPUT   MOUSE
DISK   LAPTOP   NET
FONT   MAIL   PRINTER
GAMES   MEMORY   SOFTWARE
HARDWARE   MODEM   WEB

D	E	R	D	R	A	O	B	Y	E	K	U
E	I	D	R	E	T	N	I	R	P	S	D
S	E	V	R	R	E	S	U	O	M	I	R
K	R	I	F	I	F	D	Z	M	C	D	O
T	C	B	I	O	S	E	U	E	R	O	H
O	R	A	N	V	E	S	E	M	A	G	A
P	O	T	P	A	L	N	H	A	M	R	R
R	A	I	U	T	O	I	P	Y	E	R	D
T	H	W	T	T	I	T	A	E	D	G	W
N	Z	B	R	E	T	U	P	M	O	C	A
R	E	V	L	E	M	K	L	T	M	A	R
W	A	T	F	S	O	F	T	W	A	R	E

45. STAR SIGNS

Search for the star signs in this zodiac puzzle.

ARIES   GOAT
AQUARIUS   LEO
BULL   LIBRA   SCORPIO
CAPRICORN   LION   TAURUS
CRAB   PISCES   TWINS
FISH   RAM   VIRGO
GEMINI   SAGITTARIUS   ZODIAC

S	C	O	R	P	I	O	T	L	A	M	D
A	S	A	R	D	N	W	A	R	I	E	S
G	O	A	T	A	I	W	U	A	Y	O	V
I	E	S	E	N	M	R	R	M	T	E	N
T	A	V	S	L	E	P	U	H	I	L	E
T	A	R	F	E	G	E	S	C	L	T	P
A	R	B	I	L	G	R	P	A	L	E	O
R	E	A	S	C	O	H	I	I	U	T	G
I	B	R	H	W	I	J	S	D	B	O	R
U	U	C	A	P	R	I	C	O	R	N	I
S	Q	U	E	R	T	E	E	Z	I	S	V
A	Q	U	A	R	I	U	S	H	I	P	Y

46. HERBS

Find the herbs hidden in the puzzle.

BASIL
BAY LEAF
CHERVIL
CHIVES
CORIANDER

DILL
FENNEL
MARJORAM
MINT
PARSLEY

ROSEMARY
SAGE
SAVORY
THYME

```
S E T A F A E L Y A B L
A M A R J O R A M C A R
L Y S P E P O R I C S O
R H S A T M A N N H I S
E T K I G M I X T E L E
D O F E X E E M J R K M
N R L E N N E F D V D A
A J L O E V A Z A I T R
I C I Q Z P A R S L E Y
R E D R L I F T E X E R
O S T S A V O R Y O U W
C H I V E S O N D A R O
```

47. CHRISTMAS

Find these Christmas time words.

CARDS
CAROLS
CHIMNEY
CHRISTMAS
DECEMBER
ELVES
GARLANDS

GIFTS
HOLLY
MISTLETOE
SLEIGH
TINSEL
TOYS
TREE

```
S D R A C B S U V K A Y
V E A T R R E A K F A S
M C H R I S T M A S D S
I E Q E C E B D E R Y T
S M Y E R S C A R O L S
T B J T I M H N T A T D
L E K N H G I E L S N N
E R K A S R M A E S M A
T I L E P H N P S R W L
O U V N D F E V N F A R
E L H O L L Y D I Y I A
E D H S T D B S T F I G
```

48. FESTIVE FUN

And these festive ones, too!

BAUBLES
CANDLES
CHESTNUTS
COLD
DECORATIONS
FAIRY
FEAST

LIGHTS
REINDEER
RUDOLPH
SANTA
SNOW
STAR
YULETIDE

```
R U D O L P H F A I R Y
E A R T C H J K E S W U
I F A V R T S T H G I L
N E V E Y J T S Z S H E
D S E L B U A B A T T T
E C R S I S R T N U A I
E H T F E A S T A N S D
R A T M E L E M O T N E
W T I F W M D S A S H U
O N C O L D B N M E F D
R A N F A D R D A H J K
K S N O I T A R O C E D
```

49. FIRE STATION

All the words here are linked to a fire station.

AXE
BELL
ENGINE
FIRE
FOAM

HELMETS
HOSE
LADDER
MASKS
POLE

RADIO
RESCUE
TURNTABLE
UNIFORM
WATER

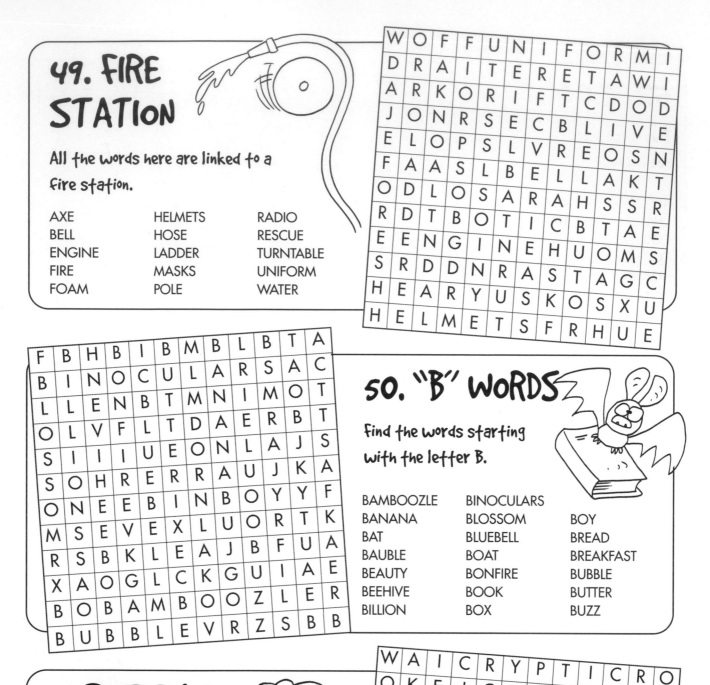

W	O	F	F	U	N	I	F	O	R	M	I
D	R	A	I	T	E	R	E	T	A	W	I
A	R	K	O	R	I	F	T	C	D	O	D
J	O	N	R	S	E	C	B	L	I	V	E
E	L	O	P	S	L	V	R	E	O	S	N
F	A	A	S	L	B	E	L	L	A	K	T
O	D	L	O	S	A	R	A	H	S	S	R
R	D	T	B	O	T	I	C	B	T	A	E
E	E	N	G	I	N	E	H	U	O	M	S
S	R	D	D	N	R	A	S	T	A	G	C
H	E	A	R	Y	U	S	K	O	S	X	U
H	E	L	M	E	T	S	F	R	H	U	E

50. "B" WORDS

Find the words starting with the letter B.

F	B	H	B	I	B	M	B	L	B	T	A
B	I	N	O	C	U	L	A	R	S	A	C
L	L	E	N	B	T	M	N	I	M	O	T
O	L	V	F	L	T	D	A	E	R	B	T
S	I	I	I	U	E	O	N	L	A	J	S
S	O	H	R	E	R	R	A	U	J	K	A
O	N	E	E	B	I	N	B	O	Y	Y	F
M	S	E	V	E	X	L	U	O	R	T	K
R	S	B	K	L	E	A	J	B	F	U	A
X	A	O	G	L	C	K	G	U	I	A	E
B	O	B	A	M	B	O	O	Z	L	E	R
B	U	B	B	L	E	V	R	Z	S	B	B

BAMBOOZLE
BANANA
BAT
BAUBLE
BEAUTY
BEEHIVE
BILLION

BINOCULARS
BLOSSOM
BLUEBELL
BOAT
BONFIRE
BOOK
BOX

BOY
BREAD
BREAKFAST
BUBBLE
BUTTER
BUZZ

51. PUZZLE WORDS

All these words have something to do with puzzles.

ANSWER
CLUES
CODE
CRYPTIC
ENIGMA
GRID

JIGSAW
LOGIC
MAZE
MIND
MYSTERY
PUZZLE

RIDDLE
QUIZ
SOLUTIONS
WORDSEARCH

W	A	I	C	R	Y	P	T	I	C	R	O
O	K	E	J	C	R	U	Z	O	O	C	E
R	Y	N	A	R	A	Z	A	Q	U	I	Z
D	N	I	M	E	B	Z	X	G	D	G	A
S	R	G	R	W	A	L	C	L	U	O	M
E	R	M	Y	S	T	E	R	Y	F	L	A
A	A	A	A	N	E	J	I	G	S	A	W
R	H	Z	D	A	I	E	D	O	C	K	O
C	R	B	R	I	V	E	D	L	L	S	O
H	P	O	T	B	R	W	L	D	U	D	F
Q	U	E	O	M	I	G	E	W	E	R	I
A	S	N	O	I	T	U	L	O	S	O	H

52. COOL!

This wordsearch is really cool.

ARCTIC
CHILLY
COLD
COOL
FREEZING
FROSTBITE
GLACIER
HAILSTONE
ICELAND
POLAR
SLEET
SNOWFLAKE
SNOWSTORM
WINTRY

I	C	H	I	L	L	Y	D	D	V	I	W
R	R	B	A	L	K	R	G	J	Y	C	I
I	A	S	N	O	W	F	L	A	K	E	N
R	L	N	I	U	N	R	L	R	O	L	T
C	O	O	E	C	O	O	L	C	A	A	R
S	P	W	V	O	Y	S	U	T	I	N	Y
T	E	S	I	L	J	T	R	I	O	D	E
E	D	T	H	D	N	B	I	C	T	L	L
E	N	O	T	S	L	I	A	H	V	E	A
L	J	R	N	I	O	T	R	H	X	S	E
S	T	M	I	O	R	E	I	C	A	L	G
B	R	U	E	G	N	I	Z	E	E	R	F

53. IT'S A JUNGLE!

Find the animals and creatures hidden here.

CHEETAH
CHIMP
COUGAR
GECKO
GIRAFFE
GORILLA
JAGUAR
MONKEY
MOSQUITO
PANTHER
TIGER
VIPER
VULTURE
ZEBRA

M	O	S	Q	U	I	T	O	L	D	G	W
O	S	T	K	T	A	K	W	I	W	O	I
N	O	R	T	K	C	A	J	K	E	R	F
K	V	T	I	E	E	F	F	A	R	I	G
E	I	H	G	R	H	O	L	R	O	L	E
Y	R	I	E	E	C	G	D	B	L	L	R
E	I	M	R	P	C	H	E	E	T	A	H
D	P	O	M	I	O	I	H	Z	U	S	W
A	C	I	F	V	U	L	T	U	R	E	H
D	H	U	S	A	G	I	R	I	L	P	A
C	R	P	A	J	A	G	U	A	R	Z	V
R	A	F	X	E	R	E	H	T	N	A	P

54. JUNGLE FUN!

Hunt for even more hidden animals and creatures.

ANTELOPE
APE
COBRA
CROCODILE
ELEPHANT
HIPPO
HYENA
LEOPARD
LION
OCELOT
PIRANHA
SNAKE
SPIDER
RHINO

S	A	N	D	S	R	U	C	O	B	R	A
P	I	R	A	N	H	A	R	D	A	X	X
I	A	R	V	A	E	D	O	N	I	H	R
D	G	H	H	K	J	T	C	S	H	L	O
E	O	A	M	E	D	B	O	P	P	I	H
R	R	N	O	O	Y	J	D	I	F	O	R
I	B	T	N	G	I	E	I	I	O	N	O
A	N	E	Y	H	L	S	L	D	C	Z	S
S	F	L	J	L	R	E	E	M	E	D	E
L	E	O	P	A	R	D	D	O	L	L	S
E	M	P	P	N	I	C	N	W	O	L	I
M	A	E	L	E	P	H	A	N	T	I	G

55. "C" WORDS

All these words begin with the letter C.

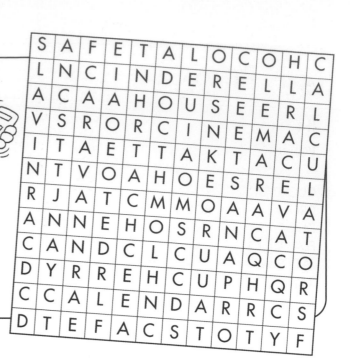

CAFE	CARTOON	CHOCOLATE
CALCULATOR	CAT	CINDERELLA
CALENDAR	CAVE	CINEMA
CARAMEL	CHARM	COCOA
CARAVAN	CHEF	COMET
CARNIVAL	CHERRY	CREAM

```
S A F E T A L O C O H C
L N C I N D E R E L L A
A C A A H O U S E E R L
V S R O R C I N E M A C
I T A E T T A K T A C U
N T V O A H O E S R E L
R J A T C M M O A A V A
A N N E H O S R N C A T
C A N D C L C U A Q C O
D Y R R E H C U P H Q R
C C A L E N D A R R C S
D T E F A C S T O T Y F
```

56. "D" WORDS

Look for the words beginning with the letter D.

```
S E L Z Z A D F R E S I
E S V D E C E M B E R F
C T R O I R S U D H U R
R G A O D A S P D O A O
E G R D A D E O A U S G
D N D L D A R K R R O H
A I C E F G T G J S N E
I W Y E M D Y N A M I C
S A L L P P A A L E D N
Y R I A D I L S L V T A
S D A N D E L I O N F D
W I D H G E O N D U C K
```

DAILY	DATE	
DAIRY	DAZZLE	
DAISY	DECEMBER	DOVE
DANCE	DESSERT	DRAWING
DANDELION	DINOSAUR	DUCK
DARK	DOODLE	DYNAMIC

57. DESERT

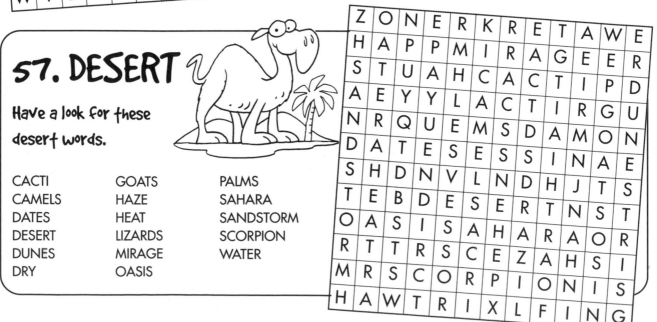

Have a look for these desert words.

CACTI	GOATS	PALMS
CAMELS	HAZE	SAHARA
DATES	HEAT	SANDSTORM
DESERT	LIZARDS	SCORPION
DUNES	MIRAGE	WATER
DRY	OASIS	

```
Z O N E R K R E T A W E
H A P P M I R A G E E R
S T U A H C A C T I P D
A E Y Y L A C T I R G U
N R Q U E M S D A M O N
D A T E S E S S I N A E
S H D N V L N D H J T S
T E B D E S E R T N S T
O A S I S A H A R A O R
R T T R S C E Z A H S I
M R S C O R P I O N I S
H A W T R I X L F I N G
```

58. BIRDS

How many birds can you spot?

CUCKOO   ROBIN
CROW   ROOK
DUCK   SPARROW
FLAMINGO   STORK
JACKDAW   SWALLOW
RAVEN   VULTURE

G	E	T	A	W	A	F	R	O	B	I	N
R	O	O	K	F	F	E	R	S	W	E	Z
A	M	T	R	O	R	S	E	T	O	K	I
V	R	E	O	E	E	R	U	T	L	U	V
E	L	Q	T	T	N	H	X	N	L	I	P
N	I	U	S	Y	K	I	E	C	A	B	M
A	N	D	J	A	C	K	D	A	W	O	T
V	S	U	Y	U	R	E	L	E	S	S	I
A	E	C	C	W	O	K	U	S	T	O	P
L	P	K	R	E	W	O	R	R	A	P	S
O	O	R	T	I	N	I	R	A	S	R	Y
O	G	N	I	M	A	L	F	L	U	P	T

59. PIZZA PICK

Pick out all the different toppings and types of pizza.

ANCHOVY   MOZZARELLA
BACON   OLIVES
CHEESE   ONIONS   PINEAPPLE
FROZEN   PAN   SAUSAGE
GARLIC   PEPPERONI   SPICY
HAM   PEPPERS   TOMATO

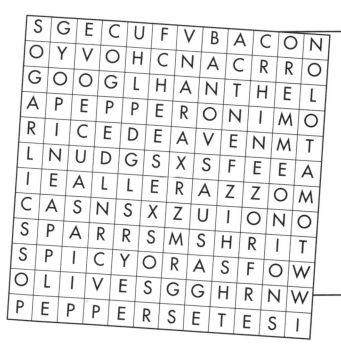

S	G	E	C	U	F	V	B	A	C	O	N
O	Y	V	O	H	C	N	A	C	R	R	O
G	O	O	G	L	H	A	N	T	H	E	L
A	P	E	P	P	E	R	O	N	I	M	O
R	I	C	E	D	E	A	V	E	N	M	T
L	N	U	D	G	S	X	S	F	E	E	A
I	E	A	L	L	E	R	A	Z	Z	O	M
C	A	S	N	S	X	Z	U	I	O	N	O
S	P	A	R	R	S	M	S	H	R	I	T
S	P	I	C	Y	O	R	A	S	F	O	W
O	L	I	V	E	S	G	G	H	R	N	W
P	E	P	P	E	R	S	E	T	E	S	I

60. SUMMER

Search for the summer words.

HAPPY   JULY
HEATWAVE   MIDSUMMER   SUMMERTIME
HOLIDAY   PICNIC   SUNSHINE
HOT   SAND   SWIMMING
JUNE   SEA   WARM

E	V	A	W	T	A	E	H	S	G	O	O
D	E	L	O	V	J	R	S	W	A	R	M
S	G	C	D	J	U	N	E	I	S	T	I
E	U	S	N	A	L	V	N	M	A	R	D
S	Y	N	A	R	Y	O	R	M	D	U	S
S	A	A	S	P	I	C	N	I	C	S	U
A	D	L	J	H	K	O	P	N	V	I	M
L	I	R	H	A	I	I	N	G	U	M	M
G	L	D	T	P	B	N	E	A	R	S	E
N	O	O	C	P	L	E	E	T	H	V	R
U	H	R	D	Y	Y	O	G	M	I	S	S
S	S	U	M	M	E	R	T	I	M	E	T

61. HALLOWEEN

It's Halloween! Can you find the ghostly words?

APPLES
BAT
CANDLES
COSTUME
GHOSTS
HALLOWEEN
LANTERN
MASK
OCTOBER
PARTY
PUMPKIN
WARLOCK
WITCH

C	U	P	U	M	P	K	I	N	G	S	H
H	C	T	I	W	H	A	P	O	H	H	K
A	P	R	I	E	M	U	T	S	O	C	B
L	A	N	T	E	R	N	O	Y	S	A	L
L	I	Y	W	N	E	A	E	Y	T	I	U
O	N	P	A	Y	T	R	A	P	S	V	E
W	C	I	R	S	L	E	C	R	O	V	F
E	D	T	L	H	S	E	L	D	N	A	C
E	O	B	O	S	E	A	E	I	B	S	I
N	L	O	C	B	S	E	L	P	P	A	R
M	A	S	K	D	E	A	V	A	L	S	E
G	I	R	L	M	L	R	H	A	F	I	M

62. SCARY STUFF!

Monsters, ghouls, and werewolves! See if you can find them.

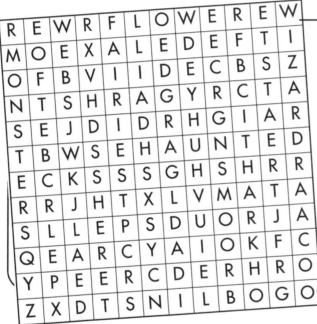

R	E	W	R	F	L	O	W	E	R	E	W
M	O	E	X	A	L	E	D	E	F	T	I
O	F	B	V	I	I	D	E	C	B	S	Z
N	T	S	H	R	A	G	Y	R	C	T	A
S	E	J	D	I	D	R	H	G	I	A	R
T	B	W	S	E	H	A	U	N	T	E	D
E	C	K	S	S	S	G	H	S	H	R	R
R	R	J	H	T	X	L	V	M	A	T	A
S	L	L	E	P	S	D	U	O	R	J	A
Q	E	A	R	C	Y	A	I	O	K	F	C
Y	P	E	E	R	C	D	E	R	H	R	O
Z	X	D	T	S	N	I	L	B	O	G	O

BEASTS
BROOMS
CREEPY
EERIE
FAIRIES
GHOULS
GOBLINS
HAUNTED
MONSTERS
SPELLS
TREATS
WEBS
WEIRD
WEREWOLF
WIZARD

63. SWEET TREATS

See how many things you can find in the shop.

BISCUITS
CUPCAKE
ECLAIR
FLAN
GATEAU
MALLOWS
MERINGUE
MUFFINS
PASTRIES
PIE
ROLLS
SCONE

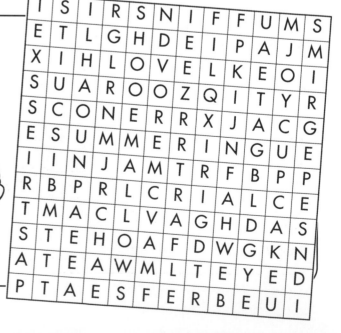

I	S	I	R	S	N	I	F	F	U	M	S
E	T	L	G	H	D	E	I	P	A	J	M
X	I	H	L	O	V	E	L	K	E	O	I
S	U	A	R	O	O	Z	Q	I	T	Y	R
S	C	O	N	E	R	R	X	J	A	C	G
E	S	U	M	M	E	R	I	N	G	U	E
I	I	N	J	A	M	T	R	F	B	P	P
R	B	P	R	L	C	R	I	A	L	C	E
T	M	A	C	L	V	A	G	H	D	A	S
S	T	E	H	O	A	F	D	W	G	K	N
A	T	E	A	W	M	L	T	E	Y	E	D
P	T	A	E	S	F	E	R	B	E	U	I

64. BAKERY

How many cakes and buns can you see?

BUNS
CAKES
CHEESECAKE
COOKIES

CRUMPETS
DOUGHNUTS
GINGERBREAD
MACAROONS

PANCAKES
PIES
SHORTBREAD
TARTS

Z	S	H	O	R	T	B	R	E	A	D	A
C	P	I	E	S	B	I	R	D	J	A	C
H	A	T	D	S	D	U	T	Y	H	E	T
M	N	T	O	P	M	I	N	U	O	R	C
A	C	R	U	M	P	E	T	S	U	B	H
C	A	I	G	L	U	U	A	E	S	R	Y
A	K	C	H	S	A	T	R	I	E	E	U
R	E	L	N	O	E	W	T	K	S	G	R
O	S	D	U	S	E	K	S	O	J	N	F
O	B	E	T	I	C	E	A	O	A	I	I
N	R	I	S	C	O	N	E	C	M	G	F
S	G	E	K	A	C	E	S	E	E	H	C

65. POST OFFICE

What can you find at the post office?

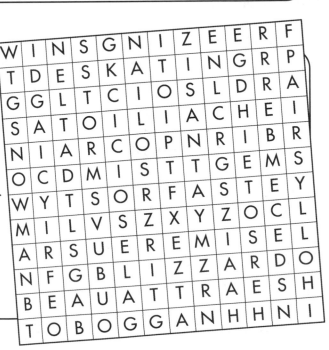

ADDRESS
CARDS
DELIVER
ENVELOPES
LETTERS

MAILBAG
MAILBOX
MESSAGE
NAMES
PACKAGE

PARCEL
STAMPS
TELEGRAMS

T	E	N	V	E	L	O	P	E	S	I	K
H	S	H	O	A	E	I	A	E	M	P	X
S	E	M	A	N	T	I	R	A	A	U	Q
A	F	M	G	H	T	I	C	A	R	D	S
D	E	L	I	V	E	R	E	D	G	S	S
W	A	R	F	L	R	B	L	B	E	T	G
S	P	M	A	T	S	E	J	R	L	E	A
T	L	O	P	I	R	N	D	E	E	D	B
H	J	E	N	B	R	D	N	N	T	O	L
O	M	E	S	S	A	G	E	B	L	E	I
R	E	G	A	K	C	A	P	I	N	K	A
F	I	F	E	V	X	O	B	L	I	A	M

66. WINTERTIME

Find the words linked to the winter season.

BLIZZARD
COLD
COZY
DECEMBER
FREEZING
FROSTY
GALES
HOLLY

ICY
RAIN
SANTA
SKATING
SKIING
SNOWMAN
STORMS
TOBOGGAN

W	I	N	S	G	N	I	Z	E	E	R	F
T	D	E	S	K	A	T	I	N	G	R	P
G	G	L	T	C	I	O	S	L	D	R	A
S	A	T	O	I	L	I	A	C	H	E	I
N	I	A	R	C	O	P	N	R	I	B	R
O	C	D	M	I	S	T	T	G	E	M	S
W	Y	T	S	O	R	F	A	S	T	E	Y
M	I	L	V	S	Z	X	Y	Z	O	C	L
A	R	S	U	E	R	E	M	I	S	E	L
N	F	G	B	L	I	Z	Z	A	R	D	O
B	E	A	U	A	T	T	R	A	E	S	H
T	O	B	O	G	G	A	N	H	H	N	I

67. CLOTHES CLUES

Find the clothes hidden in the grid.

BLOUSE
CAPE
COAT
GLOVES
HAT

JACKET
JEANS
MITTS
SCARF
SHIRT

SNEAKERS
SOCKS
TIE
TIGHTS

Grid 67:

F	A	S	H	I	M	E	S	U	O	L	B
S	O	H	W	I	G	I	R	E	A	T	C
C	O	A	T	T	W	T	R	I	H	S	E
A	M	T	E	A	F	R	O	E	O	R	D
R	S	S	K	J	E	P	A	C	Q	E	C
F	A	C	C	A	T	Y	K	L	U	N	G
T	G	L	A	N	D	S	N	Z	D	X	B
G	L	O	J	E	A	N	S	Z	C	A	J
S	O	L	V	E	T	E	E	P	U	R	H
Z	V	I	R	D	S	T	H	G	I	T	O
S	E	R	V	Y	K	L	E	W	M	N	P
T	S	S	N	E	A	K	E	R	S	E	I

Grid (left middle):

S	W	E	A	T	S	H	I	R	T	F	G
S	A	V	N	I	G	H	R	E	D	A	A
S	Q	U	O	R	S	U	M	E	B	R	L
R	A	C	R	S	S	H	J	K	T	E	O
E	A	R	A	W	E	A	N	I	P	F	S
P	B	S	K	I	R	T	N	L	O	G	H
P	L	A	U	A	D	E	I	E	C	A	E
I	A	S	H	S	H	O	P	U	T	I	S
L	C	T	R	O	X	S	E	R	S	R	O
S	H	O	E	S	O	E	R	U	I	O	N
K	T	O	W	I	N	D	R	R	A	W	S
I	A	B	L	A	Z	E	R	T	M	E	D

68. RUMMAGE SALE

How many items of clothing can you find in the puzzle?

ANORAK
BLAZER
BOOTS
CAP
DRESS
GALOSHES
HOOD

SHOES
SKIRT
SLIPPERS
SUIT
SWEATSHIRT

69. "G" WORDS

Find the words starting with the letter G.

GALAXY
GAMES
GERBIL
GIANTS
GIGGLE
GINGER

GIRAFFE
GOAT
GOSSIP
GREAT
GREEN
GRAY

GRILL
GYM

Grid 69:

E	M	P	O	C	G	R	E	E	N	G	R
L	L	I	R	G	V	E	N	S	Y	H	S
Y	E	N	J	G	A	F	U	M	P	K	C
O	B	S	E	E	Z	F	G	C	I	H	G
G	E	E	G	R	E	A	T	C	S	E	B
R	A	M	H	B	Y	R	O	A	S	D	D
A	Y	A	A	I	Y	I	T	T	O	G	G
G	I	G	G	L	E	G	I	N	G	E	R
S	O	A	V	E	A	D	X	B	E	R	A
G	I	A	N	T	S	G	A	L	A	X	Y
A	S	Q	T	I	P	A	C	E	J	C	A
A	R	V	H	G	E	H	A	W	E	H	R

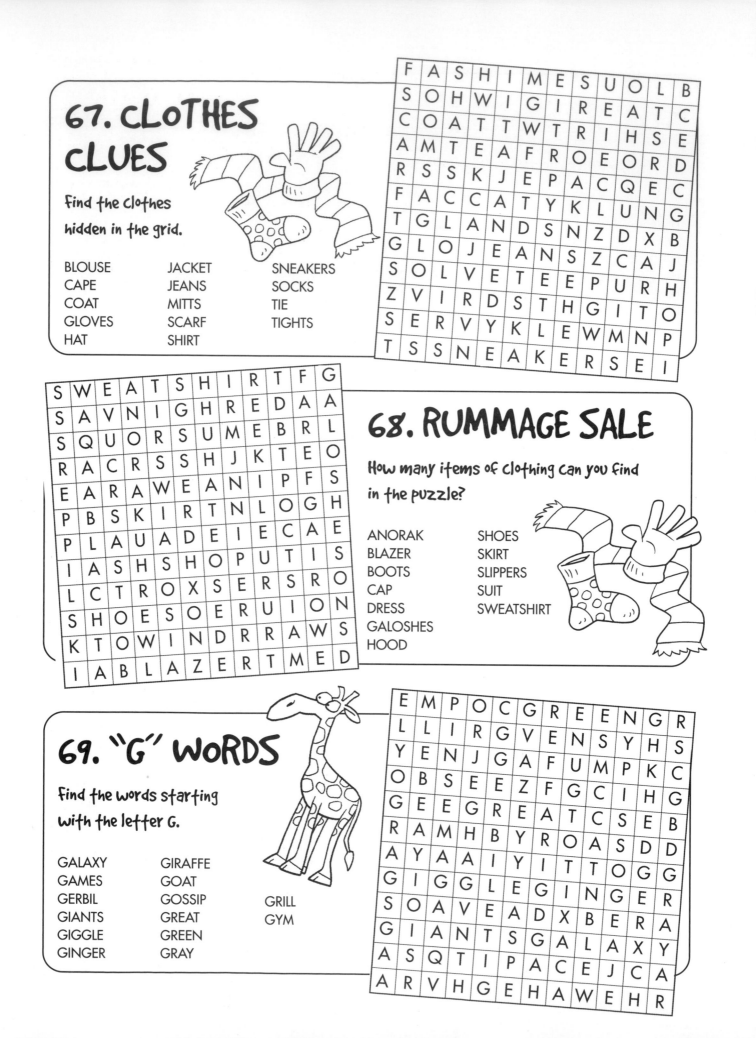

70. "H" WORDS

Find the words beginning with the letter H.

HAMBURGER
HAPPY
HARVEST
HAWK
HAZEL
HELLO

HIVE
HOBBY
HOLLY
HOMEWORK
HONEYCOMB
HORIZON

HOROSCOPE
HOUND
HURRICANE
HYENA

A	E	N	A	C	I	R	R	U	H	L	H
H	I	V	E	V	A	L	K	O	A	A	A
O	L	L	E	H	A	Z	R	E	W	N	R
R	T	H	M	A	E	D	O	S	K	E	V
O	N	H	T	Z	F	N	W	O	L	Y	E
S	D	O	S	E	P	U	E	S	L	H	S
C	C	R	U	L	E	O	M	L	P	R	T
O	R	I	G	A	M	H	O	B	B	Y	F
P	C	Z	T	O	T	H	H	O	P	P	I
E	B	O	T	I	G	S	R	I	K	P	N
H	O	N	E	Y	C	O	M	B	F	A	B
Z	I	R	E	G	R	U	B	M	A	H	E

71. SPY SEARCH

Find the spy words hidden in the grid.

ACTION
ADVENTURE
AGENT
CAMOUFLAGE
CIPHER

CODE
DISGUISE
EXCITEMENT
GADGETS
HIDDEN

MISSION
SECRET
SPYGLASS
SURVEILLANCE

S	U	R	V	E	I	L	L	A	N	C	E
P	S	S	T	E	G	D	A	G	A	O	R
Y	T	R	O	R	D	B	E	E	R	D	U
G	A	E	L	A	I	R	H	N	A	E	T
L	R	H	I	D	D	E	N	T	H	D	N
A	R	P	I	E	G	C	R	C	V	I	E
S	Y	I	S	H	O	J	N	I	A	S	V
S	E	C	R	E	T	R	O	V	E	G	D
S	R	G	M	I	S	S	I	O	N	U	A
P	U	Z	E	R	S	H	T	O	M	I	S
T	N	E	M	E	T	I	C	X	E	S	H
C	A	M	O	U	F	L	A	G	E	E	A

72. BIRDS

How many birds can you spot?

CRANE
EAGLE
GOOSE
JAY

KESTREL
KINGFISHER
KIWI
OSPREY

PEACOCK
PELICAN
SWAN
WADER

S	K	I	N	G	F	I	S	H	E	R	W
E	L	G	A	E	G	A	N	E	S	W	E
N	R	J	W	N	F	R	I	L	O	S	F
C	K	P	S	E	L	E	R	T	S	E	K
X	C	I	R	S	O	N	S	M	P	O	R
S	O	R	W	A	D	E	R	S	R	O	T
E	C	H	Q	I	H	E	I	V	E	V	A
E	A	Y	Z	E	P	E	J	A	Y	S	A
T	E	F	E	S	I	N	M	O	M	N	R
V	P	E	L	I	C	A	N	W	E	C	C
B	C	R	O	O	B	R	D	B	T	D	H
E	H	E	R	S	H	C	E	S	O	O	G

73. COLORFUL

There are lots of colors and shades for you to find.

AZURE
BLACK
BLUE
GREEN
GRAY
LILAC
MAROON
ORANGE
PINK
PURPLE
SCARLET
RED
VIOLET
WHITE
YELLOW

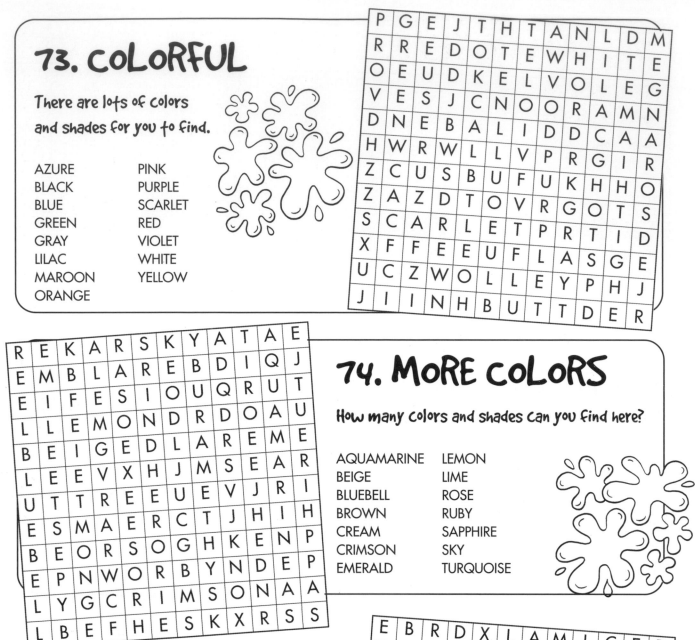

P	G	E	J	T	H	T	A	N	L	D	M
R	R	E	D	O	T	E	W	H	I	T	E
O	E	U	D	K	E	L	V	O	L	E	G
V	E	S	J	C	N	O	O	R	A	M	N
D	N	E	B	A	L	I	D	D	C	A	A
H	W	R	W	L	L	V	P	R	G	I	R
Z	C	U	S	B	U	F	U	K	H	H	O
Z	A	Z	D	T	O	V	R	G	O	T	S
S	C	A	R	L	E	T	P	R	T	I	D
X	F	F	E	E	U	F	L	A	S	G	E
U	C	Z	W	O	L	L	E	Y	P	H	J
J	I	I	N	H	B	U	T	T	D	E	R

74. MORE COLORS

How many colors and shades can you find here?

AQUAMARINE
BEIGE
BLUEBELL
BROWN
CREAM
CRIMSON
EMERALD
LEMON
LIME
ROSE
RUBY
SAPPHIRE
SKY
TURQUOISE

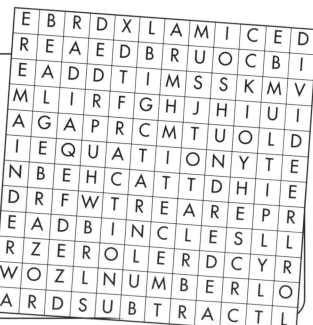

R	E	K	A	R	S	K	Y	A	T	A	E
E	M	B	L	A	R	E	B	D	I	Q	J
E	I	F	E	S	I	O	U	Q	R	U	T
L	L	E	M	O	N	D	R	D	O	A	U
B	E	I	G	E	D	L	A	R	E	M	E
L	E	E	V	X	H	J	M	S	E	A	R
U	T	T	R	E	E	U	E	V	J	R	I
E	S	M	A	E	R	C	T	J	H	I	H
B	E	O	R	S	O	G	H	K	E	N	P
E	P	N	W	O	R	B	Y	N	D	E	P
L	Y	G	C	R	I	M	S	O	N	A	A
L	B	E	F	H	E	S	K	X	R	S	S

75. MAD MATH

Find the math words in the puzzle.

ADD
ALGEBRA
DECIMAL
DIVIDE
EQUATION
FRACTION
HUNDRED
MULTIPLY
NUMBER
ONE
REMAINDER
SUBTRACT
SUM
TOTAL
ZERO

E	B	R	D	X	L	A	M	I	C	E	D
R	E	A	E	D	B	R	U	O	C	B	I
E	A	D	D	T	I	M	S	S	K	M	V
M	L	I	R	F	G	H	J	H	I	U	I
A	G	A	P	R	C	M	T	U	O	L	D
I	E	Q	U	A	T	I	O	N	Y	T	E
N	B	E	H	C	A	T	T	D	H	I	E
D	R	F	W	T	R	E	A	R	E	P	R
E	A	D	B	I	N	C	L	E	S	L	L
R	Z	E	R	O	L	E	R	D	C	Y	R
W	O	Z	L	N	U	M	B	E	R	L	O
A	R	D	S	U	B	T	R	A	C	T	L

76. NATURE TRAIL

follow the nature trail and see what you can find.

BEES
CATS
COUNTRY
FLOWERS
GLADE
GRASS
HEDGE
HONEY
MOSS
POND
ROBIN
SEA
SUNSHINE
TREES
WASP
WATERFALL
WEATHER
WOOD

Grid 76:

S	H	O	P	P	H	D	E	S	T	A	C
I	E	G	S	U	R	K	L	S	A	M	O
R	D	A	M	Y	G	U	L	O	W	R	U
U	W	O	O	D	R	D	A	M	D	M	N
B	E	C	S	E	A	Z	F	I	N	F	T
E	A	T	E	S	S	H	R	T	O	E	R
Y	T	R	E	E	S	S	E	O	P	D	Y
E	H	Z	G	R	R	A	T	W	B	E	R
N	E	O	D	X	B	F	A	L	M	I	A
O	R	O	G	S	R	E	W	O	L	F	N
H	E	D	G	E	X	F	E	D	A	L	G
G	E	N	I	H	S	N	U	S	O	N	E

77. "S" WORDS

These words start with the letter S.

SATELLITE
SATURDAY
SCHOOL
SCIENCE
SECRET
SHARK
SKELETON
SORCERER
SPACE
SPIDER
SPY
STAR
SUGAR
SUN

Grid 77:

S	A	T	E	L	L	I	T	E	V	A	R
J	O	M	Y	A	D	R	U	T	A	S	O
S	S	R	H	C	H	S	H	A	R	K	A
S	P	I	D	E	R	S	E	C	R	E	T
I	A	H	T	H	M	S	T	R	S	L	T
S	C	I	E	N	C	E	F	A	V	E	C
R	E	V	L	H	S	B	T	T	A	T	A
O	B	N	O	T	A	U	A	S	V	O	S
A	R	O	W	I	R	E	N	Z	A	N	U
S	L	D	C	D	B	A	T	S	Z	I	G
M	P	N	A	F	E	J	A	C	K	I	A
A	F	Y	G	S	O	R	C	E	R	E	R

78. "T" WORDS

These words start with the letter T.

TABBY
TARTAN
TEA
TEDDY
THISTLE
THREE
THUNDER
TIDDLYWINKS
TIGER
TORNADO
TOYS
TREASURE
TRICK
TROLL
TROPICS
TWILIGHT
TWINKLE

Grid 78:

E	T	I	S	T	H	T	A	R	T	A	N
T	I	D	D	L	Y	W	I	N	K	S	E
O	G	B	E	T	S	I	T	P	U	X	R
R	E	E	T	R	O	L	L	N	E	X	U
N	R	A	H	I	J	I	D	E	I	Z	S
A	E	T	U	C	O	G	R	M	R	L	A
D	Z	W	N	K	T	H	I	S	T	L	E
O	E	I	D	H	T	T	Y	W	F	E	R
S	N	N	E	G	G	D	I	B	Y	O	T
Y	A	K	R	L	D	V	M	P	B	F	T
O	I	L	A	E	S	O	W	O	O	A	F
T	D	E	T	K	S	C	I	P	O	R	T

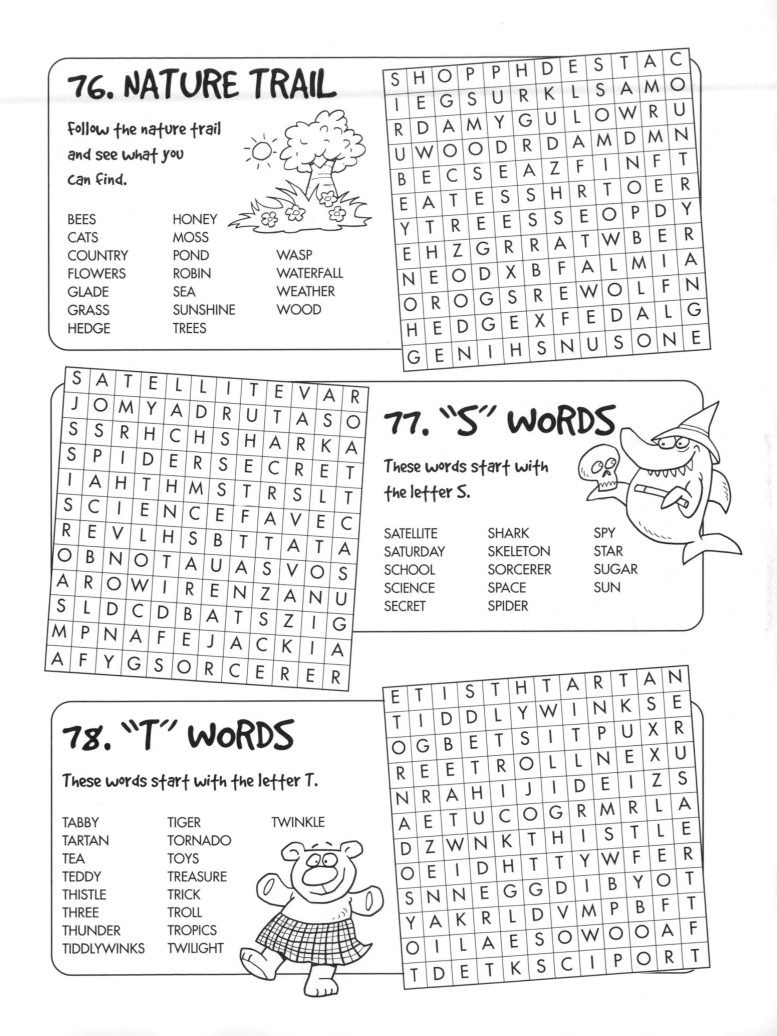

79. SPRING

The words here are to do with spring.

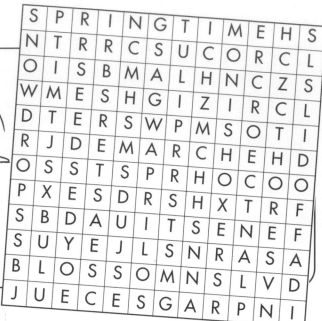

APRIL
BLOSSOM
BUDS
CROCUS
DAFFODILS

EASTER
LAMBS
MARCH
NEST
PLANT

SEEDS
SNOWDROPS
SPRINGTIME
TULIP

S		S	P	R	I	N	G	T	I	M	E	H	S
N	T	R	R	C	S	U	C	O	R	C	L		
O	I	S	B	M	A	L	H	N	C	Z	S		
W	M	E	S	H	G	I	Z	I	R	C	L		
D	T	E	R	S	W	P	M	S	O	T	I		
R	J	D	E	M	A	R	C	H	E	H	D		
O	S	S	T	S	P	R	H	O	C	O	O		
P	X	E	S	D	R	S	H	X	T	R	F		
S	B	D	A	U	I	T	S	E	N	E	F		
S	U	Y	E	J	L	S	N	R	A	S	A		
B	L	O	S	S	O	M	N	S	L	V	D		
J	U	E	C	E	S	G	A	R	P	N	I		

R	E	M	R	A	F	B	A	R	L	E	Y
E	L	F	W	I	A	F	P	E	G	A	Z
B	M	A	R	L	F	H	P	A	H	C	A
M	N	S	E	I	O	G	L	J	E	H	R
E	G	S	L	L	G	L	E	A	V	E	S
T	N	R	D	E	G	C	S	F	F	S	T
P	I	E	A	P	Y	R	N	T	R	T	S
E	W	B	U	O	O	Z	A	A	E	N	E
S	O	O	T	A	E	H	W	C	S	U	V
A	L	T	U	P	R	V	E	S	A	T	R
R	P	C	M	S	M	N	C	T	V	S	A
T	W	O	N	E	E	W	O	L	L	A	H

80. FALL

These words are linked to fall.

APPLES
AUTUMN
BALES
BARLEY
CHESTNUTS
FOGGY
HALLOWEEN

HARVEST
HAY
LEAVES
OCTOBER
PLOWING
SEPTEMBER
WHEAT

81. BIRDS

How many birds can you spot?

ALBATROSS
BUZZARD
CORMORANT
EMU

FALCON
GOLDFINCH
HERON
OSTRICH

PENGUIN
PETREL
SWIFT
WOODCOCK

A	D	R	A	Z	Z	U	B	L	U	E	T
P	P	P	G	O	L	D	F	I	N	C	H
C	L	E	M	K	C	R	A	S	I	N	M
O	S	T	R	I	C	H	L	I	U	A	S
R	E	R	O	N	P	O	C	R	K	Q	S
M	S	E	E	H	E	R	O	N	C	U	O
O	A	L	Y	M	N	W	N	G	O	I	R
R	R	O	U	K	G	O	I	F	C	P	T
A	G	L	W	O	U	W	I	G	D	P	A
N	R	D	O	R	I	F	O	R	O	Z	B
T	F	I	W	S	N	W	O	N	O	I	L
E	A	T	E	R	E	F	R	I	W	X	A

82. JEWELRY STORE

See what you can find hidden in the jeweler's store.

AQUAMARINE
BANGLES
BRACELET
BROOCH
CHAINS
CRYSTAL
GARNET
GOLD
NECKLACES
PIN
PLATINUM
RINGS
SILVER
TIARA
WATCHES

```
D I A M T N A D N E P O
W D S T E N R A G O L D
A W O R K A R T E N A D
T E L E C A R B N E T S
C T B R O O C H I V I A
H O L I G T I A R A N R
E M I N I D R E A T U C
S E L G N A B S M D M H
C R Y S T A L D A H N A
H P R E S E Z E U E S I
A S I L V E R D Q Q X N
I N S N E C K L A C E S
```

83. AMUSEMENT PARK

Find the funfair words.

AMUSEMENTS
ARCADE
BURGERS
CAROUSEL
COCONUTS
DODGEMS
FAIRGROUND
FUNHOUSE
MIRRORS
MUSIC
POPCORN
PRIZES
STALLS
SWINGS

```
D O D G E M S H O W W A
N K I T L E S U O R A C
U D B U R G E R S L L T
O F C A T S A D I T T I
R U T W I W R T A T X D
G N S E Z I R P S C E V
R H L G R N W O T I R E
I O L G H G E P D S E A
A U A M U S I C B U S X
F S T U N O C O C M O S
G E S T Z M I R R O R S
A M U S E M E N T S J G
```

84. ICE CREAM

Find the hidden ice cream words, flavors, and toppings.

BANANA
CARAMEL
CHOCOLATE
CONE
FUDGE
MINT
NUTS
PARFAIT
POPSICLE
RASPBERRY
STRAWBERRY
SUNDAE
SYRUP
TOPPING
WAFER
VANILLA

```
N R T O P P I N G C E D
P U R N A A N A N A B W
O G T Z I N T L J R R S
P I N S T M S L A A X T
S Y R U P I U I C M G R
I T H N B M T N K E E A
C F U D G E I A S L E W
L I M A E L A V T R N B
E M I E W A F E R L O E
P O R H E S R C T O C R
C H O C O L A T E M N R
S G F R A S P B E R R Y
```

85. XYZ WORDS

These words start with the letters X, Y, and Z.

XENON
XMAS
YACHT
YELLOW
YOYO
YULETIDE

YUMMY
ZEBRA
ZERO
ZILLION
ZIP
ZIRCON

ZODIAC
ZOMBIE
ZONE
ZOO

Y	A	C	H	T	Z	O	D	I	A	C	L
U	A	B	Z	O	I	S	Z	Y	R	K	E
L	C	H	O	R	P	G	L	O	B	A	H
E	D	X	M	A	S	Y	W	W	E	E	H
T	C	R	B	P	G	E	N	O	Z	S	S
I	H	O	I	X	S	L	I	P	T	D	N
D	J	K	E	A	E	L	B	I	H	F	O
E	I	N	P	I	Y	O	Y	O	C	K	C
S	O	A	P	S	U	W	M	D	R	B	R
N	O	I	L	L	I	Z	M	E	D	E	I
T	S	E	T	E	R	R	U	A	N	E	Z
E	N	O	H	P	O	L	Y	X	A	N	R

86. SHIPS

Find the ships and boats hidden in the puzzle.

CANAL BOAT
CANOE
DINGHY
FERRY
GALLEON

JUNK
KETCH
SCHOONER
SHIP
SLOOP

TANKER
TRAWLER
TUG
YACHT

T	R	E	K	N	A	T	A	L	L	A	C
F	E	R	R	Y	Z	U	U	Y	I	T	A
A	S	H	I	P	I	S	A	G	R	C	N
T	C	R	H	D	E	O	N	A	C	A	A
E	H	D	H	J	C	T	W	L	R	R	L
S	O	H	X	T	D	L	E	L	P	B	B
E	O	D	E	D	E	A	V	E	K	C	O
I	N	I	J	R	H	P	O	O	L	S	A
M	E	N	A	U	Y	E	G	N	C	N	T
W	R	G	D	T	N	O	O	T	N	O	B
G	R	H	C	T	E	K	E	T	I	R	Y
A	B	Y	A	C	H	T	W	H	I	Z	E

87. WHAT'S IN THE BEDROOM?

Look for the words linked to the bedroom.

BED
CLOCK
CLOSET
DESK
DRESSER
GAMES
LAMP

LIGHT
MATTRESS
PICTURES
PILLOW
QUILT
SHEETS
TOYS

E	S	E	M	A	G	R	S	N	X	R	R
C	H	U	I	R	P	P	A	R	Y	E	E
D	E	M	I	T	L	I	U	Q	J	S	A
B	E	D	A	R	I	L	Y	W	E	S	H
S	T	I	R	H	G	L	A	L	O	E	S
N	S	B	E	N	H	O	J	M	K	R	E
J	U	P	I	R	T	W	L	N	P	D	R
M	A	T	T	R	E	S	S	M	E	O	U
R	U	R	O	U	I	X	J	S	A	T	T
S	R	V	J	Y	L	E	K	C	O	L	C
I	M	A	R	R	S	Z	O	L	R	J	I
C	L	O	S	E	T	B	E	H	G	A	P

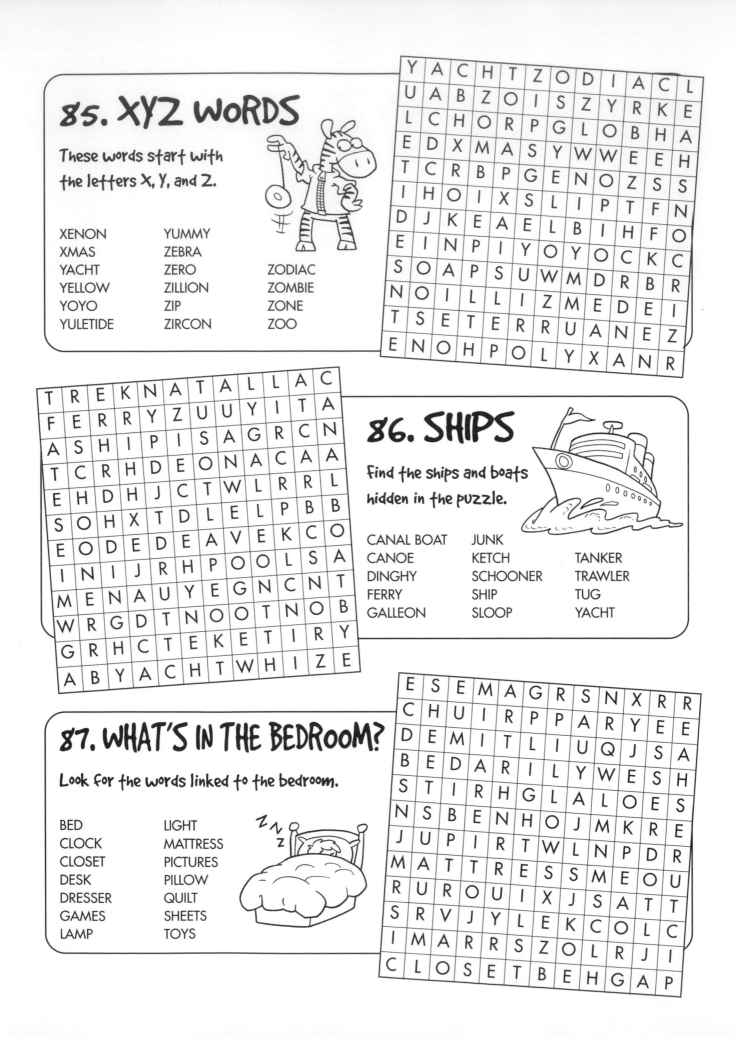

88. MONTHS OF THE YEAR

Find the twelve months of the year.

APRIL
AUGUST
DECEMBER
FEBRUARY
JANUARY
JULY

JUNE
MARCH
MAY
NOVEMBER
OCTOBER
SEPTEMBER

```
B L E R E Y E T H E A R
A D E C E M B E R S Y J
R T H K O M V S E G Y M
M A R G G A B Z B A R S
A P R I L D D O M I A E
R U R O C T O B E R U P
C R G A J V X Z V R R T
H T H U R D A U O Y B E
V N M W S A J U N E E M
S H I P R T U I I G F B
G R E X I S L T H S P E
J A N U A R Y H C B G R
```

89. NUMBERS

There are lots of numbers to discover.

EIGHT
ELEVEN
FIVE
FOUR
MILLION
NINE

ONE
SEVEN
SIX
TEN
THIRTEEN
THOUSAND

THREE
TWELVE
TWENTY
TWO

```
P L E Y M I L L I O N T
R A E L E V E N E V E V
B K E S W J E R U O F S
E V L E W T E X T I I C
T E Q U D K T N W I V N
S E R T E V H N E V E S
E I G H T Z I M N D U J
N X X R R N R C T I B N
A T R E E R T I Y I K M
D W L E W R E S H K P D
H O N E E G E S H R J B
T H O U S A N D A R I G
```

90. IN THE BACKYARD

These things are found in the backyard.

BIRDS
BUGS
FLOWERS
GRASS
HERBS
INSECTS
LAWN
LEAVES

POND
SHED
SLUGS
SNAILS
STONES
TREES
WEEDS

```
C H H I I G R E A L R C
A O E S S R E W O L F S
P R R R G A C V U A A N
R N B U G S U N D W I V
D C S I G S P V E N I M
B S F I R G S E D B N S
S J P O N D D I D O S Q
L V I Z E S S T O N E S
I Z N H O U S R P C C O
A A S M P N S E A I T R
N E S S E V A E L T S D
S G U L S E E S R Y R Z
```

91. 4TH JULY

These things are all to do with Independence Day.

BAND
DAZZLE
DISPLAY
FOURTH

FIREWORKS
FLAG
GLITTER
JULY

PARADE
ROCKET
WHIZZ

R	Y	A	L	P	S	I	D	T	O	R	F
A	E	U	Q	P	H	K	R	J	R	D	I
H	R	R	G	A	N	P	O	W	D	E	R
N	B	O	N	R	I	R	E	Q	A	I	E
S	A	C	A	A	H	E	S	J	Z	G	W
P	N	K	I	D	W	H	I	Z	Z	M	O
A	D	E	V	E	S	E	M	A	L	F	R
R	Z	T	N	O	V	E	M	J	E	R	K
G	H	H	A	V	E	N	M	W	U	D	S
A	J	P	G	L	I	T	T	E	R	L	R
L	F	T	H	G	I	N	E	W	E	D	Y
F	V	H	T	R	U	O	F	J	K	R	E

---

92. CATS

Find the cats in the puzzle.

CHEETAH
COUGAR
JAGUAR
~~LEOPARD~~
~~LION~~

LYNX
OCELOT
PANTHER
PUMA
SABERTOOTH

TABBY
TIGER
WILDCAT

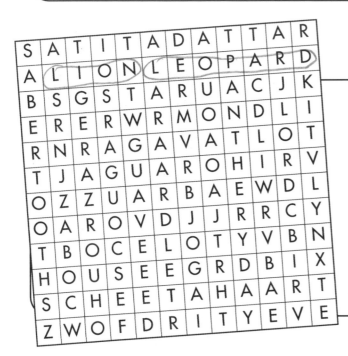

S	A	T	I	T	A	D	A	T	T	A	R
A	L	I	O	N	L	E	O	P	A	R	D
B	S	G	S	T	A	R	U	A	C	J	K
E	R	E	R	W	R	M	O	N	D	L	I
R	N	R	A	G	A	V	A	T	L	O	T
T	J	A	G	U	A	R	O	H	I	R	V
O	Z	Z	U	A	R	B	A	E	W	D	L
O	A	R	O	V	D	J	J	R	R	C	Y
T	B	O	C	E	L	O	T	Y	V	B	N
H	O	U	S	E	E	G	R	D	B	I	X
S	C	H	E	E	T	A	H	A	A	R	T
Z	W	O	F	D	R	I	T	Y	E	V	E

---

93. SHOWTIME

Find the words that are linked to theater shows.

ACTOR
AUDIENCE
BALCONY
CHORUS
DANCERS

ENTERTAIN
FOYER
LIGHTS
MUSIC
SEATS

SHOW
STAGE
TICKETS

T	E	N	T	E	R	T	A	I	N	W	R
R	R	O	F	F	B	A	T	C	O	W	G
D	A	Z	Z	O	A	E	Q	H	A	I	D
B	I	C	X	Y	L	P	S	O	E	S	A
N	I	P	L	E	C	R	I	R	C	C	N
T	S	T	E	R	O	I	N	U	N	I	C
I	A	S	F	T	N	H	G	S	E	S	E
C	R	E	C	G	Y	T	E	Y	I	U	R
K	I	A	C	R	A	N	R	D	D	M	S
E	S	T	A	G	E	H	S	S	U	A	R
T	R	S	F	J	A	C	P	L	A	Y	A
S	T	H	G	I	L	R	E	C	S	N	M

94. VOLCANO

Find the volcanic words.

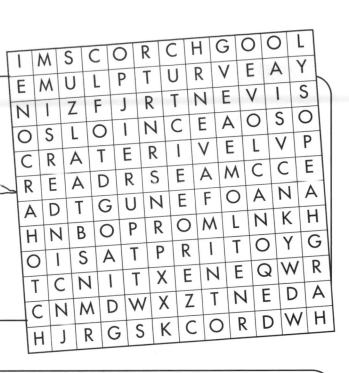

CINDER
CONE
CRATER
ERUPT
EXTINCT

FIRE
FLOW
HOT
LAVA
MOLTEN

PLUME
ROCKS
SCORCH
VENT
VOLCANO

I	M	S	C	O	R	C	H	G	O	O	L
E	M	U	L	P	T	U	R	V	E	A	Y
N	I	Z	F	J	R	T	N	E	V	I	S
O	S	L	O	I	N	C	E	A	O	S	O
C	R	A	T	E	R	I	V	E	L	V	P
R	E	A	D	R	S	E	A	M	C	C	E
A	D	T	G	U	N	E	F	O	A	N	A
H	N	B	O	P	R	O	M	L	N	K	H
O	I	S	A	T	P	R	I	T	O	Y	G
T	C	N	I	T	X	E	N	E	Q	W	R
C	N	M	D	W	X	Z	T	N	E	D	A
H	J	R	G	S	K	C	O	R	D	W	H

95. MUDDLE MIX-UP

All these words are muddled, befuddled, and crazy!

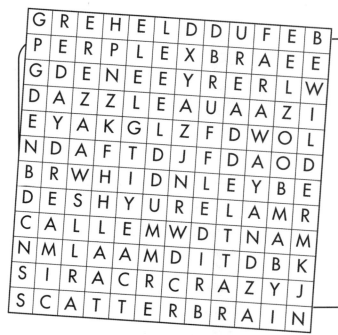

G	R	E	H	E	L	D	D	U	F	E	B
P	E	R	P	L	E	X	B	R	A	E	E
G	D	E	N	E	E	Y	R	E	R	L	W
D	A	Z	Z	L	E	A	U	A	A	Z	I
E	Y	A	K	G	L	Z	F	D	W	O	L
N	D	A	F	T	D	J	F	D	A	O	D
B	R	W	H	I	D	N	L	E	Y	B	E
D	E	S	H	Y	U	R	E	L	A	M	R
C	A	L	L	E	M	W	D	T	N	A	M
N	M	L	A	A	M	D	I	T	D	B	K
S	I	R	A	C	R	C	R	A	Z	Y	J
S	C	A	T	T	E	R	B	R	A	I	N

BAMBOOZLE
BEFUDDLE
BEWILDER
CRAZY
DAFT
DAYDREAM
DAZE

DAZZLE
MUDDLE
PERPLEX
RATTLED
RUFFLED
SCATTERBRAIN
SILLY

96. REALLY BIG!

All the words here are really big.

ASTRONOMIC
BIG
BURLY
GIANT
GIGANTIC
GRAND
ENORMOUS
HERCULEAN
JUMBO
LARGE

MAMMOTH
MONSTER
VAST

H	E	R	C	U	L	E	A	N	A	N	R
Z	G	I	G	A	N	T	I	C	A	T	Y
H	R	Z	I	H	V	M	A	V	J	E	S
E	A	A	R	G	A	T	J	U	M	B	O
E	N	B	I	G	S	R	C	N	A	U	D
S	D	B	D	I	T	O	R	J	M	R	Q
R	A	M	S	A	J	V	R	G	M	L	U
I	G	M	O	N	S	T	E	R	O	Y	L
W	R	H	J	T	I	M	W	O	T	U	A
I	E	N	O	R	M	O	U	S	H	E	R
D	H	D	E	N	J	U	E	Q	U	X	G
A	S	T	R	O	N	O	M	I	C	L	E

97. GAMES

Find the game words.

- BACKGAMMON
- BATTLESHIPS
- BOGGLE
- CHECKERS
- CHESS
- CLUE
- DOMINOES
- LUDO
- MONOPOLY
- TIDDLYWINKS

```
B A C K G A M M O N S T
A A R V A L O R J S I I
T R A E E L N O R Z C D
T R I X I A O V B R L D
L C R E S B P I O D U L
E A R H G L O V G I E Y
S B E P C V L S G P D W
H F B H A R Y Y L A O I
I S E S R E K C E H C N
P S T R O N S H E H G K
S X N I M R E T S A M S
G D O M I N O E S T D G
```

98. THE ENTERTAINERS

These people entertain us.

- ACROBAT
- ACTOR
- ARTIST
- BUSKER
- CARTOONIST
- CLOWN
- DANCER
- DAREDEVIL
- ILLUSIONIST
- JUGGLER
- SINGER
- STORYTELLER

```
T S I N O I S U L L I P
R C Z R O T C A Z O O I
E A L S I A R T I S T E
L R S O D A C R O B A T
L T Q U W I D G N E R D
E O E R Y N C J A R E C
T O R J A N N V C M K N
Y N E R R E G N I S S C
R I C O R R E L G G U J
O S N L L S B M A S B N
T T A S I D B G M I R C
S I D A R E D E V I L N
```

99. YOUNG CREATURES

Can you find the young animals?

- BUNNY
- CALF
- CHICK
- DUCKLING
- FAWN
- FLEDGLING
- FOAL
- JOEY
- KITTEN
- LAMB
- OWLET
- PIGLET
- PUP

```
D I Y E O J L H C B A R
P E C E C N J I Z Z D D
M B K C I H C O R E U C
N C N M U P K R P C C G
S A W R E B W U A S K N
E L R S H J P S B R L I
D F A W N S I S M T I L
T O N L R S G E A I N G
B U N N Y F L R L F G D
J I X F H F E D I A S E
N E Y J D R T E L W O L
N E T T I K A R V J Z F
```

100. DOUBLE "G"

Find the words with a double letter G.

BAGGAGE | GIGGLE
CRAGGY | GOGGLES | RAGGED
DOGGY | JOGGER | RUGGED
EGGS | LUGGAGE | SWAGGER
FOGGY | NUGGET | WIGGLE

Word search grid (Double G):

F D E G G U R A E R O N
O R H V X B A G G A G E
G I J R C S G M G E M N
G L O W D A G R S E K T
Y G G A R C E R I G W Y
R S G J I X D B L A I F
E E E S T O O T O G G V
G D R A G Z O E V G G Y
G E R G R A T G A U L M
A Y Y R A G I G G L E A
W E G J Y H X U A H C R
S E L G G O G N H E N T

101. FURRY CREATURES AND HAIRY MONSTERS

Word search grid (Furry Creatures):

T I M W O L F H O U N D
B R B O R I I G A M E S
T C M E C A P O O D L E
D H C B A T R R N J K P
P T P Z T R Y I H C D E
B E A V E R G L L S X E
U S N A S U R L A W L H
F E D L L S S A R T I S
F H A C H G X D E H B C
A E R V K O R D E L R D
L S F X F L O W E R E W
O S A H U S K Y E S G R

BEAR | GERBIL | POODLE
BEAVER | GORILLA | SHEEP
BUFFALO | HUSKY | WALRUS
CAT | LION | WEREWOLF
FOX | PANDA | WOLFHOUND

ANSWERS

1. FISHY TAILS

```
T P Y E H C Z S Q U I D
H R O A B A L O E H T L
H A D D O C K L W F F M
V W G N I R R E H C A L
S N R L O T O M Z C L E
E S A L M O N E L V X R
S M M O V J O S K A T E
M O T B E O B L S E I K
A D A S C A M P I N S C
L R G T U R B O T S T A
C S L E S S U M E I N M
F T S R E T S Y O R B D
```

2. DESSERT DELIGHT

```
C H E E S E C A K E J A
U N L S O T N G H P K C
S E M O L I N A G I I J
T A O B F T G H O R O O
A C U A E T A G I K F S
R S S C W C T S F L A N
D U S X O Z P O L A O L
E N E I E C E R E E G O
D D P C P K E B A V E L
Z A P P Y P I E W L P L
T E E A G E J T V M N E
F R M E R I N G U E W J
```

3. SUPERSTARS

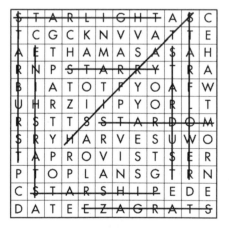

```
S T A R L I G H T A S C
T C G C K N V V A T T E
A E T H A M A S A S A H
R N P S T A R R Y T R A
B I A T O T F Y O A F W
U H R Z I I P Y O R L T
R S T T S S T A R D O M
S R Y H A R V E S U W O
T A P R O V I S T S E R
P T O P L A N S G T T N
C S T A R S H I P E D E
D A T E E Z A G R A T S
```

4. SPACE MISSION

```
A I A M P O T C O M E T
S U N A U R T I N O M E
A P E R O C K E T O D L
T I S S R P U C K N E E
S T A R B L A U T G H S
R E T B I A S O M S O C
G R U M T N H U S B N O
A B R K E E N M A R V P
L U N E P T U N E R E E
A U R O R A S E V Y N M
X S A T U S U N A R U E
Y T U R U N I V E R S E
```

5. MAGIC WORDSEARCH

```
P K H S L L E P S H A R
H C A U L D R O N R V Y
S I L W I S H T P P A Z
I R L O N E C C A M P
N T O A V B R O O M O U
A Z W S C E Y N Z T E M
V U E W W A R L O C K P
C R E T I N C L O A K
W E N S T W Z O O P A
A B R A C A D A B R A N
N A R C H A R M B C L
D I S A P P E A R D D E
```

6. SCHOOL IS COOL!

```
O X C C U H T A M A R W
L C A L C U L A T O R I
D O E A R A O S S R E B
E M M S A C C S V A H H
K P A S K S E D R C A C
R U S K O O B M N E A C
O T L N A S B N A E K
W E A S U E L B D T B
E R C H U N D Y P O O
M A N C T R A R T N O A
O L E Y U I R A T G I R
H C P L A Y G R O U N D
```

9. TREASURE CHEST

```
D A Z Z A M E T H Y S T
R R Z A E K E G A N D U
U D I A M O N D S T O R
B R R P E L O N S N I Q
Y W C K R E B M A A O U
B C O C A S C O P D P O
A H N Z G T L P N A U
N L O G D J N C H E Z S
G A V V S H E I P A E
I R T E L E C A R B A T
E O A J M I N T E D A J
E C A L K C E N A C G O
```

11. COLOR CRAZY

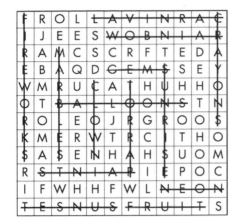

```
F R O L L A V I N R A C
I J E E S W O B N I A R
R A M C S C R F T E D A
E B A Q D G E M S S E Y
W M R U C A T H U H H O
O T B A L L O O N S T N
R O L E O J R G R O O S
K M E R W T R C I T H O
S A S E N H A H S U O M
R S T N I A P I E P O C
I F W H H F W L N E O N
T E S N U S F R U I T S
```

7. WHAT'S THE BUZZ?

```
R U Z I W O E L B R A W
B U Z Z E O F F R E D O
E T R G I K C A U Q A O
L C J R A A C R L T A F
L A I E E M O O W F E V
O C P W L S K S Q F L E
W K R A D A W G R U N T
P L A P E S U N G H B
Z E T U S N A R L E B R
Q U Q I P Y T O W A J O
A S N I F F T O O H O N
C H I R P F Y Q H I S S
```

10. FAB FRUIT

```
C R O O R A N G E Y E S
H A B A N A N A A T L T
E S N O O R Y P N Q P R
R E J O V A R B W Q P A
R S T P L U M O T T A W
Y R R E B E S O O G E B
S H R A N O M E L D N E
C A G R A P E S O F I R
I W I K I R I W I R P R
F A T R A S P B E R R Y
T O C I R P A A R H A Y
D P E A C H S E T A D O
```

12. CANDY STORE

```
C A N D Y B R L Y T L S
A E T T E B R E H S O U
R I U Q C E K I T S L I
A S G U M D R O P S L C
M X R T I A R T W O O
E F T F N S E H N C P R
L G O S T H C C S S O I
S V F I S M M S S V P C
I X F R S N B B W O S E
E J E G D U F O S E Z E
G U E E T A L O C O N C
M A R S H M A L L O W C
```

8. HAUNTED HOUSE

```
G A R G O Y L E S P I E
H A P P A M S P O O K S
S O N E Y L I H P T O N
P S E R I P M A V S S M
E A Y R N T W N O S C O
C A L G H O S T S S A N
T I H L Q W O E E R S
E C K O R O E M E I V T
C E U O Q A S H B E E
S K M L W U L L K M C R
F T U S K E L E T O N S
F L O W E R E W A Z H P
```

13. FLOWER GARDEN

```
M A R I G O L D B O R O
D C A L B A E D L R O J
V B U T T E R C U P S K
A R V T H A S T E T E S
E O Q D S T W E B I V U
P O C A L I L V E M T C
T G W A R R E L B S O
E F Y S N A P U L E E R
E R P Y G O O O E I C C
W O P Z O I N M A V L E
S N O W D R O P M I L Y
T M P K C O H Y L L O H
```

14. TREEHOUSE

T	R	H	C	R	I	B	I	S	C	K	S

Grid:
```
T R H C R I B I S C K S
E E C H E S T N U T A T
H U H W C D C A P U R S
B O E T G P A L M K T E
I S R S R A T R W M E R
U E R R A L P O P O O O
N B Y L U H I W I H K M
L E Q U K R S A S T E A
A F I Z A A E N H M I C
W I L L O W C R H U I Y
A R L A R O Z O O L A S
A P P L E B R A E P I E
```

15. SEASHORE SEARCH

```
O S E L T S A C D N A S
S T S W I U G A V E E
C A H U C R D A V D W A
W R E R W A V E S R S W
O F S F C R E P S U P E
T I R O C K P O O L P E
V S H O L I D O S C I D
I H I S H D T A O B S X
K F P S L K S K Y A I U
O S W I M M E R S R E T
S H E L L S F I V C S P
M A J H S I F Y L L E J
```

16. WILD WEATHER

```
H U R R I C A N E R R I
A C Y C L O N E R D T R
I S O W O R D C A S S E
L T R O R I B C V E E
S N O W L Y B M N W R Z
T O R N A D O B C E E
O S D E J N U H O T D N
R D B R O H A P E N G
M B C V F W P Z I O U Z
M Y D U O L C Y W I H S
I C A C G L F R O S T S
L I G H T N I N G O G G
```

17. FUNNY WORDS

```
S N I G G E R H G A G C
W A V E R C C A Y K I T
E W K A L A J O K E S E
L A U G H T E P T U U M
T I W I V B S Z L W O H
R C W G B O T Q M K R Y
A L Y G I C A R T O O N
H E N L J X D O Y R M U
C O M E D Y J J J E A U P
A V L O Z Y N N U F H M
B R I D A Y L R O R F N
Y S U O I R A L I H J O
```

18. ANIMALS

```
S T S C C G H E O O P V
T A H D O G S Y T T L A
I R E I W R A E S R O H
B V E T H D E K O P C A
E B P I G I R N U I N M
A V C A M O T O A R V S
R R E A X S T D F C A T
E Y S N E K C I H C S E
S S K C U D H S R O U R
O Z E H F S B M A L A M
M I C E I L A T T E Y P
P R O G G O A T S N Q M
```

19. TOYS!

```
O T A O B O O C K I B E
O R R I K N B F E E B T
R A T T L E H O U Z I T
Q U V S N O Y A R C M
S N O W B R I O X X Y O
R I A D O L L Y M K C O
S O W O N L H O P C L N
K H E I M A U W A A E B
A I O T A B S B I L B O
T M C G B A I T N T H N
E B O A P R V E T I K N
S E M A G A Z Y S K N E
```

20. GROCERY STORE

```
I T W B I S C U I T S S
E F F O C H T K L I M
E A V I E R S W S E R A
N C G H A E U S U G A R
M S T R P P M Z I G T M
S A E E M P S Y U S I A
C D L C H E E S E X O L
S C R D H P G C A S L A
O E M A R G A R I N E D
U C R E T T U B T A G E
P Z E R G W H J L E O O
T A V B H N O C A B B A
```

21. VEGETABLE PATCH

```
J E Z U C C H I N I V E
O E R T S Q U A S H I R
F S S K A L E F R E D E
E I L O C C O R B O E W
S S E D E A U O A L N O
E P G A A R W N O D J
O A B U R N P C E F
T N B E L O Z O O E Q I
A A B E T T K N K B X
T C A T F F J S F B S U
O H C E K O H C I T R A
P A S T U O R P S Z X C
```

22. OCEANS AND SEAS

```
D E R A H O U B L A C K
R E F B I A T E R R T G
E C A S P I A N O C H P
F T C P P U F W T I P A
C L D J I V G L P I C
T A E K E W A K C N A
I A N T A R C T I C A F
A B F L Q X G D M I A
D I K M R Y I A A D C
R E C A R I B B E A N I
D V U G N S Z J D W I L N
A T H T R O N K T I M O
```

25. BIRDS

```
A C T I C B U N S X Z N
P A R R O T Q R E N V I
R N A T W L A P W I N G
D A R E I B E E F O G H
R R C N B N T X W I N T
A Y H N C O E W D I R
B A A R M P I G E O N
K R A J A N T A R T G
C W O P S G O G H R S A
A C A T X P W B L O R L
L A T H W N A D O V E
B U D G I E E W N W F R
```

23. WHAT'S IN THE BATHROOM?

```
T H I M B L V K N I S U
O S E L I T E W S T P Q
P U R R S H A M P O O H
H R Q U H S A U R I N T
O B W S O A P T S L G A
R H W R W A N T I E E B
D E T O W E L C H I T G E
E O E D R L H A F U O L
N O F A U C E T G H I B
T T O O T H P A S T E B
A C A T Y H O T F A U U
M I R R O R F A T B O B
```

24. WHAT'S IN THE KITCHEN?

```
R O L P D O T R I F E C
E V S T O V E E B R I I
F E K P K E E D E E A N
R P C I O N S N L E L K
I W J S E R E A Z H A
G N P G R I L L C E O Y
E C O J P U T B K R B L
R E T S A O T O P P U S
A C S S N O T H A T I
N V A R S S G E H E R N
O X I I P E E L T T E K
R Z E V A W O R C I M K
```

26. GO NUTS!

```
G R M A N H C A S H E W
N X A A L L R T R E U A
B A C O R N L B F U E L
A E A G O F I O I R G N
I S D Z H A Z E L I G U
E E A E A H A I B R T
A L M O N D R P E U D S
N I I T S T B H R N H W
U A A B F S D P T O J R
T N T U N T S E H C K H
G P I S T A C H I O S D
T U N D N U O R G C W R
```

27. PRIVATE DETECTIVE

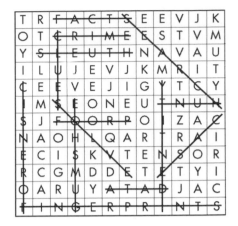

```
T R F A C T S E E V J K
O T C R I M E E S T V M
Y S L E U T H N A V A U
I L U J E V J K M R I T
C E E V E J I G Y T G Y
I M S E O N E U N U T
S J F O R P O Z A C
N A O H L Q A R R A I
E C I S K V T E N S O R
R C G M D D E T T Y I
O A R U Y A T A D J A C
F I N G E R P R I N T S
```

28. ROBOTS

```
S H I S L O R T N O E S
P T E C H N O L O G Y S
D V N O U F B H E R B E
V N I M H G O H O R O C
H K H P S D T M A X R O
U W C U E C E B A R G R
M S A T D M A R G O R P
A X M E C I T E R E U E
N I D R B J U N E I E J
O E C I T S I R U T U F
N T E L L I G E N C E
D I O R D N A S T E R Z
```

29. AROUND THE WORLD

```
S P A I N Y I N A P A J
W K I C O M M M J F M R
E E S E S O U S X E E D
D C S L P N A T I R B
E D U A L O G H P W U
N S R N A R L O Y A C Z
E C M D V W E U G C A E
C H O A C A B S E I S S
N I T A L Y E E V R R C
A N D R H I T R E F R I
R A U S T R A L I A
F R O I L Y N A M R E G
```

30. GLOBE TROTTERS

```
I A V A L L C A N A D A
N H M E X I C O F I N U
D U Y O R Z N R O B A S
I N E K R A M N E D L T
A G K G R R E A T N R R
X A R E X B W D H A E Z
E R U T D F E Z A L Z A
C Y T R U E T E N T R V
E P O R T U G A L I R V
E Q E R C V G H A F W A
R C H O L L A N D S L
G R E E N L A N D J R O
```

33. GOBBLEDYGOOK

```
Z A N P P Y L L I S Y O
A N S A B R B B U H R O
G O B B L E D Y G O O K F
M N O W T B L A G H T F
M S C A R T E B T S L B
A E H F A B L E M T A
L N A F L E T B I U N E
I S F L E S E T P C T
M E Q I V A A L U E H
A U N N R G L D T U
Z I B R R P I B D U R
F L A P D O O D L E I R
```

31. CREEPY-CRAWLY

```
B I R F S L U G A L O R
C E G R E A C U T Y O A
O K E X D G U B Y D A L
C A A T I Q I O T R S L
K K R R L M R O W I C
R D W A E E W L E F G P
O O I J S P I D E R B R
A K G A P T O V V W X E
C A Y P A R A S T E T
H T A R A N T U L A R A
A H E D E P I T N E C
J N O I P R O C S Z O I
```

32. INCREDIBLE INSECTS!

```
F I R E F L Y T H O C E
P R I B C Z W T A N G
E S H O R N E T R E P D
A S T I R S H I J J O
I G M O O C W C I T N M
T R D O P A R K V T M A
P E D O T I U Q S O M R
E T P Z O H I V S B V T
P I S S I G M T O E T O
T F A H A R L O C U S T
X L W A F R E R S U S
I Y L F R E T T U B U H
```

35. "A" WORDS

```
A S T R O N A U T G O R
S P R V E A T D R C J N
T A Q U A M A R I N E C
R P A T A D O R C A B E
O R A C U E A W T K L D
N I A R C R T C S J O S
O L O P A A Z U R E A
M R A N A L B A G S R
Y O D I D O S O U O S A
F W D N O Z A M A L V S
D L S C I T R O L W K
M M N B B S A L T A Q A
```

34. MUSICAL INSTRUMENTS

```
B R I P J U S O O Z A K
A G U I T A R S R I E E
C T N A A R U O E P N Y
E R N W T L I D M I B
N I L O I V E L R W R O
O R A I T I S R O Q U A
M B A N J O O L C U O R
R E Q D F L U T E O B D
A L R E F A Y R I M R
H L U T E I T G N S A A
L S V E S H O P I E T T
O S C S E P I P C A B H
```

36. MORE "A" WORDS

```
H E R E H P S O M T A U
A M I L K I R O S E R H
D N O M L A A R C T C
V B E W A A P P L E T O
E U A S T E R O I D H U
N Z N T M C T T A M S
T Z E I A R C A D E E R
U R S T P K O H A W T C
R A N E R A T K I T Z
E S E I O N N O I T C A
A T O M N R U B U A S Q
A L P H A B E T K A J U
```

37. BIRTHDAYS!

```
S R I B O G I F T S N S
I C I N G O R D E N U F
N W H I T E B L A O C K
S C E L E B R A T E H
N H A P P Y C H D A R O
G E K S T N E S E R P R
M E E R Y A W O R O L P
U S T A N D R A S C L A
S L A R T S G A M E S R
C R O F R I E N D S
C A N D L E S W F G H Y
```

38. DOGS

```
R E L G A E D D B P W Y
O G J A L S A T I O N O
T O N S O S S X H M W A
T E A M V H S C T E O B
W E M H H E E A M R L E
E R R I E E T S I A F S
I S E S R P O J H N H E
L A B R A D O R T I O N
E Z O L G O R M T A U E
R D D R I C R O C N N K
A R D N U H S H C A D E
A S E T T E R H A P I P
```

39. MORE DOGS

```
A D O G I L E I N A P S
C A I R E D A L E I O T
D L E E A D E R S T O B
N M A V C R O I L C D L
U A U B O X E R A H L O
O T B U L L D O G I E E
H I K L S C U E H I D
Y A W H P E T U U H
E N C O E T E A C A L
R M P U T Y K S U H A U
G E R B I E F O P U C N
N E W F O U N D L A N D
```

40. TRAIN STATION

```
B S E G A I R R A C H W
R E A D S T E K C I T H
S D R I V E R I V A I I
R E E A W I F E A L M S
E A P S I G N A L S E T
F V E E I L D R O J I T
F I E S T B S D E P A E
U P L A T F O R M D B P
B D S U N N E A W S L P
A S U R E T N U H S E A
W O R G H O R G S Q U I
T A S R E G N E S S A P
```

41. FOOTBALL CRAZY

```
R S T B S L P A S S E E
I M E T U H U E D S N
T L C W E V E O F O U D
L M K I N E L F E R B Z
I R L H T M D R D S O
K R E I I A D E E B E N
S E F K N N U L E O S E
T F T O U C H D O W N I
N E F L A G C I K A E O
I R A R E E R O C S F N
O E C O A C H K N E A
P E N A L T Y E K E D F
```

42. COWBOY RANCH

```
R E G N A R D R H A W R
A S C A R F B R O N C O
R T R U E B E X R I O U
S E I R I A R P S E V J
T R O U G H V E E A C B
E E C A T T L E L G F E
T W O D B A V H O U S A
S E W I X O B S R E S H
O I B S V R L S P A H C
N E O A E V U P A R K N
S D Y D S L A R I A T A
J O J E L D D A S W O R
```

43. CIRCUS

```
E L G G U J I G Z I P Z
L W I P T R A P E Z E B
E C M A G I C R T D Y I
P J R F E N P J A C T S
H G N I C C I R B E E H
A S D F N E O F O O S O
N E O R D S B K R W U W
S E S R O H Z C N J S
S A R E S D S T A S G K
R O G W J A E W E B E E
L I O N S R T Q V N F N
T R A I N E R R A R T O
```

44. COMPUTERS

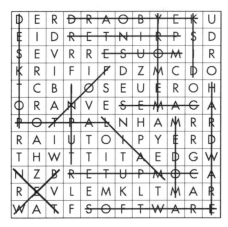

```
D E R D R A O B Y E K U
E I D R E T N I R P S D
S E V R R E S U O M R
K R I F I F D Z M C D O
T C B I O S E U E R O H
O R A N V E S E M A G A
T O T P A L N H A M R R
R A I U T O I P Y E R D
T H W T I T A E D G W
N Z B R E T U P M O C A
R X V L E M K L T M A R
W A T F S O F T W A R E
```

45. STAR SIGNS

```
S C O R P I O T Y A M D
A S A R D N W A R I E S
G O A T A W U A Y O V
I E S E N M R R M T E N
T A V S L E P U H I L E
A R F E G E S C L T P
A R B L G R P A L E O
R E A S C O H U T G
B R H W I J S D B O R
U C A P R I C O R N
S Q U E R T E E Z I S V
A Q U A R I U S H I P Y
```

46. HERBS

```
S E T A F A E L Y A B L
A M A R J O R A M C A R
L Y S P E P O R C S O
R H S A T M A N N H I S
E T K I G M I X T E L E
D O F E X E E M J R K M
N R L E N N E F D V D A
A J L O E V A Z A I T R
I C I Q Z P A R S L E Y
R E D R L I F T E X E R
O S T S A V O R Y O U W
C H I V E S O N D A R O
```

47. CHRISTMAS

```
S D R A C B S U V K A Y
V E A T R R E A K F A S
M C H R I S T M A S D S
I E Q E C E B D E R Y T
S M Y E R S C A R O L S
T B J T I M H N T A T D
L E K N H G E I S N N
E R K A S R M A E S M A
I L E P H N P S R W L
O U V N D F E V N F A R
L L H O L L Y D I Y I A
E D H S T D B S T F I G
```

48. FESTIVE FUN

```
R U D O L P H F A I R Y
E A R T C H J K E S W U
I F A V R T S T H C I L
N E V E Y J T S Z S H E
D S E L B U A B A T T
E C R S I S R T N U A
E H T F E A S T A N S D
R A T M E L E M O T N E
W T I F W M D S A S H U
O N C O L D B M E F D
R A N F A D R D A H J K
K S N O I T A R O C E D
```

49. FIRE STATION

```
W O F F U N I F O R M I
D R A T E R E T A W I
A R K O R I F T C D O D
J O N R S E C B L V E
E I O P S L V R E O S N
F A A S L B E L L A K T
O D L O S A R A H S S R
R D T B O T I C B T A E
E E N G I N E H U O M S
S R D D N R A S T X G C
H E A R Y U S K O S X U
H E L M E T S P R H U E
```

50. "B" WORDS

```
F B H B I B M B L B T A
B N O C U L A R S A C
L L E N B T M N I M O T
O L V F L T D A E R B
S I I U E O N L A J S
S O H R E R R A U J K A
O N E E B I N B O Y E
M S E V E X L U O R T K
R S B K E A J B F U A
X A O G L C K G U I A E
B O B A M B O O Z L E R
B U B B L E V R Z S B B
```

51. PUZZLE WORDS

```
W A I C R Y P T I C R O
O K E J C R U Z O O C E
R Y N A R A Z A Q U T Z
D N I M E B Z X G D G A
S R G R W A L C L U O M
E R M Y S T E R Y F I A
A A A N E J I G S A W
R H Z D A I E D O C K O
C R B R I V E D L L S O
H P O T B R W L D U D F
Q U E O M I G E W E R I
A S N O I T U L O S O H
```

52. COOL!

```
I C H I L L Y D D V W
R R B A L K R G J Y C
I A S N O W F L A K E N
R L N I U N R L R O L T
C O O E C O O L C A A R
S P W V O Y S U T I N Y
T E S I L J T R I O D E
E D T H D N B I C T L L
E N O T S L A H V E A
L J R N I O T R H X S E
S T M I O R E I C A L G
B R U E G N I Z E E R F
```

53. IT'S A JUNGLE!

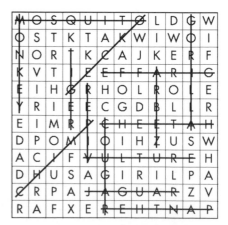

```
M O S Q U I T O L D G W
O S T K T A K W I W O I
N O R T K C A J K E R F
K V T I E F F A R I G
E I H G R H O L R O L E
Y R I E E C G D B L L R
E I M R Y C H E E T A H
D P O M I O I H Z U S W
A C I F V U L T U R E H
D H U S A G I R I L P A
Q R P A J A G U A R Z V
R A F X E R E H T N A P
```

54. JUNGLE FUN!

```
S A N D S R U C O B R A
P I R A N H A R D A X X
I A R V A E D O N I H R
D G H H K J T C S H I O
E O A M E D B O P P I H
R R N O O Y J D I F O R
I B T N G I E I I O N O
A N E Y H L S I D C Z S
S F L J L R E E M E D E
L E O P A R D D O L L S
E M P P N I C N W O L I
M A E L E P H A N T I G
```

57. DESERT

```
Z O N E R K R E T A W E
H A R P M I R A G E E R
S T U A H C A C T I P D
A E Y Y L A C T I R G U
N R Q U E M S D A M O N
D A T E S E S S I N A E
S H D N V L N D H J N S
T E B D E S E R T N S T
O A S I S A H A R A O R
R T T R S C E Z A H S I
M R S C O R P I O N S I
H A W T R I X L F I N G
```

55. "C" WORDS

```
S A F E T A L O C O H C
I N C I N D E R E L L A
A C A A H O U S E E R L
V S P O R C I N E M A C
I T A E T T A K T A C U
N T V O A H O E S R E L
R J A T C M M O O R N T
A N N E H O S R N G A T
C A N D C L O U A Q C O
D Y R R E H C U P H Q R
C C A L E N D A R R C S
D T E F A C S T O T Y F
```

56. "D" WORDS

```
S E L Z Z A D F R E S I
E S V D E C E M B E R F
C T R Q I R S U D H U R
E G R A O D A S P D O A G
D N D L D A R K R R O H
A I C E F G T G J S N E
W Y E M D Y N A M I C E
S A L L P P A A L E D N
Y R A D I L S L V T A
S D A N D E L I O N F D
W I D H G E O N D U C K
```

58. BIRDS

```
G E T A W A F R O B I N
R O O K F F E R S W E Z
A M T R O R S E T O K I
V R E O E E R U T L U V
E L Q T T N H X N L I P
N I U S Y K I E C A B M
A N D J A C K D A W O T
V S U Y U R E L E S S I
A E C C W O K U S T O P
L P K R E W O R R A P S
O O R T I N I R A S R Y
O G N I M A L F L U P T
```

59. PIZZA PICK

```
S G E C U F V B A C O N
O Y V O H C N A C R R O
G O O G L H A N T H E L
A P E P P E R O N I M O
R I C E D E A V E N M T
L N U D G S X S F E E A
I E A L L E R A Z Z O M
C A S M S X Z U I O N O
S P A R R M S H R I H
S P I C Y O R A O F O W
O L I V E S G G H R N W
P E P P E R S E T E S I
```

60. SUMMER

```
E V A W T A E H S G O O
D E L O V J R S W A R M
X G C D J U N E I S T
E U S N A L V N M A R D
S Y N A R Y O R M D U S
S A A S P I C N I C S U
A D L J H K O P N V I M
L R H A I N G U M M
G L D T P B N E A R S E
N O O C P L E E T H V R
U H R D Y Y O G M I S S
S S U M M E R T I M E T
```

61. HALLOWEEN

```
C U P U M P K I N G S H
H C T I W H A P O H H K
A P R I E M U T S O C B
L A N T E R N O Y S A L
L I Y W N E A E Y I U
O N P A Y T R A P S V E
W C I R S L E C R O V F
E D T I H S E L D N A C
E O B O S E A E I B S I
N L O C B S E L P P A R
M A S K D E A V A L S E
G I R L M L R H A F I M
```

62. SCARY STUFF!

```
R E W R F L O W E R E W
M O E X A L E D E F T I
O F B V I D E C B S Z
N T S H R A G Y R C T A
S E J D D R H G I A R
T B W S E H A U N T E D
E C K S S G H S H R R
R R J H T X L V M A T A
S L L E P S D U O R J A
Q E A R C Y A I O K F C
Y P E E R C D E R H R O
Z X D T S N I L R O G O
```

63. SWEET TREATS

```
I S I R S N I F F U M S
E T L G H D E I P A J M
X I H L O V E L K E O I
S U A R O O Z Q I T Y R
S C O N E R R X J A C G
E S U M M E R I N G U E
I N J A M T R F B P P
R B P R L C R I A L E
T M A C L V A G H D A S
S T E H O A F D W G K N
A T E A W M L T E Y E D
P T A E S F E R B E U I
```

64. BAKERY

```
Z S H O R T B R E A D A
C P I E S B I R D J A C
H A T D S D U T Y H E T
M N T O P M I N U O R C
A C R U M P E T S U B H
C A I G L U U A E S R Y
A K C H S A T R E E U
R E L N O E W T K S G R
O S D U S E K S O J R
O B E T I C E A O A I
N R I S C O N E C M G F
S G E K A C E S E E H C
```

65. POST OFFICE

```
T E N V E L O P E S I K
H S H O A E I A E M P X
S E M A N T I R A A U Q
A F M G H T I C A R D S
D E L I V E R E D G S S
W A R F L R B I B E T G
S P M A T S E J R L E A
T L O P I R N D E E D B
H J E N B R D N N T O L
O M E S S A G E B L E
R E G A K C A P I N K A
F I F E V X O B L I A M
```

66. WINTERTIME

```
W I N S G N I Z E E R F
T D E S K A T I N G R P
G G L T C I O S L D R A
S A T O I L I A C H E I
N I A R C O P H R I B R
O C D M I S T T G E M S
W Y T S O R F A S T E Y
M I L V S Z X Y Z O C L
A R S U E R E M I S E L
N F G B L I Z Z A R D O
B E A U A T T R A E S H
T O B O G G A N H H N I
```

67. CLOTHES CLUES

```
F A S H I M E S U O L B
S O H W I G I R E A T C
C O A T T W F R I H S E
A M T E A F R O E O R D
R S S K J E P A C Q E C
F A C C A T Y K L U N G
T G L A N D S N Z D X B
G L O J E A N S Z C A J
S O L V E T E E P U R H
Z V I R D S T H G I T O
S E R V Y K L E W M N P
T S S N E A K E R S E I
```

68. RUMMAGE SALE

```
S W E A T S H I R T F G
S A V N I G H R E D A A
S Q U O R S U M E B R L
R A C R S S H J K T E O
E A R A W E A N I P F S
P B S K I R T N L O G H
P L A U A D E T E C A E
I A S H S H O P U T I S
L C T R O X S E R S R O
S H O E S O E R U I O N
K T O W I N D R R A W S
I A B L A Z E R T M E D
```

69. "G" WORDS

```
E M P O C G R E E N G R
L L I R G V E N S Y H S
Y E N J G A F U M P K C
O B S E E Z F G C H G
G E E G R E A T C S E B
R A M H B Y R O A S D D
A Y A A I Y I T T O G G
G I G G L E G I N G E R
S O A V E A D X B E R A
G I A N T S G A L A X Y
A S Q T I P A C E J C A
A R V H G E H A W E H R
```

70. "H" WORDS

```
A E N A C I R R U H L L H
H I V E V A L K O A A N R
O L L E H A Z R E W N R V
R T H M A E D O S K E V
O N H T Z F N W O L Y
S D O S E P U E S L H S
C C R U L E O M L P R T
O R I G A M E H O B B Y F
P C Z T O T H O P P I N
E B O T I G S R I K E N
H O N E Y C O M B F A B
Z I R E G R U B M A H E
```

71. SPY SEARCH

```
S U R V E I L L A N C E
P S S T E G D A G A O R
Y T R O R D B E E R D U
G A E L A I R H N A E T
L R H I D D E N T H D N
A R P I E G C R C V I E
S Y I S H O J N I A S V
S E C R E T R O V E G D
S R G M I S S I O N U A
P U Z E R S H T O M I S
T N E M E T I C X E S H
C A M O U F L A G E E A
```

72. BIRDS

```
S K I N G F I S H E R W
E L G A E G A N E S W E
N R J W N F R I L O S F
C K P S E L E R T S E K
X C I R S O N S M P O R
S O R W A D E R S R O T
E C H Q I H E I V E V A
E A Y Z E P E J A Y S A
T E F E S I N M O M N R
V P E L I C A N W E C C
B C R O O B R D B T D H
E H E R S H C E S O O G
```

73. COLORFUL

```
P G E J T H T A N L D M
R R E D O T E W H I T E
O E U D K E L V O L E G
V E S J C H O O R A M N
D N E B A L D D C A A
H W R W L L V R R G I R
Z C U S B U F U K H H O
Z A Z D T O V R G O T S
S C A R L E T P R T I D
X F F E E U F L A S G E
U C Z W O L L E Y P H J
J I I N H B U T T D E R
```

74. MORE COLORS

```
R E K A R S K Y A T A E
E M B L A R E B D I Q J
E L F E S I O U Q R U T
L L E M O N D R D O A U
E B E I G E D L A R E M E
L E E V X H J M S E A R
U T T R E E U E V J R I
E S M A E R C T J H I H
B E O R S O G H K E N P
E P N W O R B Y N D E P
L Y G C R I M S O N A A
B E F H E S K X R S S
```

75. MAD MATH

```
E B R D X L A M I C E D
R E A E D B R U O C B I
E A D D T I M S S K M V
M L I R F G H J H I U
A G A P R C M T W O L D
L E Q U A T I O N Y T E
N B E H C A T T D H I
D R F W T R E A R E P R
E A D B U N C L E S L L
R Z E R O L E R D C Y R
W O Z L N U M B E R L O
A R D S U B T R A C T L
```

76. NATURE TRAIL

```
S H O P P H D E S T A C
I E G S U R K L S A M O
R D A M Y G U L O W R U
U W O O D R A D M D M N
B E C S E A Z F I N F T
E A T E S S H R T O E R
Y T R E E S S E O P D Y
E H Z G R R A T W B E R
N E O D X B F A L M I A
O R O G S R E W O L F N
H E D G E X F E D A L G
G E N I H S N U S O N E
```

77. "S" WORDS

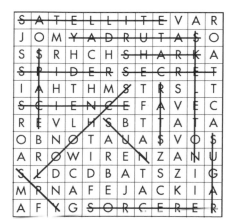

```
S A T E L L I T E V A R
J O M Y A D R U T A S O
S S R H C H S H A R K A
S P I D E R S E C R E T
I A H T H M S T R S L T
S C I E N C E F A V E C
R E V L H S B T A T A
O B N O T A U A S V O S
A R O W I R E N Z A N U
S L D C D B A T S Z I G
M R N A F E J A C K I
A F Y G S O R C E R E R
```

78. "T" WORDS

```
E T I S T H T A R T A N
T D D L Y W I N K S E
O G B E T S I T P U X R
R E E T R O L L N Z X U
N R A H I J I D E I Z S
A E T U C O G R M R L A
D Z W N K T H I S T L E
O E D H T T W F E R
S N N E G G D I B Y O T
Y A K R L D V M P B F T
O I L A E S O W O O A F
T D E T K S C I P O R T
```

79. SPRING

```
S P R I N G T I M E H S
N T R R C S U C O R C L
O I S B M A L H N C Z S
W M E S H G I Z I R C L
D T E R S W P M S O T
R J D E M A R C H E H D
O S S T S P R H O C O O
P X E S D R S H X T R F
S B D A U I T S E N E F
S U Y E J J S N R A S A
B L O S S O M N S L V D
J U E C E S G A R P N I
```

80. FALL

```
R E M R A F B A R L E Y
E L F W I A F P E G A Z
B M A R L F H P A H C A
M N S E I O G L J E H R
E G S L L G L E A V E S
T N R D E G C S F F S T
E P A E P Y R N T R T S
E W B U O O Z A A E N E
S O O T A E H W C S U V
A L T U P R V E S A T R
A R P C M S M N C T V S
T W O N E E W O L L A H
```

81. BIRDS

```
A D R A Z Z U B L U E T
P P P G O L D F I N C H
C L E M K C R A S I N M
O S T R I C H I U A S
R E R O N P O C R K Q S
M S E E H E R O N C U O
O A L Y M N W N G O I R
R R O U K G O I F C P T
A G L W O U W I G D P A
N R D O R F O R O Z B
T F I W S N W O N O I L
E A T E R E F R I W X A
```

82. JEWELRY STORE

```
D I A M T N A D N E P O
W D S T E N R A G O L D
A W O R K A R T E N A D
T E L E C A R B N E T S
C T B R O O C H I V I A
H O L I G T I A R A N R
E M I N I D R E A T U C
S E L G N A B S M D M H
C R Y S T A L D A H N A
H R R E S E Z E U E S
A S I L V E R D Q Q X N
I N S N E C K L A C E S
```

83. AMUSEMENT PARK

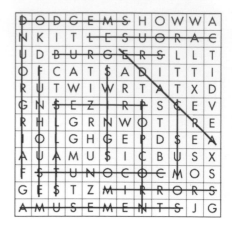

```
D O D G E M S H O W W A
N K I T L E S U O R A C
U D B U R G E R S L L T
O F C A T S A D I T T I
R U T W I W R T A T X D
G N S E Z R P S C E V
R H L G R N W O T R E
I O L G H G E P D S E A
A U A M U S I C B U S X
F S T U N O C O C M O S
G E S T Z M I R R O R S
A M U S E M E N T S J G
```

84. ICE CREAM

```
N R T O P P I N G C E D
P U R N A A N A N A B W
O G T Z I N T L J R R S
P I N S T M S L A A X T
S Y R U P I U I C M G R
I T H N B M I N K E E A
C F U D G E I A S L E W
L I M A E L A V T R N B
E M I E W A F E R L O E
P O R H E S R C T O C R
C H O C O L A T E M N R
S G F R A S P B E R R Y
```

85. XYZ WORDS

```
Y A C H T Z O D I A C L
U A B Z O S Z Y R K E
L C H O R P G L O B H A
E D X M A S Y W W E E H
T C R B P G E N O Z S
H O X S L I P T F N
D J K E A E L B I H F O
E I N P I Y O Y C K C
S O A P S U W M D R B R
X O I L L I Z M E D E I
T S E T E R R U A N E Z
E N O H P O L Y X A N R
```

86. SHIPS

```
T R E K N A T A L L A C
F E R R Y Z U U Y I T A
A S H I P I S A G R C N
T C R H D E O N A C A A
E H D H J C T W L R R L
S O H X T D L E L P B B
E O D E D E A V E K C O
I N U Y R H P O O L S A
M E N A U Y E G N C N T
W R G D T N O O T N O B
G R H C T E K E T I R Y
A B Y A C H T W H I Z E
```

87. WHAT'S IN THE BEDROOM?

```
E S E M A G R S N X R R
C H U I R P P A R Y E E
D E M I T I L U Q J S A
B E D A R I Y W E S H
S T I R H G A L O E S
N S B E N H O J M K R E
J U P I R T W L N R D R
M A T T R E S S M E O U
R U R Q U I X J S A T T
S R V J Y L E K C O L C
I M A R R S Z O L R J
C L O S E T B E H G A P
```

88. MONTHS OF THE YEAR

```
B L E R E Y E T H E A R
A D E C E M B E R S Y J
R T H K O M V S E G Y M
M A R G G A B Z B A R S
X A P R I L D D O M I A E
R U R O C T O B E R U P
C R G A J V X Z Y R R T
H T H U R D A U O Y B E
V N M W S A J U N E E M
S H I P R T U I I G F B
G R E X I S L T H S P E
J A N U A R Y H C B G R
```

89. NUMBERS

```
P L E Y M I L L I O N T
R A E L E V E N E V E V
B K E S W J E R U O F S
E V L E W T E X T I I C
T E Q U D K T N W I V N
S E R T E V H M E V E S
E I G H T Z M N D U J
N X X R R N R C T I B N
A T R E E R T I Y I K M
D W L E W R E S H K P D
H O N E E G E S H R J B
T H O U S A N D A R I G
```

90. IN THE BACKYARD

```
C H I I G R E A L R C
A O E S S R E W O L F S
P R R R G A C V U A A N
R N R U G S U N D W I V
D C S I G S P V E N I M
B S F I R G S E D B N S
S J P O N D I D O S Q
L V I Z E S S T O N E S
I Z N H O U S R P C C O
A A S M P N S E A I T R
N E S S E V A E L T S D
S G U L S E E S R Y R Z
```

91. 4TH JULY

```
R Y A L P S I D T O R F
A E U Q P H K R J R D
H R R G A N P O W D E R
S A C A A H E S J Z G W
P N K I D W H I Z Z M O
A D E V E S E M A L F R
R Z T N O V E M Y E R K
G H H A V E N M W U D S
A J P G L I T T E R L R
L F T H G I N E W E D Y
F V H T R U O F J K R E
```

92. CATS

```
S A T I T A D A T T A R
A L O N L E O P A R D
B S G S T A R U A C J K
E R E R W R M O N D L I
R N R A G A V A T L O T
L J A G U A R O H I R V
O Z Z U A R B A E W D L
O A R O V D J J R R C Y
T B O C E L O T Y V B N
H O U S E E G R D B I X
S C H E E T A H A A R T
Z W O F D R I T Y E V E
```

93. SHOWTIME

```
T E N T E R T A I N W R
R R O F F B A T C O W G
D A Z Z O A E Q H A I D
B I C X Y L P S O E S A
N I P L E C R I R C C
I S T E R O I N U N I C
A S F N H G S E S E
C R E C G Y T E Y I U R
K I A C R A N R D D M S
E S T A G E H S S U A R
T R S F J A C P L A Y A
S T H G I L R E C S N M
```

94. VOLCANO

```
I M S C O R C H G O O L
E M U L P T U R V E A Y
N I Z F J R T N E X I S
O S L O I N C E A O S O
C R A T E R I V E L V P
R E A D R S E A M C C E
A D T G U N E T O A N A
H N B O P R O M N K H
O I S A T P R I T Q Y G
T C N I T X E N E Q W R
C N M D W X Z T N E D A
H J R G S K C O R D W H
```

95. MUDDLE MIX-UP

```
G R E H E L D D U F E B
P E R P L E X B R A E E
G D E N Z E Y R E R L W
D A Z Z L E A U A A Z I
E Y A K G L Z F D W O L
N B A F T D J F D A O D
B R W H I D N L E Y B E
D E S H Y U R E L A M R
C A L L E M W D T N A M
N M L A A M D I T D B K
S I R A C R C R A Z Y J
S C A T T E R B R A I N
```

96. REALLY BIG!

```
H E R C U L E A N A N R
Z C G I G A N T I C A T Y
H R Z I H V M A V J E S
E A A R G A T J U M B O
E N B I G S R C N A U D
S D B D I T O R J M R Q
R A M S A J V R G M L U
I G M O N S T E R O Y L
W R H J T I M W O T U A
I E N O R M O U S H E R
D H D E N J U E Q U X G
A S T R O N O M I C L E
```

97. GAMES

```
B A C K G A M M O N S T
A A R V A L O R J S I I
T R A E E L N O R Z C D
R I X I A O V B R L D
L C R E S B P I O D U L
E A R H G L O V G I E Y
S B E P C V L S G P D W
H F B H A R Y Y L A O I
I S E S R E K C E H C N
P S T R O N S H E H G K
S X N I M R E T S A M S
G D O M I N O E S T D G
```

98. THE ENTERTAINERS

```
T S I N O I S U L L I P
R C Z R O T C A Z O O I
E A L S I A R T I S T E
L R S O D A C R O B A T
L T Q U W I D G N E R D
E O E R Y N C J A R E C
T O R J A N N V C M K N
Y N E R R E G N I S S C
R I C O R R E L G G U J
O S N L L S B M A S B
T T A S I D B G M I R C
S I D A R E D E V I L N
```

99. YOUNG CREATURES

```
D I Y E O J L H C B A R
P E C E C N J I Z Z D D
M B K C I H C O R E U C
N C N M U P K R P C C G
S A W R E B W U A S K N
E L R S H J S B R L
D F A W N S I S M T L
T O N L R S G E A I N G
B U N N Y F L R Y F G D
J I X F H F E D I A S E
N E Y J D R T E L W O L
N E T T I K A R V J Z R
```

100. DOUBLE "G"

```
F D E G G U R A E R O N
O R H V X B A G G A G E
G I J R C S G M G E M N
G L O W D A G R S E K T
Y G G A R C E R I G W Y
R S G J I X D B L A F
E E S T O O T O G G V
G D R A G Z O E V G G V
G E R G R A T G A U L M
A Y Y R A G I G G L E A
W E G J Y H X U A H C R
S E L G G O G N H E N T
```

101. FURRY CREATURES AND HAIRY MONSTERS

```
T I M W O L F H O U N D
B R B O R I L G A M E S
T C M E C A P O O D L E
D H C B A T R R N J K P
P T P Z T R Y I H C D E
B E A V E R G L L S X E
U S N A S U R T A W L H
F E D L L S S A R T S
F H A C H G X D E H B C
A E R V K O R D E L R D
L S F X F L O W E R E W
O S A H U S K Y E S G R
```

PICTURE PUZZLES

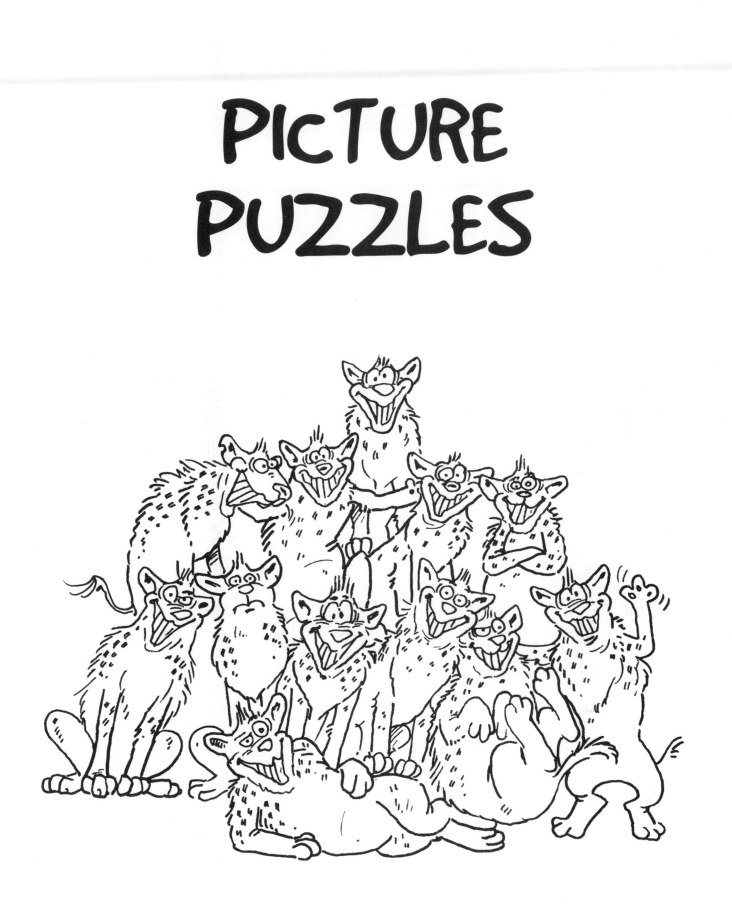

1. Freaky Footprints

Which monster left this footprint?

1.　　2.　　3.　　4.　　5.

2. Mumbo Jumbo

Spot the difference between the six elephants. Who is the odd one out?

1.　2.　3.　4.　5.　6.

3. Shadow Bats

Which shadow matches the vampire bat?

1.　2.　3.　4.　5.

4. Crossroads

You're lost! Study the clues to find which road to take.

Clues

1. Avoid hens, cows, and sheep.
2. Don't go North.
3. Head for the hills.
4. Go the opposite way from the wood.

5. Speedboat

Which skier is attached to the speedboat?

6. Jaws

Which shark took a bite out of the raft?

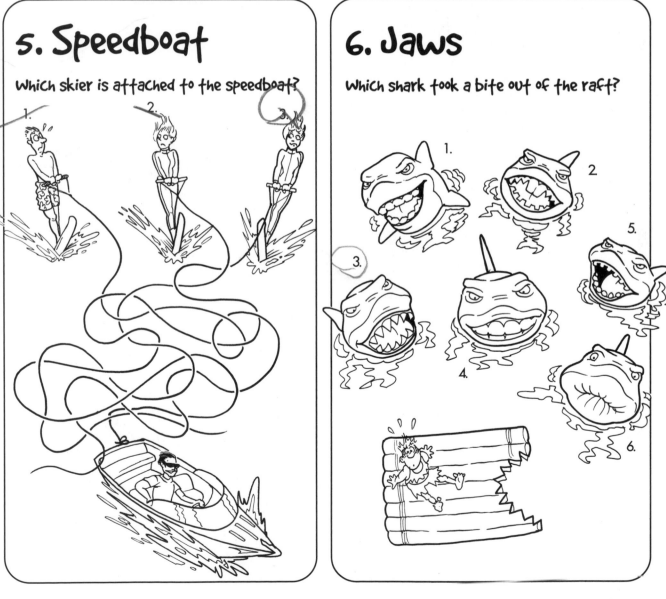

7. Haunted House

Circle the ten spooks hiding in the haunted house.

8. Mystery Tour

Which route should the mystery tour bus take to get out of the maze?

9. Spider's Web

Which spider's web trail leads to the center of the web?

10. Snakes Alive

Which snake has a rattle on the end of its tail?

11. Silly Sheep

How many sheep are there in the picture?

12. Spot the Difference

Spot the dog has lost seven spots. Circle where they are missing.

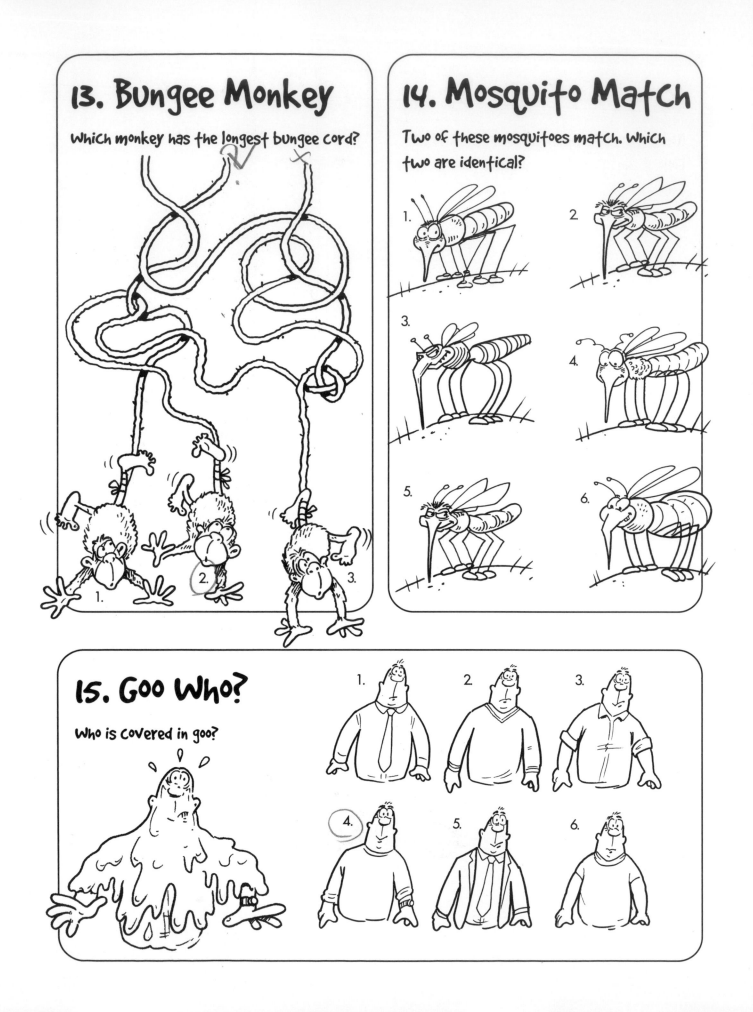

16. Alien Eyeballs

How many eyeballs does the alien have? Follow the eyeball trails to see which ones are connected to its head.

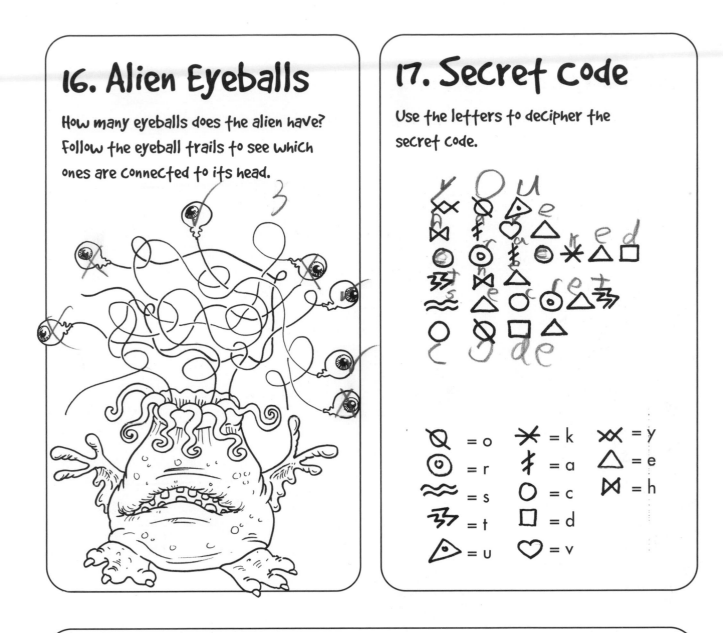

17. Secret Code

Use the letters to decipher the secret code.

⊘ = o	✳ = k	⋈ = y
⊙ = r	⨍ = a	△ = e
≈ = s	○ = c	⋈ = h
⚡ = t	□ = d	
▷ = u	♡ = v	

18. Snowbody There

Oh yes there is! Five polar bears are hiding in the snowscene. Can you find them?

19. Cat Splat

Which splat mark did the crazy cat make?

1.
2.
3.
4.
5.
6.

20. Witches' Hats

Draw three straight lines across the box to leave three different witches' hats in each part.

21. Top Secret

Use the secret code to read the message on the computer.

⟋ = a
@ = s
✓ = d
✳ = e
▽ = g
Ⅱ = h
▱ = i

♡ = m
▢ = o
〰 = r
◎ = c
◯ = t
▽ = u
= w

22. Mummy Mummy!

Can you spot the two identical mummies?

1. 2 3. 4. 5 6.

23. Bubble Trouble

Oops! Someone has used too much bubble bath. Who is it?

1. 2 3. 4. 5.

24. Laughing Hyenas

How many hyenas are smiling in the picture?

25. Blackout!

How many animals are hiding in the dark?

15

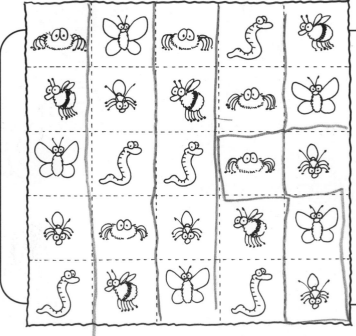

26. Howl at the Moon

Can you spot the two pictures that are identical?

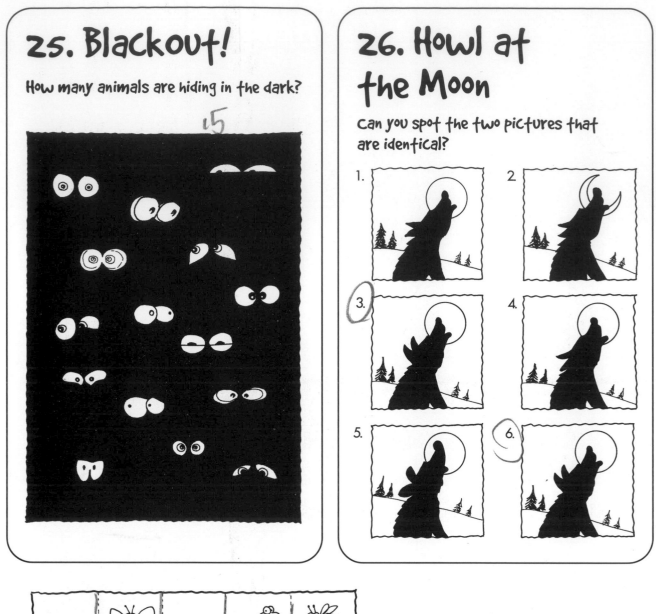

1.

2.

3.

4.

5.

6.

27. Bugs!

Draw along the dotted lines to form five equal-sized portions. Each portion should contain only one of each bug.

28. Mad Mars

Is there life on Mars? How many Martians can you see?

29. Wizard!

Can you help the wizard find his way out of the maze?

30. Crazy Castle

Which road leads to the crazy castle?

31. Computer Connection

Which game controller is connected to the computer?

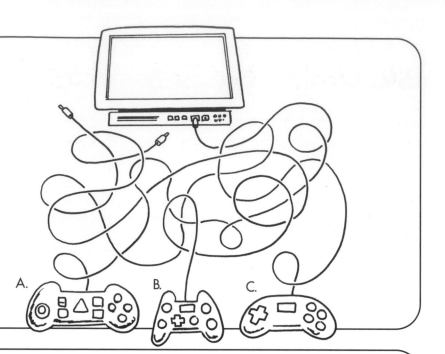

A.   B.   C.

32. Nine Dots

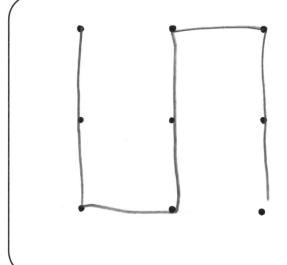

Use a pencil to join all nine dots without lifting your pencil off the page and without going back on any lines you've made. You can only draw four lines.

33. Over the Waves

Shade in all the shapes marked with a dot to find the shape hidden in the picture.

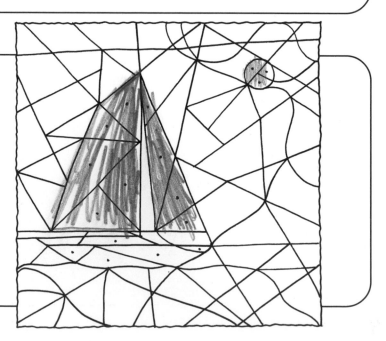

34. Under the Sea

Shade in all the shapes marked with a dot to find the shape hidden in the picture.

35. River Rapids

Which river rapid will take you safely to the lagoon?

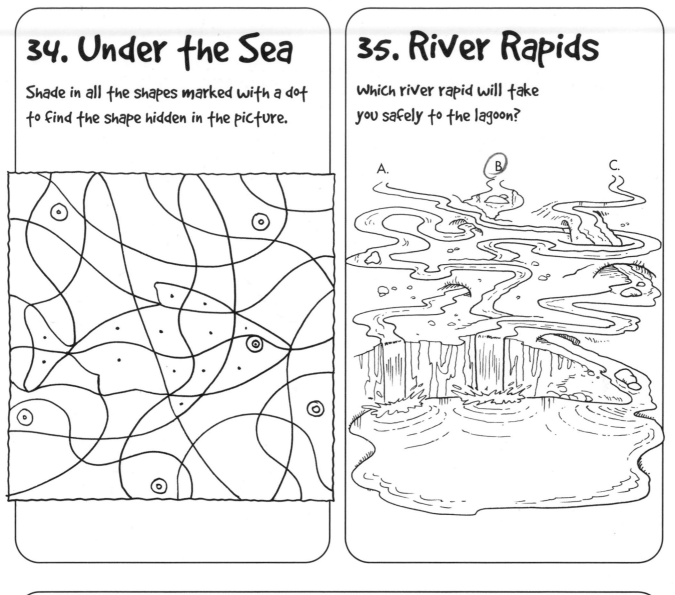

36. Sailing Boat

Without lifting your pencil off the page, start at the big dot and join the dots to make a sailing boat.

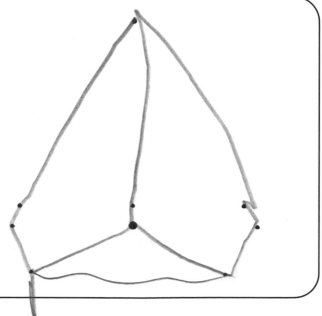

37. Clown Shapes

How many circles, triangles, and squares can you see in the picture of the clown?

†4
S13
∞8

38. Envelope

Join the dots without lifting your pencil off the paper (and without going back over any lines) to draw an envelope.

39. Manic Monkeys

How many monkeys are there in the picture? 14

40. Space Rocket

Two of these rockets are the same. Can you spot them?

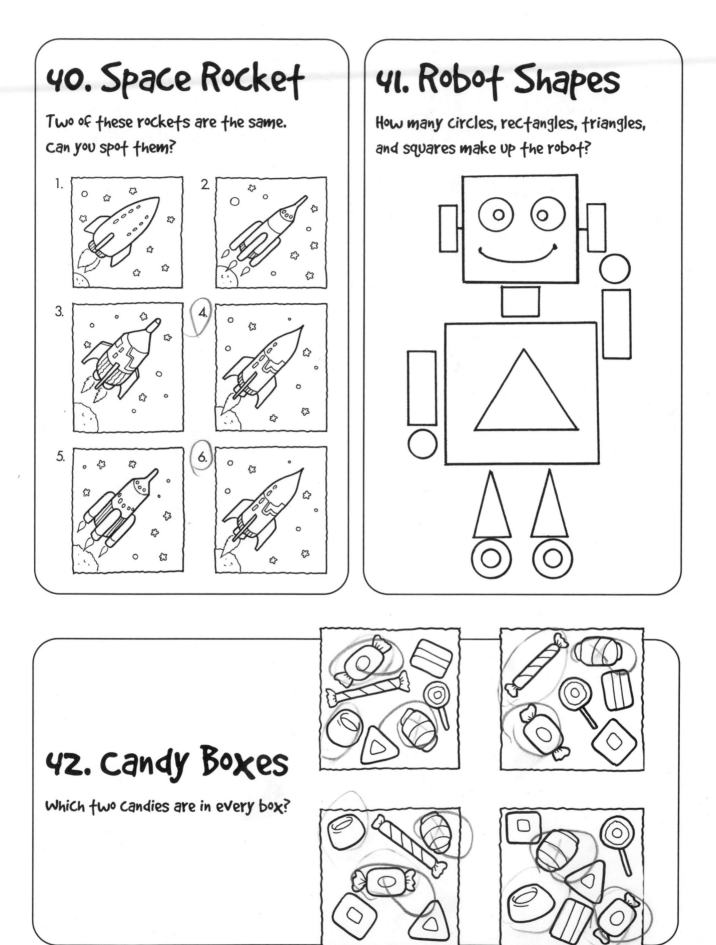

41. Robot Shapes

How many circles, rectangles, triangles, and squares make up the robot?

42. Candy Boxes

Which two candies are in every box?

43. Shadow Match

Draw lines to join each item to its matching shadow.

44. Strawberry Patch

How many strawberries are there in the strawberry patch?

22

45. Dog and Bone

This dog has lost his bone. Can you help him find it?

1.   2.   3.   4.

46. Teddy's Bedroom

Spot the ten differences in the picture. Circle them with a pencil.

47. Snowman

Which snowman is the odd one out?

1.

2.

3.

4.

5.

6.

48. Cake Puzzle

Draw two straight lines across the box to leave three different cakes in each part.

49. Flight of Fright

Shade in all the shapes marked with a dot to find the shape hidden in the picture.

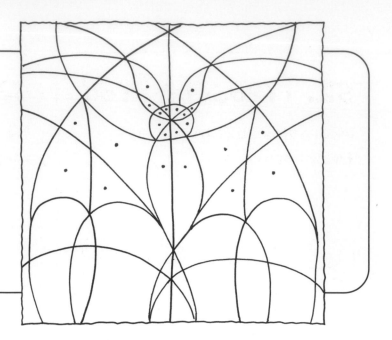

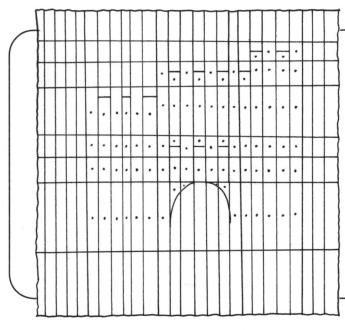

50. Fit for a King

Shade in all the shapes marked with a dot to find the shape hidden in the picture.

51. Top Secret

Follow the lines to find the key that opens the top secret file.

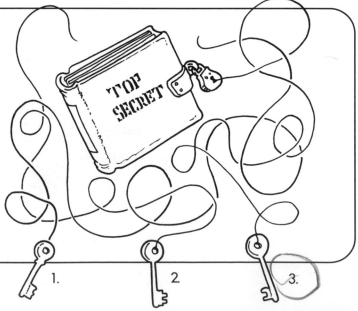

1.

2.

3.

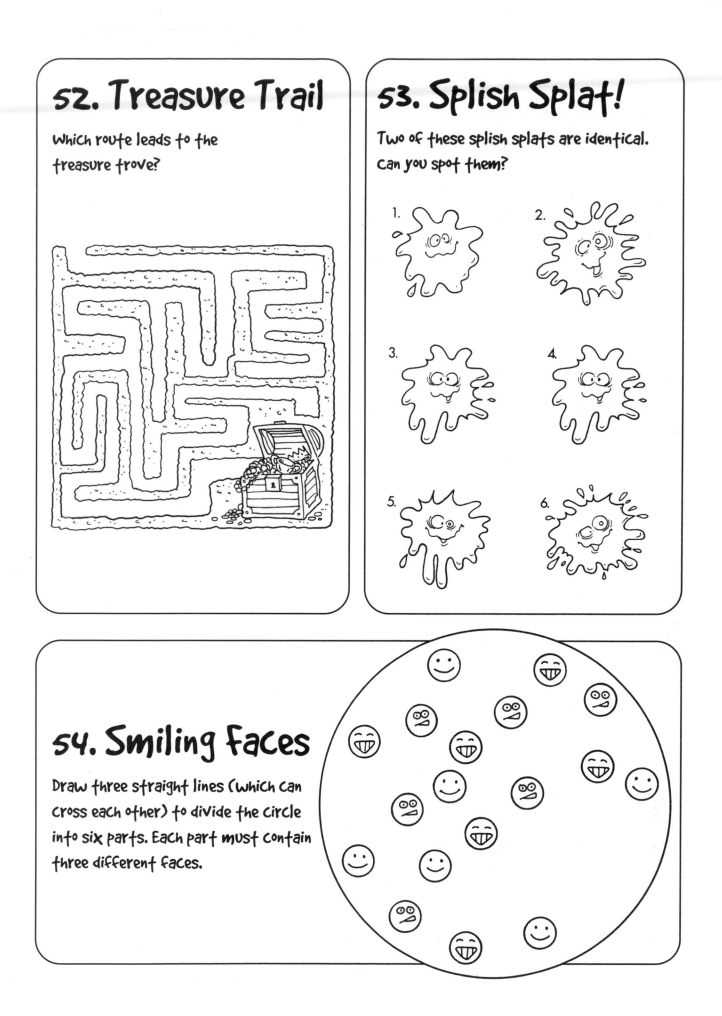

52. Treasure Trail

Which route leads to the treasure trove?

53. Splish Splat!

Two of these splish splats are identical. Can you spot them?

1.
2.
3.
4.
5.
6.

54. Smiling Faces

Draw three straight lines (which can cross each other) to divide the circle into six parts. Each part must contain three different faces.

55. High-Five Spider

Can you spot the ten differences between these two pictures?

56. Bats' Castle

How many bats are hiding in and around the castle?

57. Star Gazing

How many stars can you see in the picture?

58. Alien Adventure

Which route should the alien spaceship take to reach its home planet?

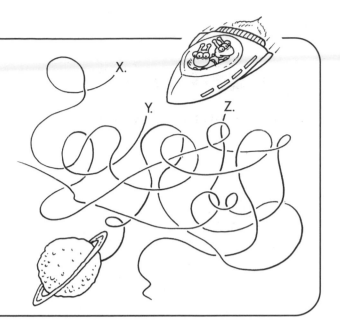

59. Blast Off

Shade in all the shapes marked with a dot to find the shape hidden in the picture.

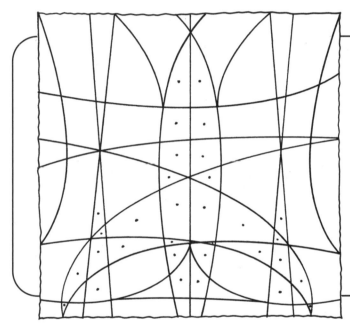

60. Kick It

Shade in all the shapes marked with a dot to find the shape hidden in the picture.

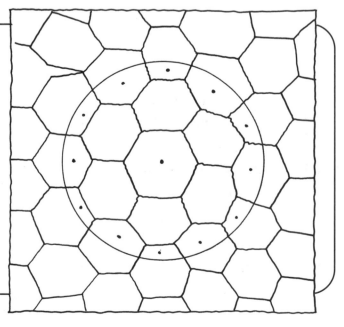

61. Cat Calling

Who is the cat phoning? Follow the lines to find out if it is the duck, the gerbil, or the dog.

62. Oodles of Doodles

Two of these doodles are identical.
Which two?

1.
2.
3.
4.
5.
6.

63. Jungle Trap

You are trapped in the jungle.
Can you find your way out?

START

64. Sun, Moon and Stars

Draw three straight lines (which can cross each other) to divide the box into five parts. Each part must contain one sun, one moon, and one star.

65. Zippy the Snail

Zippy is in a hurry to get out of the snail maze. Which route is the fastest?

66. Cat Nap

How many cats are napping in this picture?

67. Wibbly Wobbly

Two of these wibbly wobbly men are identical. Can you spot them?

1.

2.

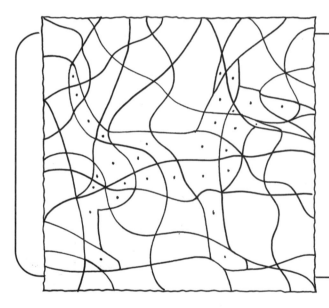

3.

4.

5.

6.

68. Walkies

Shade in the shapes marked with a dot to find the shape hidden in the picture.

69. Home Sweet Home

Shade in all the shapes marked with a dot to find the shape hidden in the picture.

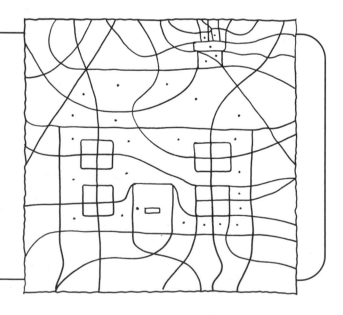

70. Shadow Shark

Which shadow belongs to the shark?

71. Beware of the Werewolf

Which shadow matches the werewolf?

72. Splatman

Which shadow matches Splatman?

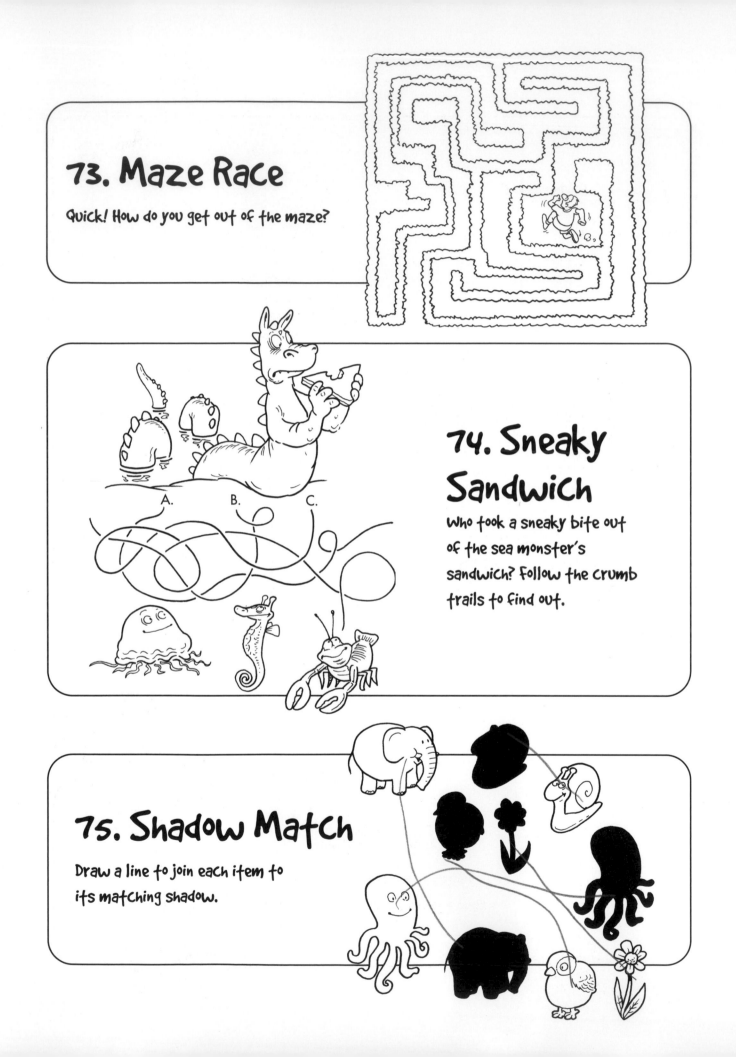

73. Maze Race

Quick! How do you get out of the maze?

74. Sneaky Sandwich

Who took a sneaky bite out of the sea monster's sandwich? Follow the crumb trails to find out.

A.   B.   C.

75. Shadow Match

Draw a line to join each item to its matching shadow.

76. Fast Fly

What's the quickest route for the fly to take to reach the flowers?

77. Growly Grizzly

Which growly grizzly silhouette matches the real one?

78. Oops!

There are ten differences between these pictures. Can you spot them?

79. Farm Fun

How many animals can you see in the picture?

80. Wrong Way

One creature in every row is pointing in the opposite direction. Circle the odd one out in each row.

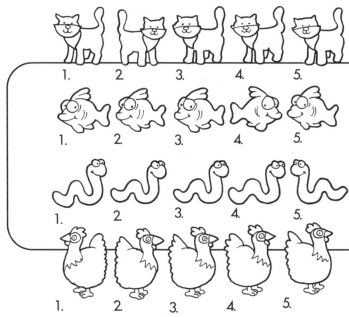

1.   2.   3.   4.   5.

1.   2.   3.   4.   5.

1.   2.   3.   4.   5.

1.   2.   3.   4.   5.

81. Teddy Bears

How many teddy bears are there in this picture?

82. Snowflakes

Two of these snowflake pictures match. Which two?

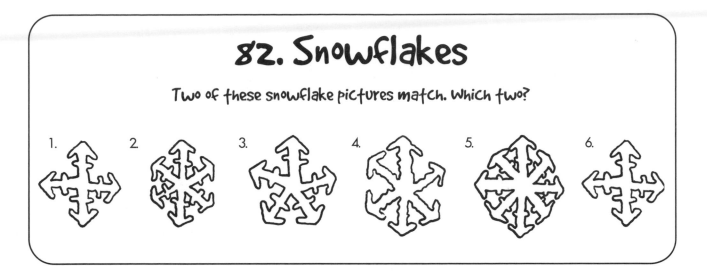

83. Fruity Split

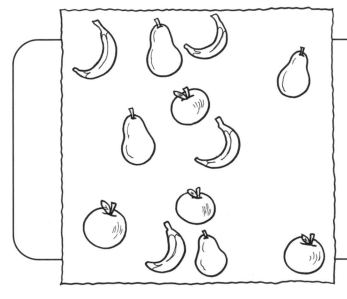

Draw two straight lines (which can cross each other) to divide the box into four parts. Each part must contain one banana, one apple, and one pear.

84. Squeaky Floorboards

Shh! Keep quiet! What is the only way to get out of the maze without stepping on the squeaky floorboards?

85. Vulture Trouble

Which vulture is the odd one out?

1. 2. 3. 4. 5. 6.

86. Kitty Tree

How many cats are hiding up and around the tree?

87. Ancient Book

What is the secret message written in the book? Use the letter code to find out.

☐ = a   ◉ = p
∿ = b   ♡ = r
△ = e   ▱ = s
⅄ = g   ○ = t
▽ = k   ✦ = u
ϟ = l   ✳ = z
▯ = o

88. Busy Bees

Draw lines to join each pair of bees.

89. Squid's Hid

Shade in the parts that have a dot to reveal the hidden image.

90. Rocket Science

Which cord leads to the space rocket?

91. Bathtime Tiger

There are ten differences between these two pictures. Can you spot them?

92. Private Detective

Which trail leads to the secret footprints?

93. Find the Fairies

Seven little fairies are hiding in the woods. Can you find them?

94. Lion Match

Two of these lions are the same. Which two?

95. Gift Box

Draw three straight lines across the box to divide it into four parts. Each part must contain three different presents.

96. Zany Zebras

How many zebras are there in the picture?

97. Duck!

Which pond contains the most ducks?

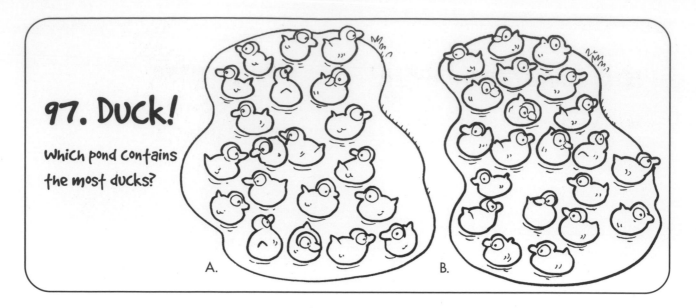

A.

B.

98. Fall Leaves

Follow the leaf trail and look at the leaf pattern. Which leaf comes next?

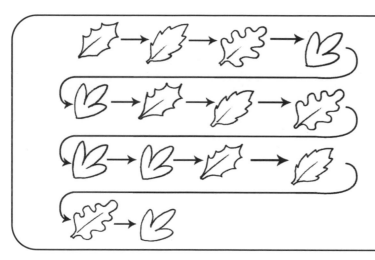

99. Secret Agent

Can you help the secret agent out of the maze?

100. Which Witch?

Which witch does this shadow belong to?

1.

2.

3.

4.

5.

101. Halloween Party

How many ghosts, skeletons, cats, and pumpkins can you see at the Halloween party?

ANSWERS

1. Freaky Footprints

5.

2. Mumbo Jumbo

3.

3. Shadow Bats

4.

4. Crossroads

Highlands

5. Speedboat

Skier number 3

6. Jaws

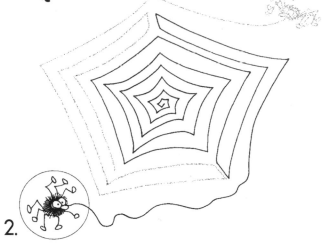

Shark number 3

7. Haunted House

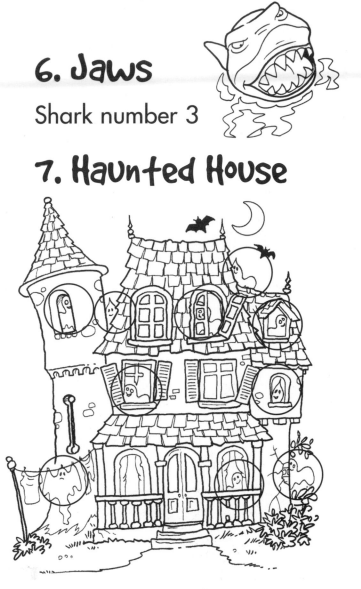

8. Mystery Tour

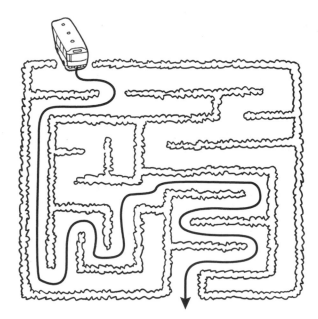

9. Spider's Web

2.

10. Snakes Alive

Snake number 2

11. Silly Sheep

16 sheep

12. Spot the Difference

13. Bungee Monkey

Monkey number 2

14. Mosquito Match

Mosquito numbers
2 and 5

15. Goo Who?

Number 4

16. Alien Eyeballs

There are three eyeballs

17. Secret Code

You
have
cracked
the
secret
code

18. Snowbody There

19. Cat Splat

Shadow number 5

20. Witches' Hats

21. Top Secret

Use this code to write
other messages

22. Mummy Mummy!

Mummies number 1 and 6

23. Bubble Trouble

Number 4, the lion

24. Laughing Hyenas

11 Hyenas

25. Blackout!

15 animals

26. Howl at the Moon

Pictures 3 and 6 match

27. Bugs!

28. Mad Mars

10 Martians

29. Wizard!

30. Crazy Castle

Road A

31. Computer Connection

Controller A

32. Nine Dots

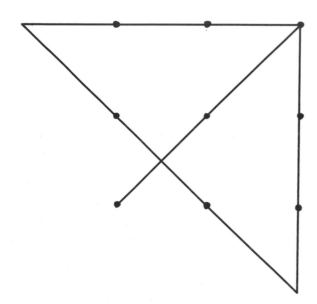

33. Over the Waves

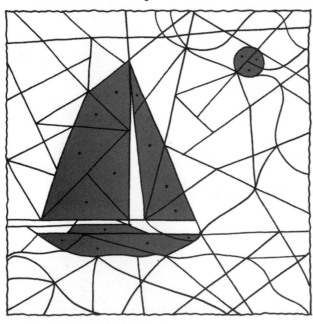

34. Under the Sea

35. River Rapids

River B

36. Sailing Boat

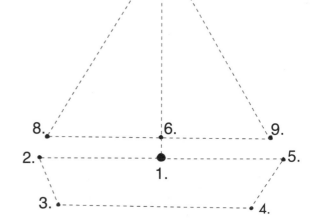

1–2–3–4–5–1–6–7–8–9–7

37. Clown Shapes

12 circles
4 triangles
14 squares

38. Envelope

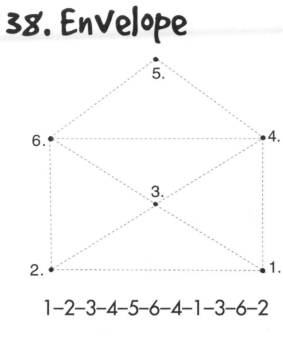

1–2–3–4–5–6–4–1–3–6–2

39. Manic Monkeys

14 monkeys

40. Space Rocket

Rockets 4 and 6

41. Robot Shapes

10 circles
4 rectangles
3 triangles
3 squares

42. Candy Boxes

43. Shadow Match

44. Strawberry Patch

22 strawberries

45. Dog and Bone

Route 1

46. Teddy's Bedroom

47. Snowman

Snowman number 4

48. Cake Puzzle

49. Flight of Fright

50. Fit for a King

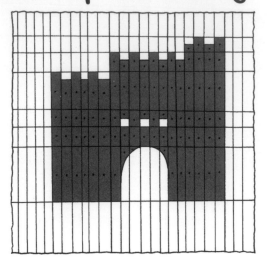

51. Top Secret

Key 3

52. Treasure Trail

53. Splish Splat!

Splish Splats 3 and 4

54. Smiling Faces

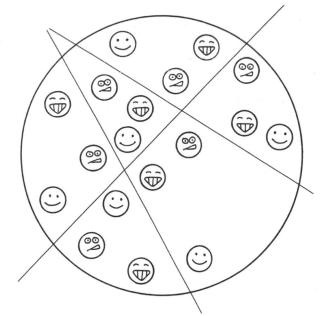

55. High-five Spider

56. Bats' Castle

18 bats

57. Star Gazing

32 stars

58. Alien Adventure

Route Z

59. Blast off

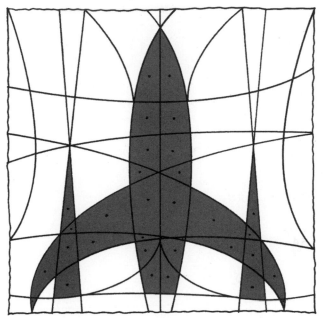

60. Kick It

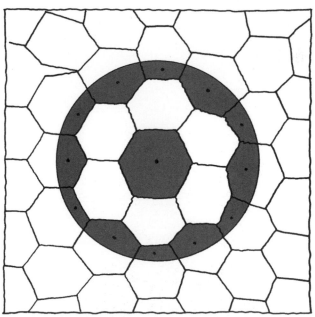

61. Cat Calling

The gerbil

62. Oodles of Doodles

Doodles 1 and 5

63. Jungle Trap

64. Sun, Moon and Stars

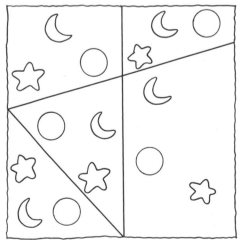

65. Zippy the Snail

Route C

66. Cat Nap

14 cats napping

67. Wibbly Wobbly

Wibbly wobbly men 4 and 6

68. Walkies

69. Home Sweet Home

70. Shadow Shark

Shadow 4

71. Beware of the Werewolf

Shadow 4

72. Splatman

Shadow 3

73. Maze Race

74. Sneaky Sandwich

Trail C, lobster

75. Shadow Match

76. Fast Fly

Route 1

77. Growly Grizzly

Growly grizzly number 1

78. Oops!

79. Farm Fun

20 animals

80. Wrong Way

Cat 2	Fish 4
Worm 5	Chicken 1

81. Teddy Bears

18 teddy bears

82. Snowflakes

Pictures 1 and 6

83. Fruity Split

84. Squeaky Floorboards

85. Vulture Trouble

Vulture 4

86. Kitty Tree

14 cats

87. Ancient Book

puzzle
books
are
great

88. Busy Bees

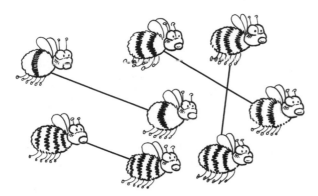

89. Squid's Hid

90. Rocket Science

Cord 1

91. Bathtime Tiger

92. Private Detective

Trail 2

93. Find the Fairies

94. Lion Match

Lions 3 and 5

95. Gift Box

96. Zany Zebra

16 zebras

97. Duck!

Pond A has 20 ducks but pond B has 21.

98. Fall Leaves

99. Secret Agent

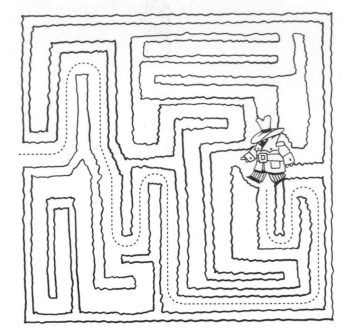

100. Which Witch?

Witch number 5

101. Halloween Party

11 ghosts
4 skeletons
8 pumpkins
2 cats

BRAINBENDER PUZZLES

1. Paintbrush Puzzle

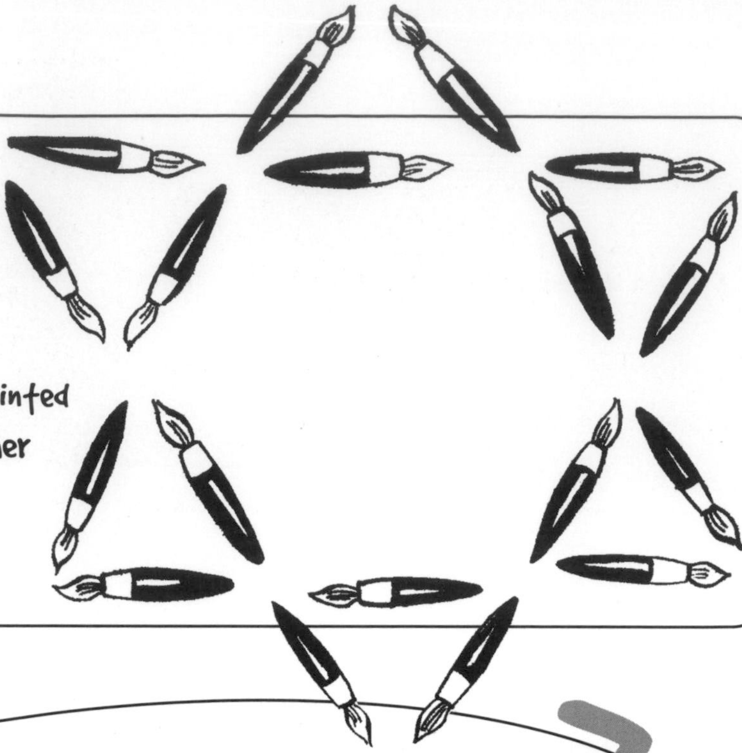

There are eight triangles in this six-pointed star. Move two brushes to make another six-pointed star, but with only six visible triangles.

2. Logic Puzzler

What is it about you that changes every year, always going up and never coming down?

3. Anagram Antics

Unscramble each of these words to find something in the picture.

CORS SISS
HARM ME
ROT RAP
TO CORD

4. Number Search

Two numbers between one and twenty are missing from the box. Can you find them?

5. Baffling Bet

A man was sitting in a cafe enjoying a drink when the waiter came over to him and said "I'll bet you $2 that if you give me $2, I will give you $3 in return." The man was puzzled as he thought about it. Should he accept the bet or not?

6. Word Play

Look at the clues and see if you can make new words by changing just one letter in each of these words.

Change FORK to a kind of meat.
Change SHOW to the opposite of fast.
Change HARD to a thick type of paper.

7. Age Question

When asked how old she was, Rosie replied "In two years I will be twice as old as I was five years ago." How old is she?

8. Number Cross

Fill in the numbers in the number grid by solving the clues.

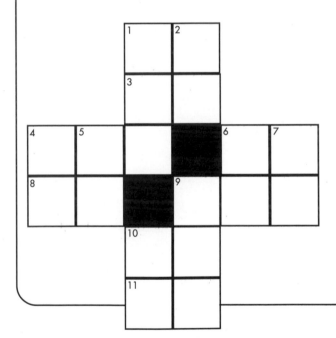

Across

1. Number of days in three weeks.
3. Six times seven.
4. 888 divided by four.
6. Half of seventy-six.
8. Four times seventeen.
9. Seven down plus eleven across.
10. 125 divided by five.
11. Eight + fourteen + eighteen.

Down

1. 121 doubled.
2. Thirty-six divided by three.
4. Half of fifty-two.
5. Eight across minus eleven across.
6. Four times eight.
7. Three across plus six across.
9. Half of 300.
10. Number of hours in a day.

9. Driving Dilemma

Bill was sitting in his car on an ordinary road pointing north. He turns to his friend and says "Even though we are pointing north, I can drive this car for one mile and end up one mile south of where we started from." How?

M	D	Y	T	A	F	W	U	Q	D	J	P
K	O	I	R	C	E	S	H	O	Z	K	S
T	B	U	J	O	C	I	G	L	B	D	Y
A	Z	Y	S	K	V	S	O	B	C	W	E
O	A	C	N	E	C	E	X	Y	I	N	K
G	I	P	L	K	F	S	N	A	C	R	N
F	O	S	J	F	T	D	D	O	F	L	O
H	R	C	A	W	I	B	K	S	I	Q	M
I	P	R	Q	U	X	N	T	H	P	L	X
K	I	Y	T	E	R	E	S	R	O	H	A
G	T	D	A	Z	C	I	O	J	U	C	B
R	W	A	C	F	L	X	B	D	R	I	B

10. Wild Wordsearch

Find these ten animals in the wordsearch.

GIRAFFE	HORSE
CAT	PIG
DOG	MONKEY
MOUSE	BIRD
LION	GOAT

11. Letter Change

Turn REAL into BELT by changing one letter at a time by following the clues.

1. Cotton and films come on this.
2. Sense of touch.
3. You walk on these.
4. A sort of pen tip.

REAL

reel
feel
feet
felt

BELT

12. Number Sequence

What's the next number in the sequence?

10 8 11 7 13 14 5

13. Ridiculous Riddle

Which source of heat is black when you buy it, red when you use it, and gray when you throw it away?

14. Alphabet Puzzle

Put a different letter or letters in front of the word AIR each time to solve the clues.

1. Strands of this are on your head.   _AIR

2. At this you can go on different rides.   _AIR

3. You sit on this.   _AIR

15. Letter Assembler

Rearrange these letters to make a ten-letter word meaning "all."

THIEVE GRYN

16. What Am I?

I am a word of five letters.
If you take away the first and last letters,
I will still sound the same.
Even if you take away the middle letter,
I will be the same as before.
What am I?

17. Mix And Match

Put the words below into their correct pairs.

Swan	Foal
Bear	Chick
Cow	Cygnet
Kangaroo	Cub
Rooster	Joey
Horse	Calf

18. Spot The Difference

Study the picture carefully for one minute. Then turn over the page and look at the same picture. Spot five things that have changed in the picture.

1. _____

2. _____

3. _____

4. _____

5. _____

19. Solve The Mystery

It's the middle of winter and five pieces of coal, a carrot, and a scarf are lying on the lawn. Nobody put them there but there is a perfectly good explanation why they are there. What is it?

20. Word Change

Look at the clues and make new words by changing just one letter in each of these words:

1. Change TALK into a story.

2. Change GATE into something found on a calendar.

3. Change FINE into a number.

21. Proverb Puzzler

Rearrange the letters to form a well-known six-word saying. As in the question, there are six letters in the first word of the answer, five letters in the second, three letters in the third, four letters in the fourth, two letters in the fifth, and three letters in the sixth.

TRIKES HILWE ETH RONI SI THO

22. Number Cruncher

The number FIVE as written using block capitals contains exactly ten strokes or segments of a straight line. Can you find a number which, when written out as words, contains as many strokes as the number says. (clue: it's between twenty and thirty.)

23. Word Wizz

Name the flowers that can be found by removing one letter from each word.

1. IRISH **2.** ROUSE
3. MASTER **4.** VIOLENT

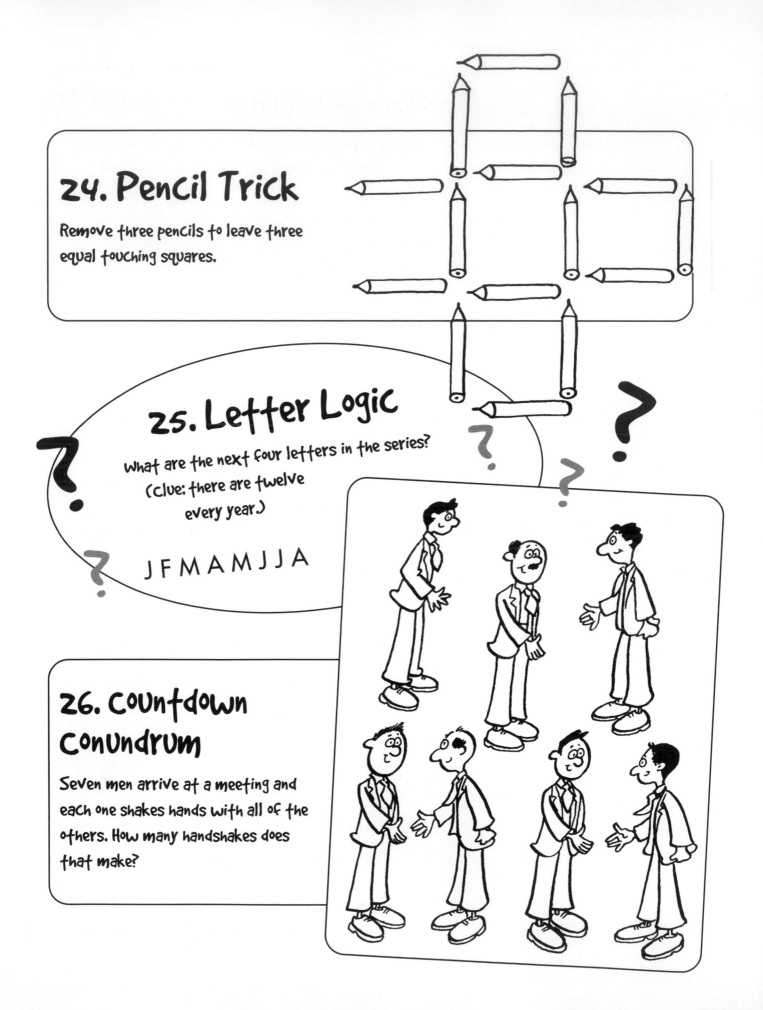

24. Pencil Trick

Remove three pencils to leave three equal touching squares.

25. Letter Logic

What are the next four letters in the series?
(clue: there are twelve every year.)

J F M A M J J A

26. Countdown Conundrum

Seven men arrive at a meeting and each one shakes hands with all of the others. How many handshakes does that make?

27. Hidden Countries

In each of the sentences below, the name of a country is hidden. For example, the sentence: "Interpol and the FBI catch criminals" contains the word Poland. Can you find them?

1. Our dog likes his food so much he eats a can a day.
2. Always use a pencil when drawing lines in diagrams.
3. The king was angry when a thief stole his painting.
4. Does the teacher teach in a classroom?
5. In anger, many people say things they don't mean.

28. Adder

Answer the clues, then create a new word by joining the two answers together. Can you think of any other words that are made up in this way?

	NOISE OF A COW
+	DANGER COLOUR
=	SECURED LIKE A BOAT

29. Tricky Words

Which word can be put before all the words below to make four new words?

FAST THROUGH DOWN AWAY

30. How Did She Do That?

A woman went outside without an umbrella or a raincoat, yet did not get wet. How's that?

31. Upside Down

Which number, written in figures, increases in value by 21 when turned upside down? (clue: it's between 60 and 70)

32. Learn The Language

Think of words ending in –GRY. Angry and hungry are two of them. There are only three words in the English language. What is the third word? The word is something that everyone uses every day. If you have read carefully what is written, it already says what it is.

33. Match Them Up

Match up the pairs with their rightful owners.

34. Mind The Gap

Which single three-letter word completes all of the following words?

_ _ _ WARD

BE _ _ _ E

_ _ _ GED

IN_ _ _ MATION

35. Oddly Enough

What is the opposite of NOT OUT?

36. Figure It Out

Andy bought a bag of apples on Monday and ate a third of them. On Tuesday he ate half of the remaining apples. On Wednesday he looked in the bag to find he only had two apples left. How many apples were originally in the bag?

37. Date Dilemma

How many days is it from Wednesday August 1st to the first Saturday in September?

38. Missing Alphabet

Find the two letters missing from the ball.

39. Catch A Cat

If six cats can catch six rats in six minutes, how many cats are needed to catch ten rats in ten minutes?

40. Deadly Decision

An explorer is caught stealing food by a tribe who order that he must die. But the tribe chief is a reasonable man and allows the explorer to choose the method by which he will be killed. The explorer is asked to make a single statement. If it is true he will be thrown off a high cliff. If it is false he will be eaten by lions. What clever statement does the explorer make that forces the chief to let him go?

41. Animal Madness

Can you name the creature missing from the nursery rhyme?

1. Mary had a little ____.

2. With a nicknack paddywhack, give the ___ a bone.

3. Pop goes the _____.

4. The ___ jumped over the moon.

42. Wise Words

What is the one thing that all people, no matter how important they are, agree is between heaven and Earth?

43. Gambling Games

Tom and Nancy are playing a game of cards for $1 a game. At the end of the evening, Tom has won three games and Nancy has won $3. How many games did they play?

44. Put Them Together

Match up these characters with their other halves.

Gretel   Jane   Hermione Granger   Gandalf   Jerry

Harry Potter   Bilbo Baggins   Tom   Tarzan   Hansel

45. About Turn

A group of soldiers were standing in the boiling hot sun, facing west. Their sergeant shouted at them: "Right Turn! About Turn! Left Turn!" What direction are they now facing? Right and left turns are both 90 degrees, and an about turn is 180 degrees.

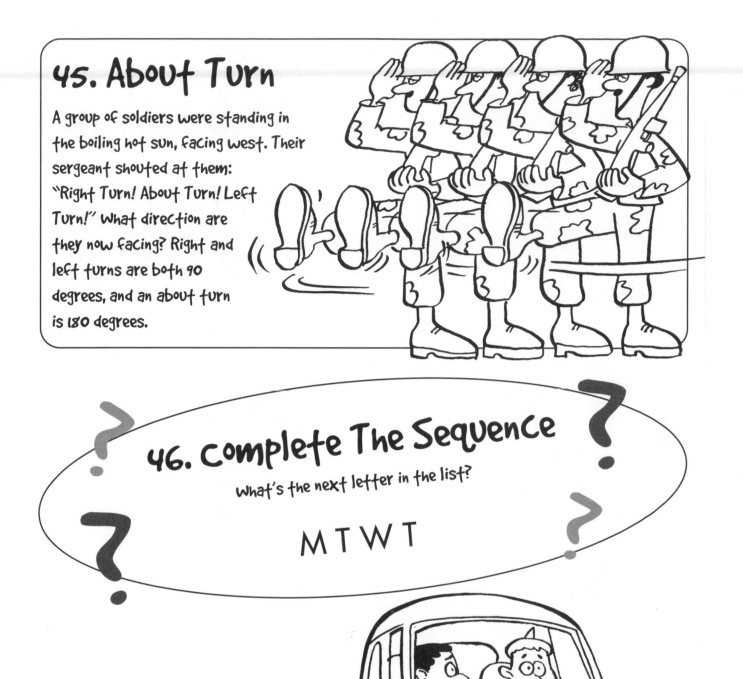

46. Complete The Sequence

what's the next letter in the list?

M T W T

47. Car Trouble

A four-wheeled car has traveled 24,000 miles and uses four tires. Each tire traveled the same distance. How far has each separate tire traveled?

48. Wacky Wordsearch

N	B	E	R	R	A	Z	I	B	M	F	C
J	P	U	V	I	Q	P	L	G	R	R	A
R	T	W	O	S	H	S	H	E	K	U	O
Q	D	F	G	N	N	A	K	E	B	D	D
A	B	C	M	I	G	J	G	G	T	E	M
Y	T	Z	F	E	J	N	P	G	N	S	Q
K	S	H	K	L	A	S	C	D	H	J	G
C	D	V	U	R	R	S	M	B	H	P	Z
A	O	N	T	D	S	H	O	A	W	N	H
W	M	S	S	W	T	B	F	Q	I	S	D
P	J	I	D	E	H	V	Z	R	D	K	D
C	W	W	E	I	R	D	M	U	B	G	O

Find the words:

STRANGE

WACKY

ODD

WEIRD

BIZARRE

RUDE

49. Number Solver

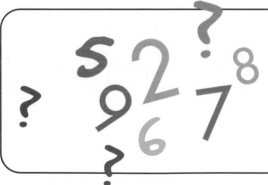

Find two whole numbers which, when multiplied together, give an answer of 61.

50. What Am I?

You use me from head to toe, the more I work the thinner I grow.
What am I?

51. Letter Game

HAND

_ _ _ _

_ _ _ _

_ _ _ _

FEET

Go from HAND to FEET by changing only one letter at a time.

1. This is found on a beach.
2. You do this to a letter.
3. You plant this to make a flower grow.
4. To take food in.

52. Picture Puzzle

Work out the saying from the picture.

ARREST

YOU'RE

53. Pencil Palaver

Take away six pencils to leave three equal-sized squares.

54. Sweet Tooth

Five children were sharing out a box of candy. Bob took five, Peter took five, Joey took five, and Danny took five. That left half the pack, which Natasha took. How many candies were there altogether?

FLUFF

IRAQI

ROBIN

SANTA

TOTAL

55. Long List

What's special about the list of words opposite? (Clue: look at the beginning and end of each word.)

56. Number Parts

Bill's number is two, Clare's number is three, and Edward's number is five. What is Donna's number?

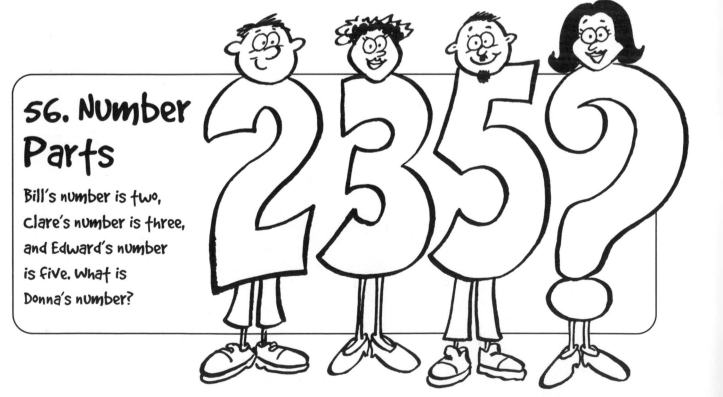

57. Body Parts

Name ten body parts that are spelt with three letters. No slang words!

58. Pictionary

Work out the saying from the picture.

59. Chocolate Challenge

One boy can eat sixteen chocolates in half a minute, and another can eat half as many in twice the length of time. How many chocolates can both boys eat between them in fifteen seconds?

60. Common Factor

What letter do the following numbers have in common?

3, 7, 10, 11, 12

61. Sleep Tight

Turn the word SLEEP into DREAM by changing one letter at a time.

1. An alarm clock makes this noise.
2. What happens when you cut yourself.
3. A species of something.
4. Eat this with jam.
5. Not looking forward to something.

SLEEP

_ _ _ _ _

_ _ _ _ _

_ _ _ _ _

_ _ _ _ _

_ _ _ _ _

DREAM

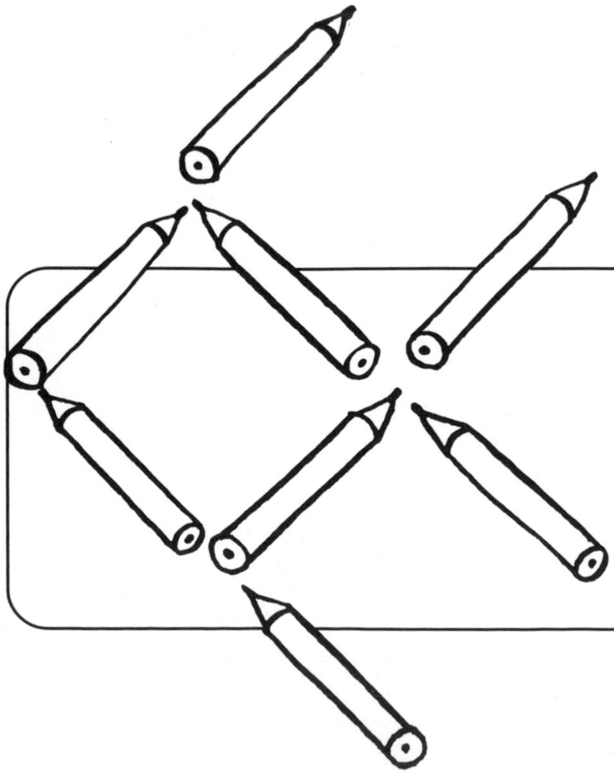

62. Sink or Swim

Reposition three pencils to make the fish swim in the opposite direction.

63. Picture Guess

Discover the saying from the picture.

64. Memory Trick

Pick a number between one and ten. Multiply by nine. Subtract five. Add the digits together and repeat this step until you have a one-digit number. For whatever number you have, pick that letter of the alphabet. E.g. A = 1, B = 2, etc.

Now think of a country beginning with that letter.

Think of an animal that begins with the second letter of the country.

Think of a color usually associated with the animal. What do you have?

65. A Dog's Life

Once there was a dog named Nelly, who lived on a farm. There were three other dogs on the farm. Their names were Blackie, Whitey, and Brownie. What do you think the fourth dog's name was?

66. Anagram Anger

Rearrange these letters to give the title of a famous wizard.

PORT TRAY HER

67. Memorize This

Look at the picture below for one minute. Then cover it up (no cheating!) and answer the questions.

1. How many loaves of bread are there in the bakery window?
2. Whose bakery is it?
3. What hairstyles do the twins have?
4. What time is it?
5. Is the toy store closed or open?

68. Odd One Out

Which of the following words doesn't belong in the group and why?

LAME   MALE   MEAL   MEAT

69. Building Split

This row of ten letters can be split into two five-letter words which are the names of two things used to make buildings. Words read from left to right and the letters are in the correct order. What are they?

B R S I T O C K N E

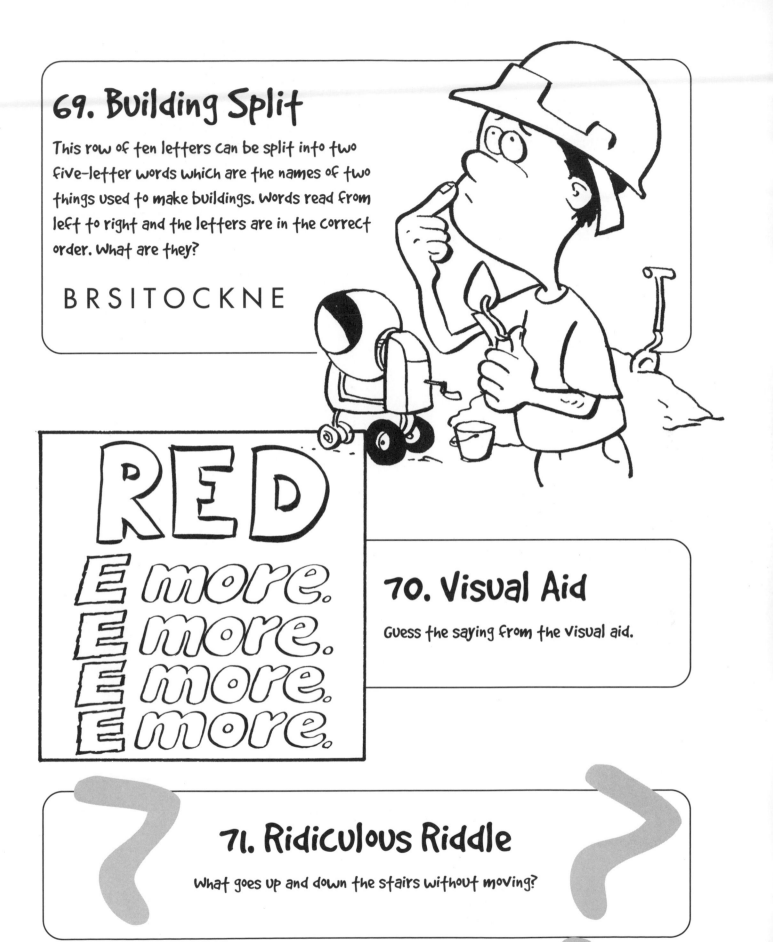

RED
E more.
E more.
E more.
E more.

70. Visual Aid

Guess the saying from the visual aid.

71. Ridiculous Riddle

What goes up and down the stairs without moving?

72. Snakes Alive

The name of a type of snake is hidden in each of the sentences below. Find them by joining words or parts of words together.

1. How sad Derek looks.
2. They stayed all night at the disco, bravely in my opinion.
3. The jumbo arrived on time.

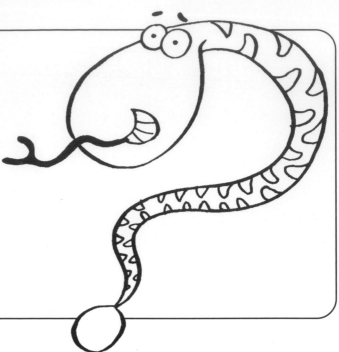

73. Flower Power

Here are the names of four flowers with the vowels removed. Can you name them?

DSY   BTTRCP   DFFDL   SNFLWR

74. Hunt The Word

The letters missing from this box make up the name of an animal. Can you name it?

75. Happy Birthday

Sally was eight the day before yesterday.

Next year she will be ten.

What is the date of Sally's birthday, and on which date would the first two things have been true?

76. Tennis Trouble

Two men were playing tennis. They played five sets and each man won three sets. How can this be possible?

77. Spoon Puzzle

Reposition six of the spoons in the pattern below to make six equal-sized diamond shapes in a star pattern.

78. What's Next?

What's the next letter in the series?

B, C, D, E, G

79. What Is It?

Guess the phrase from the picture.

Me right

80. Tall Tale

Before Mount Everest was discovered, what was the tallest mountain in the world?

81. Math Magic

Is half of two plus two equal to two or three?

82. Give Me Five

Solve the clues, so that each answer contains five letters. Write all the answers in place and the shaded squares reading down will reveal the name of a musical instrument.

1. Opposite of last.
2. Outer covering of an egg.
3. Sailing boat.
4. Bad weather.
5. Light you can carry.
6. Push this to power a bicycle.
7. Meadow.
8. Number in a trio.

1. _ _ _ _ _
2. _ _ _ _ _
3. _ _ _ _ _
4. _ _ _ _ _
5. _ _ _ _ _
6. _ _ _ _ _
7. _ _ _ _ _
8. _ _ _ _ _

83. Word Mix

Rearrange the letters of GROW NO LINSEED to spell one single word.

GROW NO
LINSEED

84. Word Ladder

Change NOSE into FAST by changing one letter at a time.

1. Misplace.
2. Opposite of found.
3. At the back.

NOSE

_ _ _ _

_ _ _ _

_ _ _ _

FAST

85. Big Is Best

Who is bigger? Mr Bigger, Mrs Bigger, or their baby?

86. The Hole Truth

If it takes three people to dig a hole, how many people does it take to dig half a hole?

87. Mathematical Equation

If five thousand, five hundred and five dollars is written as $5,505, how should twelve thousand, twelve hundred and twelve dollars be written?

88. Matchstick Marvel

Reposition four matches from this pattern to form five triangles.

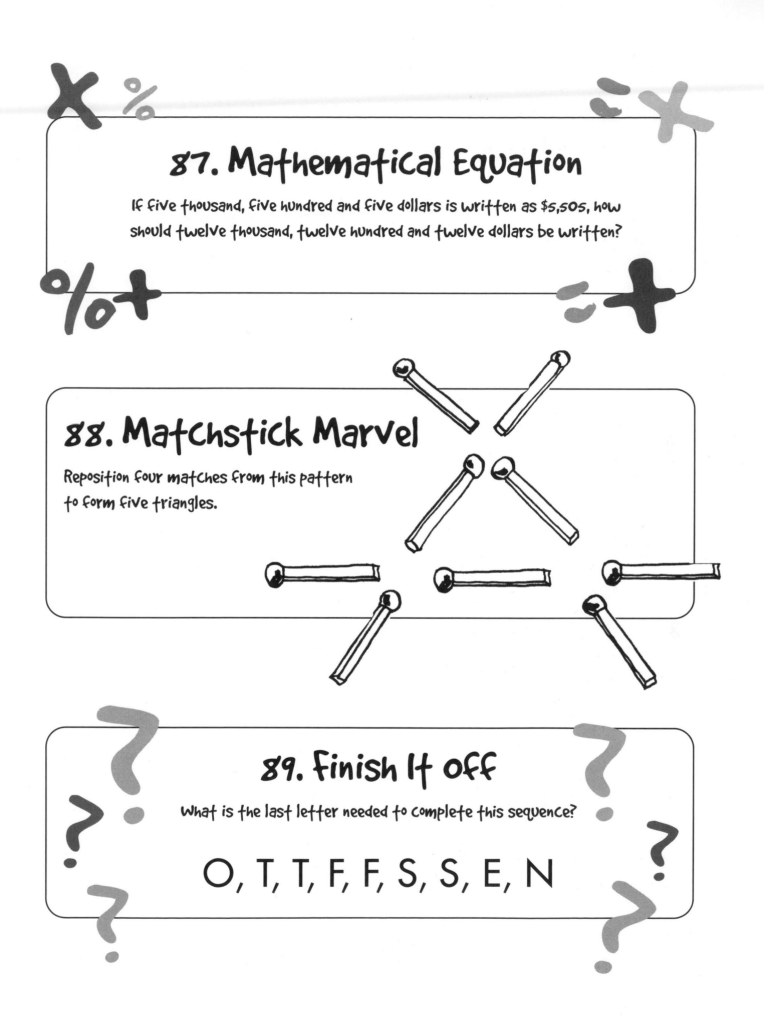

89. Finish It Off

What is the last letter needed to complete this sequence?

O, T, T, F, F, S, S, E, N

90. How Confusing

What starts with a T, ends with a T
and has T in it?

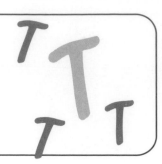

91. What Am I?

My first is in chair
But isn't in chain

My second is in pale
And also in pain

My third is in edge
But isn't in green

My fourth is in lime
But isn't in mean

My fifth's in cone
And also in round.

Do you know what I am?
I'm connected with sound!

92. Hot or cold?

What moves faster,
heat or cold?

93. Math Trick

When can you add two to eleven and get one?

94. Word Scramble

Rearrange these letters to give the names of some animals you might find at the zoo.

DANAP

KNOMEY

NAHPETLE

FEIRAGF

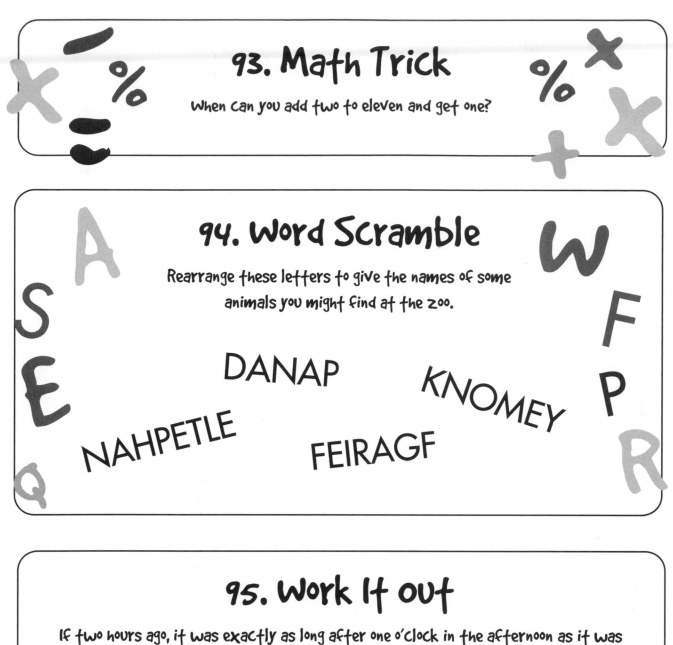

95. Work It Out

If two hours ago, it was exactly as long after one o'clock in the afternoon as it was before one o'clock in the morning, what time would it be now?

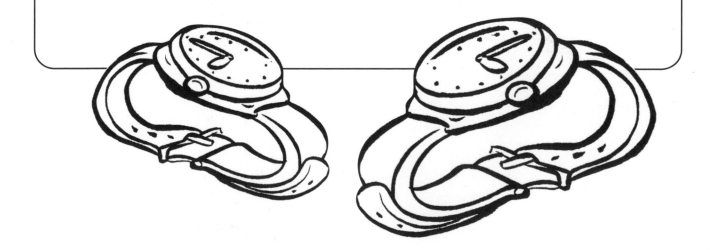

96. Animal Tracks

Make tracks and find seven different animals in the grid. Start at the letter in the top left square and move in any direction except diagonally. Every letter is used once.

```
C A M E A R
L L E B L E
I A R D E P
O P E G I H
N O R E T A
L E A P T N
```

97. Take Away

What is it that, when you take away the whole, you still have some left over?

98. Perplexing Puzzle

What is in the middle of nowhere?

99. Bowling

Four friends go bowling together. They decide that they will each play each other once.
How many games will they play?

100. Fitting In

? ? ?

What is the only other letter that fits in the following series?

B, C, D, E, I, K, O, X

? ? ?

101. Key Words

There's a problem on the keyboard of Clare's computer. She types in letters but the
screen only shows numbers! In each case the letter links to a number below it.
So, for example, 1 can stand for a Q, an A or a Z.
The number 9 could be an O or an L.
Can you work out what Clare was trying to say?

```
1 2 3 4 5 6 7 8 9 0
Q W E R T Y U I O P
A S D F G H J K L
Z X C V B N M
```

8 2165 5682 7136863
59 53 43018433

ANSWERS

1. Paintbrush Puzzle

2. Logic Puzzler

Your age.

3. Anagram Antics

Scissors

Hammer

Parrot

Doctor

4. Number Search

13 and 19

5. Baffling Bet

The man is in a no-win situation—
even if he wins the bet he still loses
$1 of his money.

6. Word Play

Pork
Slow
Card

7. Age Question

She's twelve.

8. Number Cross

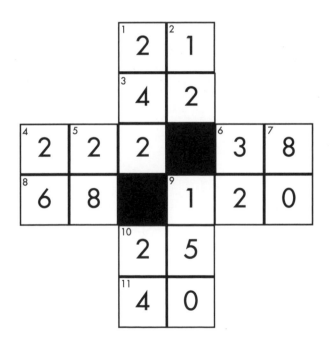

9. Driving Dilemma

Bill was driving in reverse.

10. Wild Wordsearch

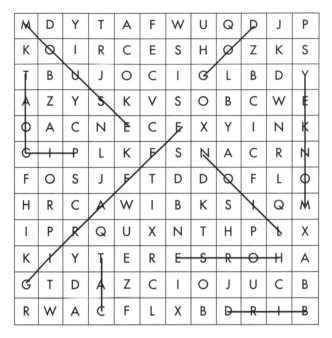

11. Letter Change

1. REEL
2. FEEL
3. FEET
4. FELT

12. Number Sequence

Fourteen—each time you add on two, then one, then two, then one and so on.

13. Ridiculous Riddle

Coal

14. Alphabet Puzzle

1. Hair
2. Fair
3. Chair

15. Letter Assembler

Everything

16. What Am I?

Empty

17. Mix And Match

Swan + cygnet
Bear + cub
Cow + calf
Kangaroo + joey
Rooster + chick
Horse + foal

18. Spot The Difference

1. The bottle of drink has gone.
2. The woman's glasses have disappeared.
3. There are now only two balloons.
4. There are only four people queuing for ice cream now.
5. There are five birds in the air now.

19. Solve The Mystery

They were used to make a snowman. The snow has melted.

20. Word Change

1. Tale
2. Date
3. Nine or Five

21. Proverb Puzzler

Strike while the iron is hot

22. Number Cruncher

TWENTY NINE

23. Word Wizz

1. IRIS 2. ROSE
3. ASTER 4. VIOLET

24. Pencil Trick

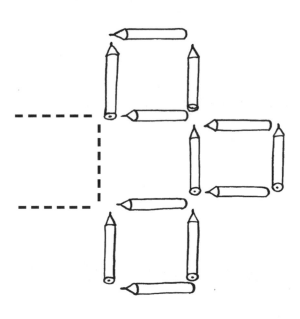

25. Letter Logic

S O N D—they are all the first
letters of months of the year

26. Countdown Conundrum

21

27. Hidden Countries

1. Canada – Our dog likes his food so
   much he eats a **can a d**ay.
2. India – Always use a pencil when
   drawing lines **in dia**grams.
3. Spain – The king was angry when a
   thief stole hi**s pain**ting.
4. China – Does the teacher tea**ch in a**
   classroom?
5. Germany – In an**ger, many** people
   say things they don't mean.

28. Adder

Moored

29. Tricky Words

They can all have the word BREAK in
front of them to make a new word.

30. How Did She Do That?

It wasn't raining.

31. Upside Down

68 (changes to 89)

32. Learn The Language

The key sentences are: There are only three words in the English language. What is the third word? The third word is "language."

33. Match Them Up

34. Mind The Gap

For

35. Oddly Enough

Out!

36. Figure It Out

He had six apples to start with and ate two apples on the first day and two on the second.

37. Date Dilemma

32—including both dates.

38. Missing Alphabet

K and R

39. Catch A Cat

Six cats

40. Deadly Decision

The explorer makes the statement: "I will be killed by the lions." Now if the chief feeds him to the lions, his statement will be true, so he should be thrown off the cliff. But if he is thrown off the cliff, his statement will be false. The chief has to let the explorer go!

41. Animal Madness

1. Lamb
2. Dog
3. Weasel
4. Cow

42. Wise Words

AND is between heaven and earth.

43. Gambling Games

They played nine games. Tom won three games and Nancy won six games.

44. Put Them Together

Hansel and Gretel
Tarzan and Jane
Harry Potter and Hermione Granger
Tom and Jerry
Bilbo Baggins and Gandalf

45. About Turn

East

46. Complete The Sequence

The next letter is F— the days of the week.

47. Car Trouble

They all traveled the same distance—24,000 miles each.

48. Wacky Wordsearch

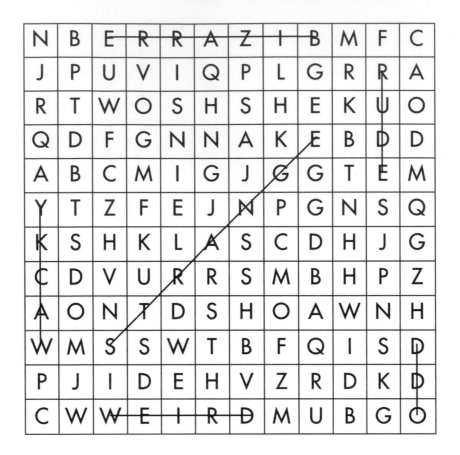

N	B	E	R	R	A	Z	I	B	M	F	C
J	P	U	V	I	Q	P	L	G	R	R	A
R	T	W	O	S	H	S	H	E	K	U	O
Q	D	F	G	N	N	A	K	E	B	D	D
A	B	C	M	I	G	J	G	G	T	E	M
Y	T	Z	F	E	J	N	P	G	N	S	Q
K	S	H	K	L	A	S	C	D	H	J	G
C	D	V	U	R	R	S	M	B	H	P	Z
A	O	N	T	D	S	H	O	A	W	N	H
W	M	S	S	W	T	B	F	Q	I	S	D
P	J	I	D	E	H	V	Z	R	D	K	D
C	W	W	E	I	R	D	M	U	B	G	O

49. Number Solver

1 x 61

50. What Am I?

A bar of soap.

51. Letter Game

1. Sand
2. Send
3. Seed
4. Feed

52. Picture Puzzle

You're under arrest.

53. Pencil Palaver

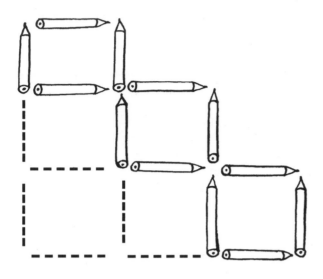

54. Sweet Tooth

40

55. Long List

The first letters in sequence, spell FIRST, the final letters spell FINAL.

56. Number Parts

Four—the first letter of the name has a value with A = 1, B = 2, etc.

57. Body Parts

Arm, Ear, Eye, Gum, Hip, Jaw, Lip, Leg, Rib, Toe.
Not: Bum, Gut, Lap!

58. Pictionary

Time after time

59. Chocolate Challenge

Ten chocolates

60. Common Factor

The only vowel they contain when written out fully is the letter E.

61. Sleep Tight

1. Bleep
2. Bleed
3. Breed
4. Bread
5. Dread

62. Sink or Swim

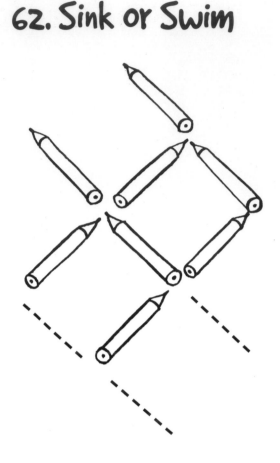

63. Picture Guess

Missing Link

64. Memory Trick

Do you have a gray elephant from Denmark? Now try it on your friends!

65. A Dog's Life

Nelly

66. Anagram Anger

Harry Potter

67. Memorize This

1. Four
2. Bernie's
3. Plaits
4. 10.30 am
5. Open

68. Odd One Out

Meat—all the others are anagrams of each other.

69. Building Split

Brick and Stone

70. Visual Aid

Ready for more.

71. Ridiculous Riddle

A carpet

72. Snakes Alive

1. Adder
2. Cobra
3. Boa

73. Flower Power

1. Daisy
2. Buttercup
3. Daffodil
4. Sunflower

74. Hunt The Word

Bear

75. Happy Birthday

Sally's birthday is December 31. The information would have been true on January 1.

76. Tennis Trouble

The two men were partners playing doubles.

77. Spoon Puzzle

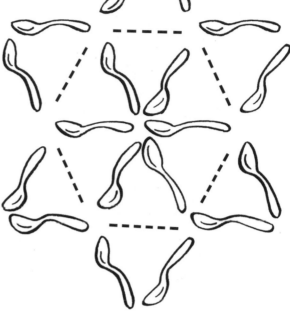

78. What's Next?

P—they all rhyme.

79. What Is It?

Right beside me

80. Tall Tale

Mount Everest—it was the tallest mountain even before it was discovered!

81. Math Magic

Three

82. Give Me Five

1. First
2. Shell
3. Yacht
4. Storm
5. Torch
6. Pedal
7. Field
8. Three

The musical instrument made
is a RECORDER

83. Word Mix

ONE SINGLE WORD

84. Word Ladder

1. Lose
2. Lost
3. Last

85. Big Is Best

The baby, because he's a
little bigger!

86. The Hole Truth

You can't dig half a hole!

87. Mathematical Equation

$13,212

88. Matchstick Marvel

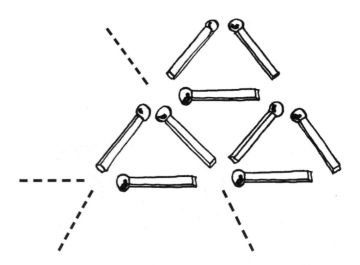

89. Finish It Off

T—the letters are the initials of the numbers one to ten.

90. How Confusing

A teapot

91. What Am I?

Radio

92. Hot or Cold

Heat—everyone can catch a cold!

93. Math Trick

When you add two hours to eleven o'clock you get one o'clock.

94. Word Scramble

Elephant
Panda
Giraffe
Monkey

95. Work It Out

Nine o'clock—since there are twelve hours between the two times, and half of that time equals six, then the halfway mark would have to be seven o'clock.
If it were seven o'clock, two hours ago, then the time would now be nine o'clock.

96. Animal Tracks

1. Camel
2. Lion
3. Leopard
4. Bear
5. Elephant
6. Tiger
7. Ape

97. Take Away

The word "wholesome."

98. Perplexing Puzzle

The Letter "H."

99. Bowling

There are six games.

100. Fitting In

H—all of the letters in the series flipped vertically look the same.

101. Key Words

I WANT THIS MACHINE TO BE REPAIRED.

Now that you've completed 101 of our brainbender puzzles it's time to find out what your score reveals about your brain's puzzle-solving ability!

1-20	You have an average puzzle solving ability.
21-40	Your performance reveals that you are a fine puzzle solver.
41-60	People with this score are often distinguished puzzle busters.
61-80	Your logical thinking makes problem solving easy.
81-101	Puzzle master—puzzles are easy for your fabulous brain.

CROSSWORD SEARCH PUZZLES

1. Mother Nature

1. A small animal with a bushy tail (8)
2. A tall plant with a trunk and branches (4)
3. A series of tunnels where rabbits live (6)
4. A small red beetle with black spots (7)
5. Season between summer and winter (4)
6. It has a soft body, no bones, and lives in the earth (4)
7. Dry soil found in the garden (5)
8. The oval nut of an oak tree (5)
9. They are flat and green and grow on branches (6)
10. A small animal with stiff spines on its back (8)

B	Q	R	S	S	Q	U	I	R	R	E	L
T	H	E	D	G	E	H	O	G	U	T	S
L	M	E	J	P	Z	R	O	L	V	Q	P
Z	I	R	J	A	C	O	R	N	L	N	Z
O	L	T	K	M	D	A	B	S	T	M	A
E	N	P	Q	A	R	N	A	B	H	L	O
A	L	A	D	Y	B	U	G	D	L	L	O
R	A	L	E	A	V	E	S	P	K	A	W
T	S	Y	L	W	A	T	S	M	R	F	D
H	R	A	D	L	Q	P	R	V	O	J	I
B	O	T	N	D	J	O	K	S	M	J	Q
N	E	R	R	A	W	V	T	W	R	L	P

D	L	H	O	S	P	I	T	A	L	F	N
T	U	O	G	E	T	T	H	A	O	I	A
I	R	W	U	O	Z	O	O	T	O	R	C
E	N	O	T	O	F	R	E	Y	P	E	U
H	T	L	P	H	E	S	O	O	G	S	L
L	A	E	M	R	C	O	U	J	N	T	O
O	E	L	Y	I	I	L	D	U	I	A	N
O	O	V	I	F	S	A	S	T	M	T	D
H	L	Y	M	H	I	N	F	I	M	I	O
C	O	F	F	I	C	E	N	C	I	O	N
S	L	C	H	U	R	C	H	O	W	N	U
P	A	L	A	C	E	C	T	I	S	N	E

2. Going Places

1. The capital city of England (6)
2. This is where firefighters work (4,7)
3. Kings live in this sort of place (6)
4. Where children go to learn new things (6)
5. A place where you can go to swim (8,4)
6. A place to go when you're very ill or hurt (8)
7. People go here to work on computers (6)
8. Where planes take off and land (7)
9. Here you can see lots of different animals (3)
10. A place where people go to worship God (6)

3. Getting Around

1. A big vehicle that carries lots of passengers (3)
2. A fast vehicle that runs on tracks (5)
3. This vehicle takes you across the sky (8)
4. A large vehicle that takes objects by road (5)
5. A two-wheeled vehicle that you pedal (4)
6. You drive this small vehicle along the road (3)
7. This vehicle carries people and objects by sea (4)
8. It's larger than a car and smaller than a lorry (3)
9. A bike with an engine (9)
10. Wheeled objects attached to feet to get around (12)

N	M	C	E	B	O	A	T	M	S	T	S
V	O	D	A	F	D	R	O	R	H	U	E
H	T	O	L	Y	I	K	C	E	P	E	T
P	O	Z	C	D	S	R	S	T	N	Q	A
B	R	N	A	A	E	L	S	A	F	L	K
A	B	I	A	N	R	C	L	Z	G	S	S
T	I	A	M	A	N	P	T	O	E	R	R
G	K	R	Y	A	R	O	R	B	E	O	E
W	E	T	N	I	A	C	U	H	K	T	L
S	L	R	A	Z	N	A	C	Y	I	A	L
U	E	A	M	E	S	R	K	E	B	P	O
B	A	I	N	A	V	O	L	I	T	O	R

4. Down on The Farm

1. Rolls around in the mud, and has a curly tail (3)
2. This animal's coat is used to make wool (5)
3. An animal with a mane and long tail (5)
4. This hopping animal has soft fur and long ears (6)
5. This animal has feathers and lays eggs (7)
6. They are good at herding sheep (4)
7. A horned animal and some have beards (4)
8. A large animal which goes "moo" (3)
9. A baby goat (3)
10. A male chicken (7)

S	R	A	B	B	I	T	U	N	T	Y	S
L	I	N	A	T	C	O	E	S	R	O	H
P	M	A	N	T	E	E	N	P	I	D	E
E	F	R	E	R	H	E	O	D	N	T	B
E	O	M	E	R	K	B	S	E	P	I	G
H	V	A	F	C	I	R	H	O	T	R	H
S	O	L	I	L	F	D	O	G	S	Z	G
T	E	H	Z	D	E	H	D	E	E	F	W
O	C	I	L	R	I	T	I	M	T	O	O
D	M	Q	T	A	O	G	T	E	H	T	C
I	I	G	T	O	N	M	A	N	N	O	I
K	R	H	R	O	O	S	T	E	R	W	S

5. fantastic food

1. A baked dessert which comes in many flavors (4)
2. These small green vegetables grow in a pod (4)
3. Finger-shaped meat which is great with mash (7)
4. You have this wobbly dessert with ice cream (5)
5. A yellow fruit with spiky green leaves on top (9)
6. Heated-up bread which has turned brown (5)
7. Sea-living food, often served with chips (4)
8. Hard-shelled food that comes from chickens (3)
9. A vegetable that can be boiled, roasted, or fried (6)
10. Breakfast food that is delicious with milk (6)

L	A	E	R	E	C	A	Y	I	M	F	I
U	Y	A	S	E	R	D	T	O	A	S	T
T	O	R	W	Q	P	O	O	A	N	N	E
O	L	L	B	H	E	K	D	J	T	P	H
L	O	A	E	G	A	S	U	A	S	I	S
L	O	S	I	T	M	C	Y	H	X	Z	I
E	H	E	P	O	T	A	T	O	B	S	F
J	P	I	N	E	A	P	P	L	E	H	A
O	R	Y	W	F	G	L	U	Y	I	K	N
T	C	A	K	E	G	U	S	O	U	T	S
K	T	O	E	G	V	C	H	P	E	A	S
L	A	T	E	R	U	A	P	L	S	E	A

6. Cool Colors

1. A mixture of red and blue (6)
2. Light red, the color of fingernails (4)
3. The darkest color (5)
4. The color of 'stop' on traffic lights (3)
5. The color of a lemon (6)
6. The lightest color (5)
7. A mixture of red and yellow (6)
8. The color of grass (5)
9. A yellow color, used to make jewelry (4)
10. Another valuable object color (6)

L	W	R	R	Q	I	E	G	N	A	R	O
G	H	M	K	E	S	T	L	R	V	T	F
E	I	G	G	H	V	I	W	J	R	Z	G
P	T	I	K	U	S	L	I	Q	I	O	R
E	E	N	T	E	R	U	I	Q	N	S	E
L	I	D	E	R	P	H	R	S	G	E	E
W	G	O	L	D	T	E	U	M	G	D	N
O	E	L	S	V	L	C	K	C	A	L	B
L	R	E	W	P	D	K	H	F	P	Z	I
L	G	B	R	X	D	N	Y	L	A	N	N
E	W	U	E	R	D	I	N	B	S	L	S
Y	P	A	V	E	R	P	O	O	A	H	T

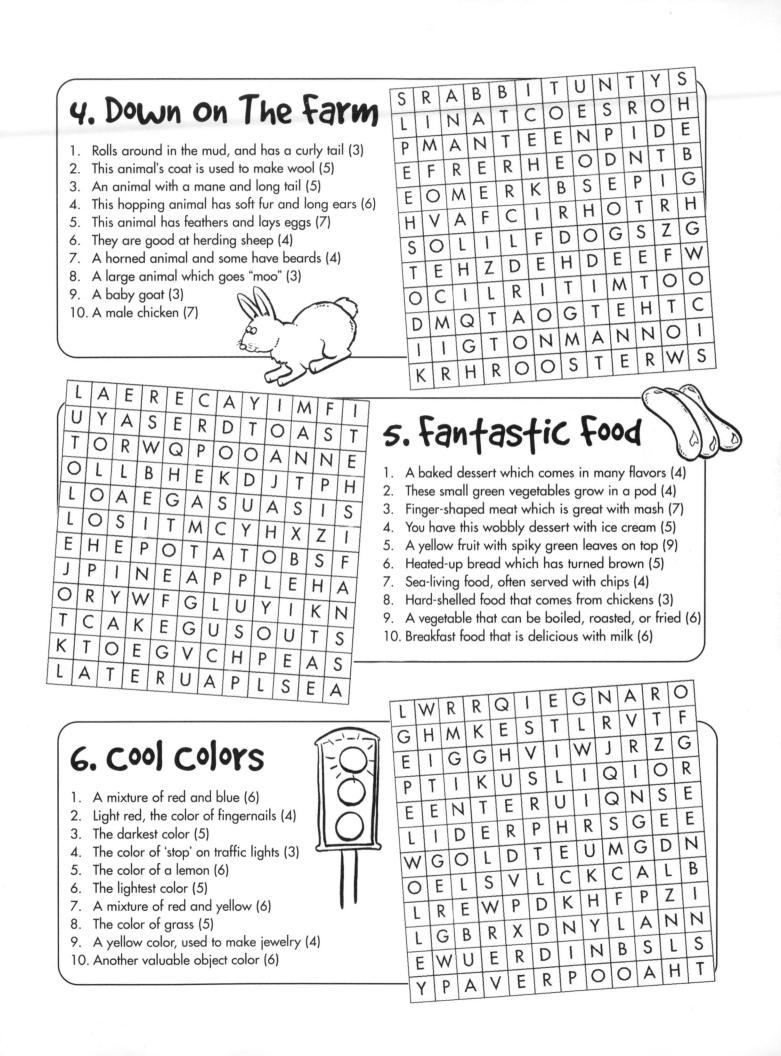

7. In The Home

1. An object you put garbage in (8)
2. Something you sleep in (3)
3. What you use to pick up dirt on the floor (6)
4. A four-legged object where food is served (5)
5. Something you lie in to wash or relax (4)
6. You need to go up these to get to the next floor (6)
7. Where books can be stored (8)
8. You heat water in this to make a cup of tea (6)
9. You watch your favorite programs on it (10)
10. A very big chair for two or three people (5)

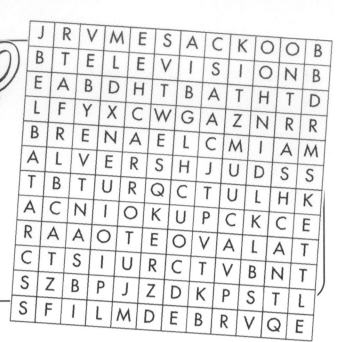

J	R	V	M	E	S	A	C	K	O	O	B
B	T	E	L	E	V	I	S	I	O	N	B
E	A	B	D	H	T	B	A	T	H	T	D
L	F	Y	X	C	W	G	A	Z	N	R	R
B	R	E	N	A	E	L	C	M	I	A	M
A	L	V	E	R	S	H	J	U	D	S	S
T	B	T	U	R	Q	C	T	U	L	H	K
A	C	N	I	O	K	U	P	C	K	C	E
R	A	A	O	T	E	O	V	A	L	A	T
C	T	S	I	U	R	C	T	V	B	N	T
S	Z	B	P	J	Z	D	K	P	S	T	L
S	F	I	L	M	D	E	B	R	V	Q	E

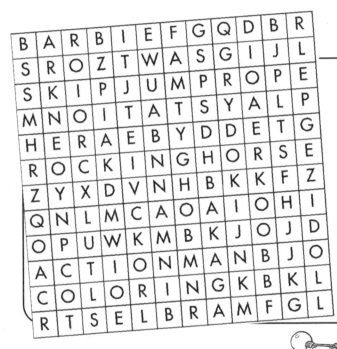

B	A	R	B	I	E	F	G	Q	D	B	R
S	R	O	Z	T	W	A	S	G	I	J	L
S	K	I	P	J	U	M	P	R	O	P	E
M	N	O	I	T	A	T	S	Y	A	L	P
H	E	R	A	E	B	Y	D	D	E	T	G
R	O	C	K	I	N	G	H	O	R	S	E
Z	Y	X	D	V	N	H	B	K	K	F	Z
Q	N	L	M	C	A	O	A	I	O	H	I
O	P	U	W	K	M	B	K	J	O	J	D
A	C	T	I	O	N	M	A	N	B	J	O
C	O	L	O	R	I	N	G	K	B	K	L
R	T	S	E	L	B	R	A	M	F	G	L

8. Toy Store

1. A book with pictures where you fill in the colors (8)
2. A furry toy animal you can cuddle (5, 4)
3. A blonde doll who has lots of different outfits (6)
4. Pieces which you put together to see a picture (6)
5. A games console on which you can play (11)
6. A wooden horse you can sit on and ride (7, 5)
7. A hero boy soldier toy you can play with (6, 3)
8. A girl toy you can dress up and style (4)
9. A piece of thick cord with handles to jump over (4, 4)
10. Round pieces of glass flicked at an opponent's (7)

9. At The Circus

1. A swing on which acrobatics are performed (7)
2. A funny person who does comical tricks (5)
3. The circle in which circus people perform (4)
4. A man who can lift heavy things (6, 3)
5. A bike with one wheel that people do tricks on (8)
6. Powdery wood used for animals to walk on (7)
7. This cold treat is sold during the interval (3, 5)
8. You buy one of these to get into the circus (6)
9. A four-legged animal that performers ride on (5)
10. The big tent where the circus is held (3, 3)

S	V	E	L	C	Y	C	I	N	U	L	D
T	R	Q	K	L	B	J	Z	G	N	I	R
R	M	S	A	W	D	U	S	T	T	V	L
O	L	P	Q	D	R	M	D	A	I	W	T
N	J	O	D	K	L	V	P	C	U	C	E
G	M	T	P	C	O	E	E	N	B	L	K
M	R	G	L	N	Z	C	Z	G	K	P	C
A	H	I	J	E	R	Q	L	J	N	R	I
N	S	B	P	E	F	I	R	A	W	O	T
B	C	A	A	D	C	B	D	Z	O	M	C
Z	R	M	T	V	R	X	L	K	L	S	T
T	I	E	S	R	O	H	W	J	C	R	O

10. Girls' Names

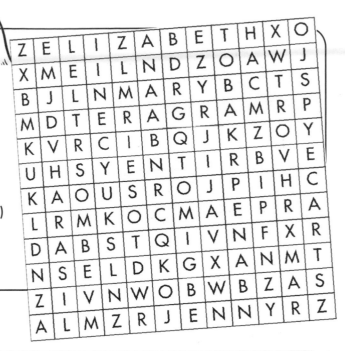

1. Short for Joanne (2)
2. Short for Jennifer (5)
3. This girl's name starts with "T" (6)
4. This name is also the name of a flower (4)
5. This woman was the mother of Jesus (4)
6. This five-letter name begins with "S" (5)
7. This name is the same when it's spelt backwards (4)
8. This name can be shortened to "Maggie" (8)
9. The Queen of England's name (9)
10. This pop star sang "Sometimes" and "Boys" (7)

Z	E	L	I	Z	A	B	E	T	H	X	O
X	M	E	I	L	N	D	Z	O	A	W	J
B	J	L	N	M	A	R	Y	B	C	T	S
M	D	T	E	R	A	G	R	A	M	R	P
K	V	R	C	I	B	Q	J	K	Z	O	Y
U	H	S	Y	E	N	T	I	R	B	V	E
K	A	O	U	S	R	O	J	P	I	H	C
L	R	M	K	O	C	M	A	E	P	R	A
D	A	B	S	T	Q	I	V	N	F	X	R
N	S	E	L	D	K	G	X	A	N	M	T
Z	I	V	N	W	O	B	W	B	Z	A	S
A	L	M	Z	R	J	E	N	N	Y	R	Z

11. At Work

B	C	N	S	T	W	R	I	T	E	R	S
F	L	O	R	I	S	T	R	U	N	A	R
S	D	O	C	T	O	R	S	U	U	R	E
R	Y	H	M	A	E	A	R	F	O	K	T
E	N	Y	C	R	I	S	L	T	B	Q	H
H	D	D	S	Z	E	O	C	O	W	V	G
C	R	K	I	S	L	A	P	L	T	B	I
A	T	N	E	D	I	S	E	R	P	E	F
E	Q	P	U	L	L	W	M	S	L	M	E
T	Z	L	W	R	E	K	M	F	K	I	R
F	X	S	R	E	M	R	A	F	Q	R	I
S	I	N	G	E	R	S	W	T	I	P	F

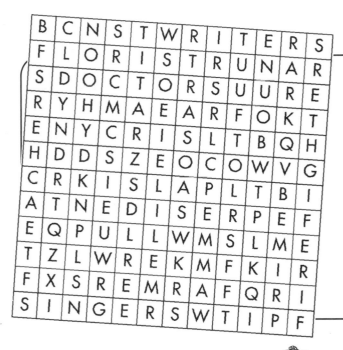

1. He runs the country (9)
2. They make ill people well again (7)
3. They help doctors (6)
4. They sing very well (7)
5. They help children to learn (8)
6. They grow crops and raise animals (7)
7. They put fires out and rescue people (12)
8. She makes up stories and poems (6)
9. She sells and arranges flowers (7)
10. He plays different parts in films or plays (5)

12. Wild Animals

1. African animal with a very long neck (7)
2. Very large animal with a trunk and tusks (8)
3. This big cat is the fastest land animal (7)
4. Black and white, this looks like a horse (5)
5. A mischievous animal, similar to humans (6)
6. A big cat with a huge roar and a fur mane (4)
7. A black and white sea bird that eats fish (7)
8. A large swimming reptile with lots of teeth (9)
9. A large, heavy animal with thick fur (4)
10. A big river animal with thick skin (12)

N	Z	R	R	A	E	B	S	E	I	D	D
Z	Y	E	U	V	X	H	U	L	L	P	C
N	B	O	B	R	I	V	M	E	X	V	R
H	L	L	D	R	P	Y	A	P	K	G	O
A	L	I	S	Z	A	K	T	H	M	I	C
T	C	U	O	L	O	N	O	A	N	R	O
E	V	K	B	N	I	M	P	N	I	A	D
E	O	A	X	U	Z	E	O	T	U	F	I
H	S	R	G	U	N	K	P	N	G	F	L
C	U	N	A	P	I	N	P	R	N	E	E
O	E	L	C	V	R	C	I	T	E	D	R
P	M	O	N	K	E	Y	H	B	B	O	L

13. Holidays

1. Presents are left in this at Christmas (8)
2. This is decorated with tinsel and baubles at Christmas (4)
3. Jewish holiday in December (8)
4. Traditional meat eaten at Thanksgiving (6)
5. You are given these at Christmas (8)
6. Father ____ , another name for Santa Claus (9)
7. Baby Jesus was laid in this (6)
8. Eat this after the main course (7)
9. These special songs are sung at Christmas (6)
10. Chocolate cake eaten at Christmas (4, 3)

C	Z	C	S	A	M	T	S	I	R	H	C
M	M	A	N	G	E	R	O	Y	X	S	R
G	P	H	B	T	C	A	R	O	L	S	E
N	U	R	I	D	U	A	C	U	M	F	H
I	D	Z	H	M	W	R	P	A	T	N	T
K	D	A	T	A	V	S	K	M	O	I	A
C	I	M	X	L	K	L	Z	E	K	H	F
O	N	P	M	E	F	K	M	S	Y	Z	A
T	G	O	E	I	B	Q	U	D	F	W	Q
S	C	R	P	O	A	X	Y	N	N	W	B
N	T	Y	U	L	E	L	O	G	A	Z	X
Q	S	T	N	E	S	E	R	P	L	H	H

14. Under The Sea

1. Shellfish with large claws (7)
2. Fishy horse (8)
3. Plant that grows in the sea (7)
4. Intelligent animal that plays in the sea (7)
5. Imaginary half-woman with a fish's tail (7)
6. A shellfish with ten legs (4)
7. There are lots of these in the sea (4)
8. Large sea fish with lots of sharp teeth (5)
9. Moving ridges of water in the sea (5)
10. Large sea animal with eight tentacles (7)

J	Y	X	H	U	P	W	M	J	H	F	F
D	C	V	N	S	H	A	R	K	Y	D	X
Y	F	U	E	K	X	X	E	F	J	P	N	P
D	D	O	L	P	H	I	N	U	D	E	U
E	Q	H	D	S	V	L	R	C	I	Q	E
E	M	K	U	C	F	E	H	D	A	H	S
W	S	W	R	J	T	L	K	F	M	M	R
A	L	A	C	S	S	U	X	E	R	V	O
E	B	X	B	V	Y	E	C	H	E	P	H
S	F	O	K	D	M	Y	V	K	M	E	A
Y	L	E	H	S	I	F	E	A	N	Q	E
O	C	T	O	P	U	S	V	H	W	J	S

15. TV characters

1. Thomas the Tank Engine's pal (5)
2. He's also known as T.C. (3, 3)
3. This builder likes to fix things (3)
4. He's a big purple dinosaur (6)
5. This powerful man is very strong (5)
6. One of the *Rugrats* (5)
7. The name of the main tank engine (6)
8. ____ Bunny (4)
9. This crime-solving dog gets very scared (6, 3)
10. Dummy-sucking *Simpsons* character (6)

N	B	O	B	F	I	X	W	T	S	A	H
P	A	S	H	L	T	C	H	J	U	F	I
L	C	U	B	O	Y	O	K	P	S	W	D
E	D	Y	M	A	M	F	T	B	E	N	L
I	K	M	Y	A	I	L	A	H	I	Y	P
G	Y	B	S	H	N	K	C	Y	B	E	I
G	N	X	P	A	S	M	P	F	S	N	U
A	S	L	M	Y	S	J	O	A	G	R	B
M	C	E	K	W	G	U	T	X	U	A	S
L	H	A	F	B	J	P	H	N	B	B	X
S	C	O	O	B	Y	D	O	O	C	Y	H
U	H	E	N	R	Y	A	N	L	A	W	G

16. Family Fun

1. The man who brings you up (3)
2. Father of your mom or dad (7)
3. Mother of your mom or dad (7)
4. The child of your aunt or uncle (6)
5. Your brother or sister's daughter (5)
6. The woman who brings you up (3)
7. Daughter of the same parents as another person (6)
8. Sister or sister-in-law of your mom or dad (6)
9. Your brother or sister's son (6)
10. Son of the same parents as another person (7)

B	E	C	E	I	N	U	I	F	K	E	M
H	R	X	A	L	C	J	I	H	Z	O	W
N	E	P	H	E	W	S	X	B	M	R	P
I	S	C	B	A	M	D	N	A	R	G	U
Z	F	O	H	I	F	G	E	M	C	E	I
E	A	U	J	R	D	L	A	W	N	L	O
I	R	S	N	E	P	A	S	H	D	H	W
T	M	I	R	T	I	U	D	P	K	A	U
N	C	N	S	S	J	H	O	N	D	K	D
U	O	A	M	I	H	Z	E	I	A	Y	X
A	B	L	X	S	D	N	P	F	W	R	K
R	B	R	O	T	H	E	R	R	U	E	G

17. Clothes

G	S	E	O	H	S	Q	I	L	U	D	L
A	K	H	V	F	Y	R	B	G	M	R	F
U	M	X	R	I	E	N	R	U	O	E	A
I	N	A	O	P	F	U	N	V	K	S	T
H	C	L	M	H	Q	D	A	S	O	S	R
S	R	U	G	B	E	M	R	K	N	O	I
Y	J	E	K	R	H	E	H	H	I	M	H
N	U	V	W	L	S	Y	X	B	H	Q	S
F	Q	E	I	T	R	T	A	O	C	F	T
M	A	V	N	A	G	T	R	I	K	S	N
R	B	A	L	K	N	M	U	V	E	O	G
Y	P	R	I	U	S	O	C	K	S	Y	X

1. Wear these to walk in (5)
2. An alternative to pants (5)
3. A top, often made of wool (6)
4. Wear these on your feet under shoes (5)
5. This top is shaped like a T (1, 5)
6. Wear these over your legs (5)
7. Wear these under your clothes (9)
8. This is a combined skirt and top (5)
9. This goes over your clothes when you go outside (4)
10. This long woolly item keeps your neck warm (5)

18. In the Backyard

1. Use this to dig (5)
2. These plants aren't wanted (5)
3. Grow plants in this building (10)
4. You cut the grass with it (9)
5. A small house for children to play in (9)
6. A ceramic or plastic object to put plants in (9)
7. A wheeled object that carries heavy things (11)
8. Paved area where people can sit (5)
9. A beautiful plant with petals (6)
10. A wooden structure to separate gardens (5)

W	R	I	R	E	W	O	M	N	W	A	L
H	Y	J	T	A	L	P	A	T	I	O	B
E	F	D	K	O	T	R	B	L	G	N	D
E	L	E	L	N	P	E	T	Y	C	Z	S
L	O	A	C	B	Z	R	J	I	D	Q	D
B	W	G	W	N	D	H	E	U	C	U	E
A	E	R	Y	I	E	E	L	W	B	J	E
R	R	J	T	D	Q	F	B	K	O	L	W
R	K	T	A	B	K	N	G	T	I	L	K
O	U	P	D	W	Y	N	A	Q	U	Z	F
W	S	R	E	S	U	O	H	Y	A	L	P
J	K	G	R	E	E	N	H	O	U	S	E

19. Space

1. Earth's only natural satellite (4)
2. Someone who goes into outer space (9)
3. Large body in space that revolves around the sun (6)
4. This explosive thing shoots into space (6)
5. Reusable spacecraft (7)
6. Bodies of gas that shine in the sky (5)
7. The moon has none of this force on it (7)
8. Includes the sun and eight planets (5, 6)
9. The planet we live on (5)
10. Heavenly body with a luminous 'tail' (5)

Q	C	H	G	T	E	K	C	O	R	I	V
B	O	M	R	L	D	Q	Z	B	A	H	O
R	M	E	A	U	W	M	G	T	S	K	L
D	E	T	V	V	B	O	E	N	T	O	G
H	T	S	I	K	L	N	X	S	R	K	E
M	Z	Y	T	G	A	R	D	G	O	S	L
O	B	S	Y	L	H	M	T	K	N	W	T
O	I	R	P	V	T	U	H	Y	A	X	T
N	U	A	T	Q	B	T	I	L	U	O	U
S	K	L	D	S	R	D	Z	D	T	R	H
Q	G	O	H	A	X	N	V	O	N	M	S
Z	R	S	E	L	S	R	A	T	S	X	D

F	O	T	R	A	E	H	S	T	U	A	R
T	C	Z	Q	H	K	E	O	D	A	E	H
E	R	L	A	T	U	L	M	Z	K	B	N
E	K	N	M	U	S	C	L	E	Q	F	V
F	D	F	C	S	Q	N	V	E	S	T	P
S	L	R	E	O	A	M	N	A	R	E	T
A	T	Y	U	S	N	O	B	C	L	E	N
C	E	P	Q	C	B	T	K	B	R	N	O
F	Z	U	K	R	L	F	A	T	Z	K	H
S	L	I	A	N	R	E	G	N	I	F	B
R	P	C	L	Q	N	O	V	R	S	H	L
K	N	O	T	T	U	B	Y	L	L	E	B

20. The Body

1. You see with these (4)
2. Allows the leg to bend (4)
3. On top of your neck (4)
4. You walk on these (4)
5. You pick things up with these (5)
6. Tissue that allows us to move (6)
7. This pumps blood around the body (5)
8. This hard material part makes up the skeleton (4)
9. Also known as the navel (5, 6)
10. They are on the end of your fingers (11)

21. Opposites

1. The opposite of cold (3)
2. The opposite of thin (3)
3. The opposite of big (5)
4. The opposite of up (4)
5. The opposite of difficult (4)
6. The opposite of quiet (4)
7. The opposite of right (4)
8. The opposite of backward (8)
9. The opposite of quickly (6)
10. The opposite of smooth (5)

Z	F	P	D	Y	L	W	O	L	S	P	E
O	R	E	S	Q	K	S	X	H	C	H	N
U	X	M	E	D	H	B	L	Y	S	A	E
D	N	K	K	T	R	D	O	X	N	K	T
N	B	T	F	U	Z	A	R	J	T	J	G
W	K	E	R	F	N	F	W	I	S	F	D
O	L	S	L	P	K	R	U	R	Q	L	S
D	X	T	D	B	O	M	G	T	O	C	M
Q	F	O	C	U	E	G	A	X	K	F	A
G	I	H	G	E	J	E	P	I	E	S	L
K	Z	H	D	N	O	F	T	K	Z	D	L
M	U	D	U	O	L	R	B	H	R	S	J

22. Magic

1. The magic word (11)
2. A magician's helper (9)
3. Pull this out of a hat (6)
4. Someone who performs magic (8)
5. Magicians perform these (6)
6. Tricks sometimes involve a pack of these (5)
7. A magic black and white stick (4)
8. Harry who is a famous young magician (6)
9. Wave this around to conceal things (12)
10. "Hey _____" is the magic saying (6)

```
F E I H C R E K D N A H
A B R A C A D A B R A M
O H N F D H S E S W Q A
T L K J H S O N N L J A
S E A B D V A M K H S R
E M W R L I R F C S S A
R D A Q C E H D I V X B
P C K I T N N S N Q K B
S F G T A E T D C M S I
L A O J O A B W N L F T
M P H V N B K D M A S A
A Q M T R I C K S J W Z
```

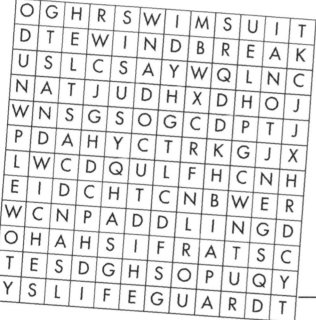

```
O G H R S W I M S U I T
D T E W I N D B R E A K
U S L C S A Y W Q L N C
N A T J U D H X D H O J
W N S G S O G C D P T J
P D A H Y C T R K G J X
L W C D Q U L F H C N H
E I D C H T C N B W E R
W C N P A D D L I N G D
O H A H S I F R A T S C
T E S D G H S O P U Q Y
Y S L I F E G U A R D T
```

23. The Beach

1. A chair you sit on on the beach (4,5)
2. Splashing in the sea (8)
3. Dry yourself off with this (5)
4. A star-shaped sea creature (8)
5. Put this up to shelter you from wind (9)
6. These popular snacks can be eaten on the beach (10)
7. A little wooden shack on the beachfront (3)
8. A castle made with a bucket and spade (10)
9. Costume ladies wear (8)
10. Someone who watches swimmers in case they get into trouble (9)

24. Time

1. Ten years (6)
2. 60 seconds (6)
3. 60 minutes (4)
4. 365 days (4)
5. Wear this on your wrist to tell the time (5)
6. There are 60 of these in one minute (7)
7. Clock that beeps when it's time to get up (5)
8. There are twelve of these in a year (6)
9. There are seven of these each week (4)
10. A clock in a tall wooden case (11)

```
O M I N U T E C P S Y T
A D M U E V W F R N X F
B S H C T A W G E M O B
S D N O C E S D H W B G
D O T N S N D R T E A P
R P X Y A C A H A Y L X
U W E F D E N N F S A G
O G V D Y M B T D U R B
H A S B A O P S N F M S
T N H E Y C D U A V X A
C B M D X W E M R N X A
S H T N O M G D G D S D
```

25. Drinks

1. Made with bags or leaves (3)
2. Apple or orange (5)
3. Ginger _____ (4)
4. Free and pure (5)
5. This type of drink has bubbles in it (10)
6. Made from beans (6)
7. Made from grapes, alcoholic (4)
8. Add this flavoring to water to make a drink (7)
9. Drink you can pour over your cereal (4)
10. Sweet that can also be a hot drink (9)

J	O	T	C	H	O	C	O	L	A	T	E
C	O	R	D	I	A	L	H	K	D	S	X
Y	C	B	E	D	A	Z	R	E	E	B	D
C	A	R	B	O	N	A	T	E	D	M	B
K	H	E	E	F	F	O	C	V	H	J	D
J	D	M	C	N	N	S	K	W	I	N	E
S	X	T	B	B	T	Y	O	N	L	H	K
S	E	B	H	I	Z	R	A	V	C	F	C
A	L	K	V	Z	B	J	R	E	T	A	W
W	N	M	I	Y	W	D	B	V	S	X	S
O	Z	F	F	M	I	L	K	N	A	O	L
I	A	S	N	M	C	J	U	I	C	E	Z

G	L	Y	T	R	O	F	Y	S	E	E	K
K	E	L	N	I	J	D	S	I	O	Y	U
O	E	P	A	L	A	D	D	E	R	S	H
U	P	L	V	B	H	X	F	D	V	W	C
H	L	L	D	Z	T	D	F	K	U	G	T
B	K	I	A	A	S	O	P	X	I	M	O
E	F	N	W	Y	R	G	O	J	N	R	C
L	D	Y	T	R	T	C	T	F	H	Y	S
L	S	H	T	A	G	I	S	X	D	F	P
I	J	I	K	V	F	I	M	T	K	F	O
G	N	I	P	P	I	K	S	E	A	N	H
P	F	N	X	Z	H	W	T	V	J	C	S

26. The Playground

1. A break between lessons when children play (8)
2. A game played with elastic (4, 6)
3. You have to touch another person in this game (3)
4. Hide and _____ (4)
5. A game where you kick a ball (8)
6. This rings to signal the end of break (4)
7. A hop, skip, and jump game (9)
8. Stuck in the ___ (3)
9. Jumping with a rope (8)
10. Snakes and _____ (7)

27. Party Time

1. Dance to this (5)
2. Eat this at the party (4)
3. A gift for the host (7)
4. A present might be carried in this (3)
5. Hope you have a _____ birthday (5)
6. You might wear this to the party (5, 5)
7. Have this treat with jello (3, 5)
8. Pass this on to get a prize (6)
9. You need one of these to go to the party (10)
10. In musical _____ you should sit down when the music stops (6)

B	Q	W	S	D	V	C	V	E	B	N	C
N	F	S	S	E	R	D	Y	C	N	A	F
P	R	E	S	E	N	T	F	D	Y	F	E
E	M	G	H	L	M	C	Y	K	H	G	F
L	K	U	C	D	F	D	S	P	W	Q	B
E	D	V	O	F	X	R	C	N	P	K	Y
C	F	O	M	Q	I	G	O	D	X	A	L
R	F	H	W	A	B	E	G	H	D	F	H
A	M	V	H	L	Y	S	U	D	G	F	K
P	D	C	N	F	M	U	S	I	C	M	G
S	N	O	I	T	A	T	I	V	N	I	A
C	I	C	E	C	R	E	A	M	Q	V	B

28. Holidays

1. Send these to your friends (9)
2. Pack your clothes in this (8)
3. Where you catch the airplane from (7)
4. A building to stay in with lots of rooms (5)
5. Use this to find your way around (3)
6. A roll-up bag you sleep in (8, 3)
7. A mobile home you can stay in (7)
8. A material home held up with poles (4)
9. Don't forget this to clean your teeth with (10)
10. We hope the weather is like this (5)

T	E	N	T	G	B	F	D	S	W	E	Q
A	M	E	K	B	N	A	V	A	R	A	C
S	L	E	E	P	I	N	G	B	A	G	F
L	P	H	S	U	R	B	H	T	O	O	T
N	O	F	J	R	H	U	Q	H	D	E	D
W	S	S	U	N	N	Y	F	G	F	S	N
G	T	B	E	M	L	D	V	A	B	A	L
Q	C	D	F	A	E	E	N	Q	R	C	W
K	A	S	D	J	H	W	T	B	U	T	K
E	R	B	P	A	M	G	E	O	D	I	J
N	D	L	F	R	M	S	H	Q	H	U	B
S	S	T	R	O	P	R	I	A	F	S	A

29. Farmyard Animals

M	J	L	N	D	F	V	H	B	C	N	X
L	N	K	T	I	K	Q	N	E	H	H	K
L	G	O	O	S	E	U	E	D	V	I	Y
A	C	E	D	U	C	K	M	D	G	K	E
M	X	J	H	X	H	I	C	L	T	K	K
A	T	C	N	X	H	B	Y	V	B	V	R
D	A	B	K	G	N	E	J	P	N	M	U
F	O	L	V	T	D	C	B	G	P	U	T
G	G	I	K	Q	M	M	J	H	Q	U	X
V	X	E	B	U	A	F	X	D	T	L	P
B	U	L	L	L	F	N	K	K	I	C	J
C	J	M	Q	G	E	T	A	C	V	F	B

1. The male of this animal is called a gander (5)
2. The male of this animal is called a billy (4)
3. This bird lives on water and quacks (4)
4. A small furry domesticated animal (3)
5. A female chicken (3)
6. A male version of a cow (4)
7. A large bird that gobbles (6)
8. A baby sheep (4)
9. A baby dog (5)
10. A mammal found on South American farms (5)

30. Bedtime

1. A girl wears this to sleep in (7)
2. Something you rest your head on (6)
3. You may drink this before you go to bed (5)
4. Pictures that you see when you are asleep (6)
5. Mommy might come and ___ you into bed (4)
6. Turn this out before you go to sleep (5)
7. Read or listen to one at bedtime (5)
8. This toy may sleep with you (5)
9. Drink this warm before bed (4)
10. Have a hug and a ____ before bed (4)

G	J	K	B	V	C	F	D	S	W	H	S
Q	E	I	T	H	G	I	N	R	T	Y	C
S	K	W	Z	C	U	I	K	L	I	M	I
K	W	I	Q	V	G	M	S	C	C	F	T
C	B	X	S	J	G	M	C	N	X	W	Q
U	T	H	R	S	A	F	W	K	A	G	J
T	E	D	Y	E	M	T	H	T	C	I	S
K	D	V	R	C	V	B	E	Z	V	H	T
G	D	D	W	U	Q	R	U	J	B	D	O
F	Y	C	H	R	X	K	C	F	S	W	R
S	B	Z	F	T	W	O	L	L	I	P	Y
X	T	H	G	I	L	Y	D	H	G	V	K

31. The Desert

1. A prairie wolf (6)
2. The sun's warmth (4)
3. A pool of water in the desert (5)
4. This animal has one or two humps (5)
5. A reptile with four legs and a long tail (6)
6. A tree with large leaves and no branches (4, 4)
7. An optical illusion caused by the atmosphere (6)
8. Fine fragments of crushed rock (4)
9. Small creature with a sting in its long tail (8)
10. There isn't much of this drink in the desert (5)

B	M	N	H	U	S	A	N	D	I	D	F
H	I	G	K	T	Y	U	G	N	H	C	O
N	R	V	B	D	L	F	C	E	U	A	T
U	A	C	H	B	I	F	R	D	S	X	N
E	G	X	E	G	Z	T	E	I	V	G	O
T	E	G	E	I	A	U	S	H	T	B	I
O	U	F	R	K	R	L	T	N	G	Y	P
Y	E	N	T	D	D	C	E	I	D	R	R
O	V	I	M	B	N	F	E	M	U	F	O
C	U	G	L	H	T	X	G	K	A	N	C
B	R	T	A	E	H	Y	V	B	G	C	S
K	D	E	P	D	R	E	T	A	W	I	H

32. Flowers

J	K	N	P	A	N	S	I	E	V	H	C
X	D	A	D	A	I	S	Y	R	F	O	J
H	R	T	N	Y	S	N	A	P	G	L	K
P	C	E	B	J	F	G	D	U	C	L	X
P	N	F	W	Z	F	K	G	C	N	Y	A
E	E	G	E	O	M	B	D	R	V	J	Y
T	V	F	N	E	L	A	M	E	N	T	L
A	K	H	S	S	X	F	P	T	Q	E	I
L	M	O	Z	B	D	R	N	T	N	S	L
J	R	D	E	P	A	T	S	U	H	G	K
X	A	T	E	U	Q	U	O	B	S	J	P
D	N	G	M	V	Q	N	G	F	A	E	L

1. A funnel-shaped flower (4)
2. An arrangement of flowers (7)
3. A flower that is named after the Sun (9)
4. A wild plant with yellow, cup-shaped flowers (9)
5. A small flower with white petals (5)
6. A colored outer part of a flower head (5)
7. A green, flat organ that grows from the stem (4)
8. Member of the violet family, with broad petals (5)
9. Rearrange the letters of "sore" to make this flower (4)
10. A prickly plant associated with Christmas (5)

33. The Letter "W"

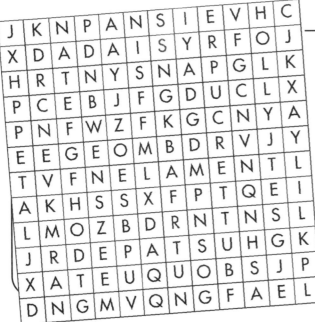

1. Opposite of man (5)
2. Opposite of black (5)
3. Wear this on your wrist (5)
4. Use a pen to do this (5)
5. It runs in streams (5)
6. Birds use them to fly (5)
7. Humpty Dumpty sat on one (4)
8. Do this to clean yourself (4)
9. Cats have them on their faces (8)
10. Keep your clothes in this cupboard (8)

W	V	H	F	W	A	T	E	R	F	D	S
A	D	C	E	D	W	R	I	T	E	W	R
L	R	T	E	S	X	W	Y	N	W	H	G
L	K	S	J	J	R	O	Y	R	E	I	S
W	N	D	F	S	H	E	R	I	A	T	W
G	F	T	G	C	I	P	K	D	K	E	C
D	X	N	A	F	S	H	R	S	G	S	V
Y	I	E	V	T	N	T	S	E	I	G	S
W	W	H	R	A	G	X	N	A	F	H	E
V	K	S	M	D	S	S	Y	C	W	T	W
T	F	O	G	A	W	A	T	C	H	T	F
S	W	A	R	D	R	O	B	E	E	A	S

34. The Letter "S"

1. You get one of these if you stay in the sun (6)
2. Wear these on your feet around the house (8)
3. The green supporting part of a plant (4)
4. A precious metal and a color (6)
5. Words and music make a _____ (4)
6. The number between six and eight (5)
7. Close your eyes and go to _____ (5)
8. A soft-bodied animal with a shell (5)
9. These twinkle in the night sky (5)
10. An apology (5)

S	D	F	G	M	H	S	L	E	E	P	J
I	K	S	E	L	S	P	C	O	S	R	S
L	E	T	I	K	U	D	I	T	J	I	T
V	S	O	R	S	O	E	A	S	S	D	S
E	D	K	O	S	W	R	A	K	R	R	I
R	W	R	Z	O	S	N	F	G	E	L	D
F	R	L	C	D	A	D	E	S	P	O	N
Y	H	J	S	T	S	K	N	D	P	H	E
G	S	R	N	U	W	A	R	A	I	C	V
I	E	U	O	J	I	L	J	S	L	G	E
K	S	Z	X	L	D	T	R	K	S	F	S
R	U	S	Y	G	N	O	S	R	O	S	H

35. Spies

K	O	S	U	N	G	L	A	S	S	E	S
L	R	E	V	O	C	R	E	D	N	U	K
A	E	N	O	H	P	L	L	E	C	O	M
R	E	D	O	C	V	J	E	A	E	R	I
S	O	T	L	A	K	F	L	T	S	L	O
J	E	W	I	P	N	L	G	B	A	A	J
F	R	A	O	N	E	T	E	R	C	E	S
K	V	R	K	R	J	J	P	W	F	N	O
C	D	A	B	T	S	R	I	S	E	B	K
A	M	M	G	P	K	L	O	E	I	P	V
L	U	E	J	F	A	V	A	M	R	K	J
B	S	I	O	W	N	M	A	T	B	G	R

1. Leaving something to be picked up later is called a dead _____ (4)
2. Spies carry important things in this (9)
3. Spies who are on a secret mission are said to have gone _____ (10)
4. To help you find your way (3)
5. Write your message in _____ to keep it secret (4)
6. Something which not many people know (6)
7. Spies wear this color to go unnoticed (5)
8. Spies wear these to cover their eyes (10)
9. Use this to get in touch with other spies (4, 5)
10. Spies use these to keep dry in the rain (8)

36. Birds

1. Powerful bird of prey (5)
2. A small brown-gray bird (7)
3. Nickname for the budgerigar (6)
4. A small bird with a red breast (5)
5. A brightly colored bird that talks (6)
6. A large blackbird with a harsh cry (4)
7. This bird lays its eggs in other birds' nests (6)
8. Large bird from Australia that doesn't fly (3)
9. A pink-feathered bird with long legs (8)
10. Can hover in the air, this bird's wings hum (11)

N	R	O	B	I	N	F	C	H	S	T	U
D	I	K	X	E	O	O	K	C	U	C	Y
W	R	A	O	G	N	I	M	A	L	F	M
S	N	I	M	O	P	K	E	N	B	O	A
H	W	F	B	N	D	T	O	R	R	A	P
Y	O	T	E	G	C	I	R	C	U	V	F
M	R	U	A	E	N	E	B	Y	P	M	H
N	R	X	G	S	O	I	I	N	U	K	E
B	A	A	L	W	H	F	M	G	T	I	X
I	P	D	E	O	K	M	A	M	D	J	F
N	S	Y	T	R	C	P	F	E	U	U	C
M	E	F	B	C	U	N	W	X	S	H	B

37. Creepy Crawlies

1. A flying insect which is black and yellow (3)
2. Rearrange the letters WIGEAR for this insect (6)
3. Small flying insect that carries disease (8)
4. Has a hard body and biting mouthparts (6)
5. A common small flying insect that buzzes (3)
6. It burrows in soil and has a long body (4)
7. A jumping insect that chirps loudly (7)
8. It has two pairs of wings, strong jaws and a sting (4)
9. An insect that can hop, walk, and fly (11)
10. This catches other insects while flying (9)

R	I	S	T	U	I	C	K	L	P	M	V
N	G	R	A	S	S	H	O	P	P	E	R
S	F	H	E	W	Q	R	G	B	B	I	W
E	M	Y	L	F	N	O	G	A	R	D	P
L	C	C	R	B	L	Z	S	K	G	L	S
R	R	K	E	E	B	R	E	C	T	G	A
W	I	T	S	U	H	I	L	F	V	K	W
O	C	I	P	E	C	N	T	K	M	H	Y
R	K	G	I	W	R	A	E	R	B	L	R
M	E	V	K	I	W	G	E	Q	F	I	N
U	T	H	R	F	T	P	B	S	Z	C	K
N	C	O	T	I	U	Q	S	O	M	U	E

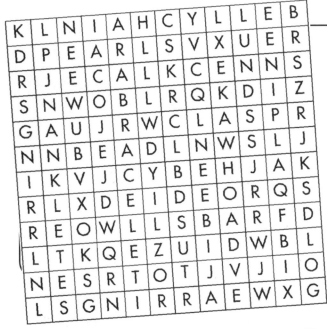

K	L	N	I	A	H	C	Y	L	L	E	B
D	P	E	A	R	L	S	V	X	U	E	R
R	J	E	C	A	L	K	C	E	N	N	S
S	N	W	O	B	L	R	Q	K	D	I	Z
G	A	U	J	R	W	C	L	A	S	P	R
N	N	B	E	A	D	L	N	W	S	L	J
I	K	V	J	C	Y	B	E	H	J	A	K
R	L	X	D	E	I	D	E	O	R	Q	S
R	E	O	W	L	L	S	B	A	R	F	D
L	T	K	Q	E	Z	U	I	D	W	B	L
N	E	S	R	T	O	T	J	V	J	I	O
L	S	G	N	I	R	R	A	E	W	X	G

38. Jewelry

1. Wear this on your wrist (8)
2. Wear this round your neck (8)
3. The fastening on a chain (5)
4. Wear this round your ankle (6)
5. These go in your ears (8)
6. Lots of jewelry is made from this precious metal (4)
7. This intricate item is worn on your head (5)
8. Wear this when you get engaged or married (4)
9. This jewelry goes round your waist (10)
10. These gems are found in oysters (6)

39. Boys' Names

1. Can be shortened to Andy (6)
2. The first man on Earth (4)
3. A shortened version of Robert (3)
4. Name that rhymes with "five" (5)
5. Little ____ who was a friend of Robin Hood (4)
6. The Prince of Wales, was married to Diana (7)
7. This piper picked a peck of pickled peppers (5)
8. Shortened version of Anthony (4)
9. Name that rhymes with "park" (4)
10. Bill is a shortened version of this name (7)

S	D	K	O	M	A	R	K	P	V	W	Q
Y	U	C	L	I	V	E	B	R	D	L	Y
B	H	N	D	H	U	G	W	F	N	D	N
V	Q	S	P	Z	I	X	H	G	N	S	O
A	R	E	L	W	K	U	I	H	V	K	T
N	P	L	H	I	D	C	O	P	B	P	D
D	W	R	S	L	B	J	O	Y	R	U	H
R	F	A	D	L	G	G	Q	V	I	N	M
E	L	H	N	I	U	H	X	B	K	L	A
W	Y	C	Z	A	P	B	O	B	D	O	D
Q	D	K	G	M	F	R	P	Z	S	W	A
B	V	D	R	E	T	E	P	I	N	Y	C

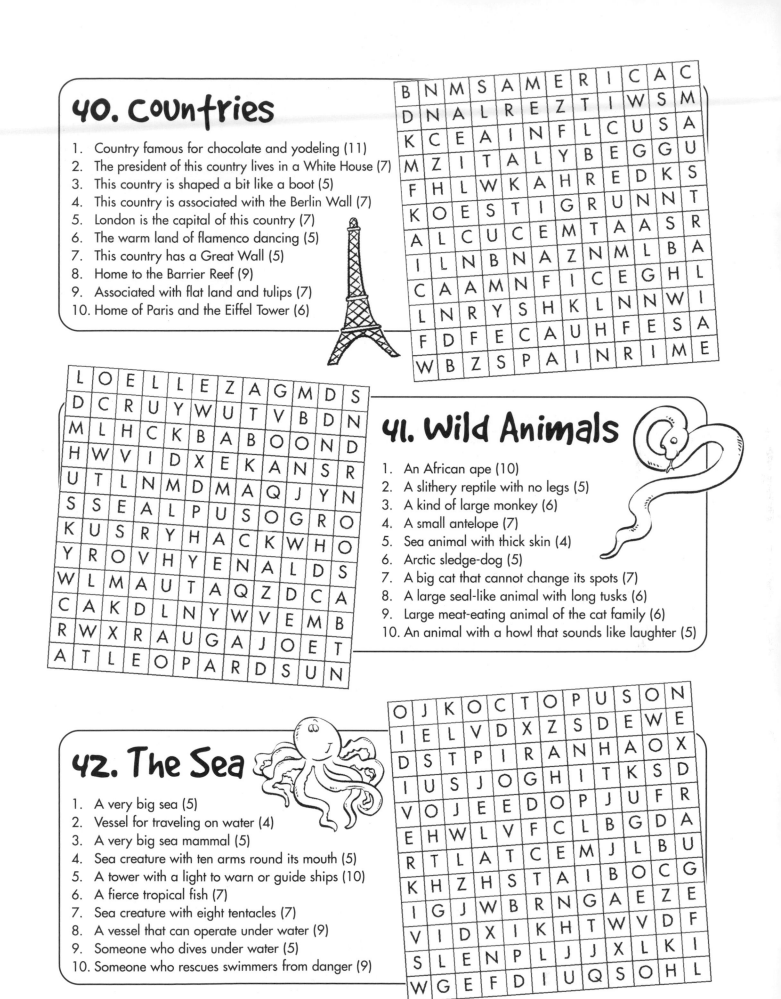

40. Countries

1. Country famous for chocolate and yodeling (11)
2. The president of this country lives in a White House (7)
3. This country is shaped a bit like a boot (5)
4. This country is associated with the Berlin Wall (7)
5. London is the capital of this country (7)
6. The warm land of flamenco dancing (5)
7. This country has a Great Wall (5)
8. Home to the Barrier Reef (9)
9. Associated with flat land and tulips (7)
10. Home of Paris and the Eiffel Tower (6)

B	N	M	S	A	M	E	R	I	C	A	C
D	N	A	L	R	E	Z	T	I	W	S	M
K	C	E	A	I	N	F	L	C	U	S	A
M	Z	I	T	A	L	Y	B	E	G	G	U
F	H	L	W	K	A	H	R	E	D	K	S
K	O	E	S	T	I	G	R	U	N	N	T
A	L	C	U	C	E	M	T	A	A	S	R
I	L	N	B	N	A	Z	N	M	L	B	A
C	A	A	M	N	F	I	C	E	G	H	L
L	N	R	Y	S	H	K	L	N	N	W	I
F	D	F	E	C	A	U	H	F	E	S	A
W	B	Z	S	P	A	I	N	R	I	M	E

L	O	E	L	L	E	Z	A	G	M	D	S
D	C	R	U	Y	W	U	T	V	B	D	N
M	L	H	C	K	B	A	B	O	O	N	D
H	W	V	I	D	X	E	K	A	N	S	R
U	T	L	N	M	D	M	A	Q	J	Y	N
S	S	E	A	L	P	U	S	O	G	R	O
K	U	S	R	Y	H	A	C	K	W	H	O
Y	R	O	V	H	Y	E	N	A	L	D	S
W	L	M	A	U	T	A	Q	Z	D	C	A
C	A	K	D	L	N	Y	W	V	E	M	B
R	W	X	R	A	U	G	A	J	O	E	T
A	T	L	E	O	P	A	R	D	S	U	N

41. Wild Animals

1. An African ape (10)
2. A slithery reptile with no legs (5)
3. A kind of large monkey (6)
4. A small antelope (7)
5. Sea animal with thick skin (4)
6. Arctic sledge-dog (5)
7. A big cat that cannot change its spots (7)
8. A large seal-like animal with long tusks (6)
9. Large meat-eating animal of the cat family (6)
10. An animal with a howl that sounds like laughter (5)

42. The Sea

1. A very big sea (5)
2. Vessel for traveling on water (4)
3. A very big sea mammal (5)
4. Sea creature with ten arms round its mouth (5)
5. A tower with a light to warn or guide ships (10)
6. A fierce tropical fish (7)
7. Sea creature with eight tentacles (7)
8. A vessel that can operate under water (9)
9. Someone who dives under water (5)
10. Someone who rescues swimmers from danger (9)

O	J	K	O	C	T	O	P	U	S	O	N
I	E	L	V	D	X	Z	S	D	E	W	E
D	S	T	P	I	R	A	N	H	A	O	X
I	U	S	J	O	G	H	I	T	K	S	D
V	O	J	E	E	D	O	P	J	U	F	R
E	H	W	L	V	F	C	L	B	G	D	A
R	T	L	A	T	C	E	M	J	L	B	U
K	H	Z	H	S	T	A	I	B	O	C	G
I	G	J	W	B	R	N	G	A	E	Z	E
V	I	D	X	I	K	H	T	W	V	D	F
S	L	E	N	P	L	J	J	X	L	K	I
W	G	E	F	D	I	U	Q	S	O	H	L

43. Weather

1. Wet drops that fall (4)
2. How hot or cold it is (11)
3. The light of the sun (8)
4. Wear these in the rain (5)
5. This can be forked or sheet (9)
6. Violent storm-wind (9)
7. Frozen white flakes (4)
8. A mass of watery vapor in the sky (5)
9. A description of the weather by an announcer (6)
10. Frozen dew or vapor (5)

I	T	E	M	P	E	R	A	T	U	R	E
H	G	O	N	S	T	G	K	M	I	E	B
V	N	B	F	R	O	S	T	R	O	N	T
O	I	M	Q	Z	V	C	G	B	V	I	H
K	N	E	N	A	C	I	R	R	U	H	S
B	T	C	I	R	E	P	O	R	T	S	O
O	H	B	G	O	C	H	F	R	C	N	I
O	G	S	T	D	N	C	S	L	I	U	K
T	I	V	N	M	U	V	K	N	Q	S	M
S	L	R	I	H	Z	O	V	B	O	N	N
E	O	Q	A	I	G	V	L	T	G	W	M
S	N	K	R	L	K	J	H	C	H	S	Z

44. Creepy Crawlies

1. A bug that walks on water (10)
2. A creature with eight legs (6)
3. This travels in armies and makes holes (3)
4. Also known as a daddy long-legs (10)
5. A beetle-like insect with a hard body (9)
6. A small, crawling insect with many legs (9)
7. Mollusk famous for being so slow (5)
8. A small, slimy animal (4)
9. A small, bloodsucking worm (5)
10. Larva of a kind of beetle that bores in wood (8)

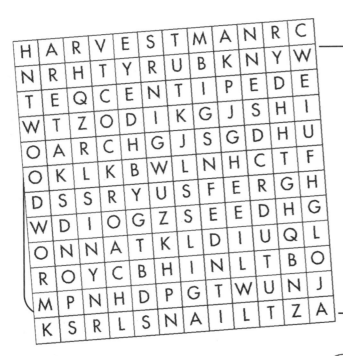

H	A	R	V	E	S	T	M	A	N	R	C
N	R	H	T	Y	R	U	B	K	N	Y	W
T	E	Q	C	E	N	T	I	P	E	D	E
W	T	Z	O	D	I	K	G	J	S	H	I
O	A	R	C	H	G	J	S	G	D	H	U
O	K	L	K	B	W	L	N	H	C	T	F
D	S	S	R	Y	U	S	F	E	R	G	H
W	D	I	O	G	Z	S	E	E	D	H	G
O	N	N	A	T	K	L	D	I	U	Q	L
R	O	Y	C	B	H	I	N	L	T	B	O
M	P	N	H	D	P	G	T	W	U	N	J
K	S	R	L	S	N	A	I	L	T	Z	A

45. Characters

1. Pumba's friend (6)
2. The cowboy from *Toy Story* (5)
3. The lovable deer (5)
4. Astronaut called Buzz (9)
5. He was friends with Tinkerbell (5, 3)
6. The female version of He-man (5)
7. Was the beauty to the beast (5)
8. The baby lion from *The Lion King* (5)
9. The lobster friend of Ariel (9)
10. The friendly giant in Harry Potter books (6)

J	O	B	I	V	H	A	G	R	I	D	R
B	E	L	L	E	A	J	E	S	O	R	W
Y	C	J	Y	D	O	O	W	D	G	A	C
I	S	R	H	G	V	Y	C	K	J	E	N
O	H	E	W	J	N	J	M	X	C	Y	A
X	E	T	A	N	A	R	B	O	B	T	I
B	R	I	S	C	P	H	A	K	R	H	T
E	A	M	R	N	R	I	M	E	D	G	S
D	Y	O	C	V	E	O	B	N	C	I	A
S	V	N	I	E	T	W	I	A	X	L	B
N	J	E	H	N	E	S	C	V	J	V	E
S	I	M	B	A	P	B	C	O	Y	I	S

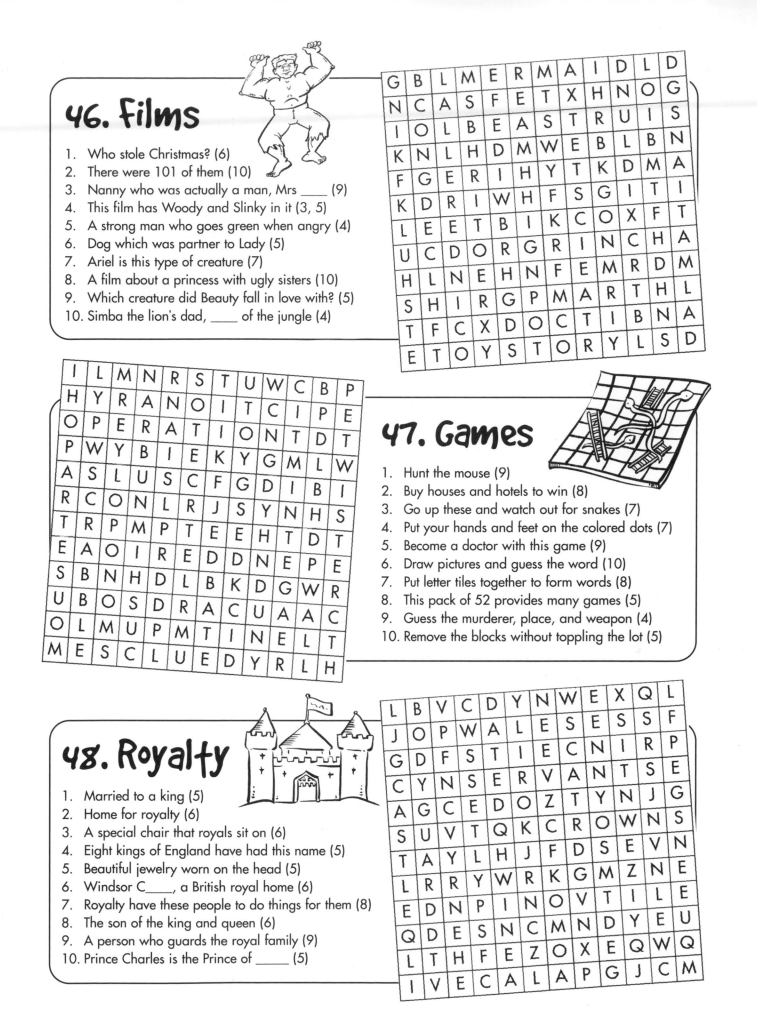

46. Films

1. Who stole Christmas? (6)
2. There were 101 of them (10)
3. Nanny who was actually a man, Mrs ____ (9)
4. This film has Woody and Slinky in it (3, 5)
5. A strong man who goes green when angry (4)
6. Dog which was partner to Lady (5)
7. Ariel is this type of creature (7)
8. A film about a princess with ugly sisters (10)
9. Which creature did Beauty fall in love with? (5)
10. Simba the lion's dad, ____ of the jungle (4)

```
G B L M E R M A I D L D
N C A S F E T X H N O G
I O L B E A S T R U I S
K N L H D M W E B L B N
F G E R I H Y T K D M A
K D R I W H F S G I T I
L E E T B I K C O X F T
U C D O R G R I N C H A
H L N E H N F E M R D M
S H I R G P M A R T H L
T F C X D O C T I B N A
E T O Y S T O R Y L S D
```

47. Games

1. Hunt the mouse (9)
2. Buy houses and hotels to win (8)
3. Go up these and watch out for snakes (7)
4. Put your hands and feet on the colored dots (7)
5. Become a doctor with this game (9)
6. Draw pictures and guess the word (10)
7. Put letter tiles together to form words (8)
8. This pack of 52 provides many games (5)
9. Guess the murderer, place, and weapon (4)
10. Remove the blocks without toppling the lot (5)

```
I L M N R S T U W C B P
H Y R A N O I T C I P E
O P E R A T I O N T D T
P W Y B I E K Y G M L W
A S L U S C F G D I B I
R C O N L R J S Y N H S
T R P M P T E E H T D T
E A O I R E D D N E P E
S B N H D L B K D G W R
U B O S D R A C U A A C
O L M U P M T I N E L T
M E S C L U E D Y R L H
```

48. Royalty

1. Married to a king (5)
2. Home for royalty (6)
3. A special chair that royals sit on (6)
4. Eight kings of England have had this name (5)
5. Beautiful jewelry worn on the head (5)
6. Windsor C____, a British royal home (6)
7. Royalty have these people to do things for them (8)
8. The son of the king and queen (6)
9. A person who guards the royal family (9)
10. Prince Charles is the Prince of ____ (5)

```
L B V C D Y N W E X Q L
J O P W A L E S E S S F
G D F S T I E C N I R P
C Y N S E R V A N T S E
A G C E D O Z T Y N J G
S U V T Q K C R O W N S
T A Y L H J F D S E V N
L R R Y W R K G M Z N E
E D N P I N O V T I L E
Q D E S N C M N D Y E U
L T H F E Z O X E Q W Q
I V E C A L A P G J C M
```

49. The Letter "P"

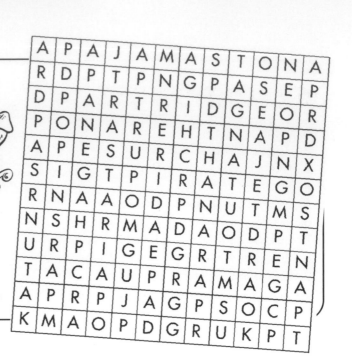

1. A yellow vegetable (7)
2. A talking bird (6)
3. Wear these on your legs (5)
4. A baby is pushed around in this (4)
5. A farmyard animal (3)
6. A bird commonly associated with a pear tree (9)
7. Wear these in bed (7)
8. An evil sailor who steals treasure (6)
9. A leopard (7)
10. Another word for a couple or two of something (4)

A	P	A	J	A	M	A	S	T	O	N	A
R	D	P	T	P	N	G	P	A	S	E	P
D	P	A	R	T	R	I	D	G	E	O	R
P	O	N	A	R	E	H	T	N	A	P	D
A	P	E	S	U	R	C	H	A	J	N	X
S	I	G	T	P	I	R	A	T	E	G	O
R	N	A	A	O	D	P	N	U	T	M	S
N	S	H	R	M	A	D	A	O	D	P	T
U	R	P	I	G	E	G	R	T	R	E	N
T	A	C	A	U	P	R	A	M	A	G	A
A	P	R	P	J	A	G	P	S	O	C	P
K	M	A	O	P	D	G	R	U	K	P	T

50. School

1. Eat this at school (6)
2. School's out! (8)
3. You may have to wear this at school (7)
4. Use this to draw straight lines (5)
5. The periods where you learn about the subjects (7)
6. Girls wear this for P.E. (8)
7. This person teaches you (7)
8. The teacher writes on this with chalk (10)
9. Work you have to do after school (8)
10. Written tests that may be longer than other tests (5)

B	L	E	S	S	O	N	S	T	J	L	I
K	U	F	O	E	R	E	H	C	A	E	T
H	B	M	I	B	V	S	W	X	M	K	T
O	L	S	T	J	L	F	S	R	D	A	N
M	A	T	U	K	G	Q	O	A	G	O	X
E	C	R	S	U	F	F	D	M	I	U	Z
W	K	I	O	T	I	B	J	T	S	W	S
O	B	K	D	N	V	I	A	T	G	M	R
R	O	S	U	M	E	C	S	S	A	Q	E
K	A	M	K	U	A	X	O	X	L	B	L
S	R	Y	J	V	W	G	E	D	S	F	U
O	D	G	I	R	E	N	N	I	D	V	R

51. Food

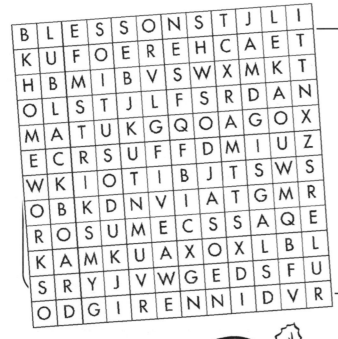

1. Menthol herb (4)
2. Part of a pig (5)
3. A beef patty in a bun with relish (6)
4. Roast dinner is usually eaten on this day (6)
5. This quick snack is made from potatoes (5)
6. Sauce made from cooked meat juices (5)
7. Sweet pudding that comes after dinner (7)
8. This round fruit grows on trees (5)
9. The inside part of a sandwich (7)
10. This fruit is often given to ill people (6)

D	E	S	S	E	R	T	L	B	U	A	G
W	R	E	A	T	H	R	W	B	M	S	R
Y	V	A	R	G	L	Y	E	L	O	H	A
A	E	H	A	Y	T	F	A	G	Y	O	P
S	U	N	D	A	Y	I	E	L	R	J	E
U	N	E	M	O	M	A	C	B	K	U	S
D	E	W	H	I	T	H	U	T	H	A	B
J	L	L	B	N	I	M	A	E	N	I	S
K	P	T	A	P	Y	F	K	D	E	I	W
E	P	S	S	I	N	S	E	L	O	B	M
I	A	P	N	G	E	N	O	C	A	B	D
Y	M	G	N	I	L	L	I	F	E	A	E

52. Christmas

1. The kissing plant (9)
2. He has a carrot for a nose (7)
3. Hang this on the tree (6)
4. Rudolph is one (8)
5. Type of song sung at Christmas (5)
6. Another name for Father Christmas (5)
7. A festive arrangement of flowers (6)
8. Santa's reindeers pull this with presents on (6)
9. Drape this over the tree (6)
10. A heavenly being that goes on top of the tree (5)

K	D	U	V	I	S	E	L	B	U	A	B
W	R	E	A	T	H	F	G	X	E	A	W
L	E	P	F	N	A	M	W	O	N	S	K
S	E	J	K	N	K	H	C	E	I	K	U
H	D	A	L	H	G	I	E	L	S	I	E
F	N	E	I	C	O	A	L	M	F	J	N
K	I	U	V	Y	T	K	H	O	N	A	F
D	E	G	W	N	S	D	E	E	R	L	Y
P	R	X	A	F	L	F	K	V	U	A	G
J	W	S	T	I	N	S	E	L	W	E	C
F	P	A	N	G	E	L	A	S	I	J	X
V	M	I	S	T	L	E	T	O	E	L	D

53. Clothes

C	A	P	R	I	E	D	C	U	R	E	R
T	O	C	Y	S	A	G	V	T	A	V	T
C	V	S	W	F	J	L	P	B	I	C	R
N	A	E	Z	T	U	O	I	X	N	T	I
J	R	M	S	Y	W	V	K	J	C	A	H
T	V	D	F	T	I	E	H	D	O	O	S
I	R	A	S	G	D	S	O	C	A	C	R
U	B	Q	G	F	C	S	W	E	T	I	E
E	A	S	F	A	J	R	U	I	S	T	D
W	C	X	E	F	V	T	F	Z	H	T	N
D	M	K	I	L	T	B	A	S	F	E	U
B	I	K	I	N	I	O	T	H	D	P	A

1. A coat to wear when it rains (8)
2. Wear this on your head (3)
3. Waist-length sleeveless jacket (4)
4. Two-piece swimming costume (6)
5. Indian women wear this (4)
6. A skirt worn under your clothes (9)
7. Wear these to keep your hands warm (6)
8. Trousers also known as pedal pushers (5)
9. Wear this under your top to stay warm (10)
10. Tartan skirt worn as part of Highland dress (4)

54. Nature

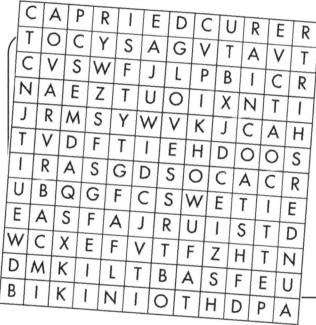

1. A large bee (9)
2. A freshwater fish (4)
3. A badger's burrow (4)
4. The edible dark berry of a bramble (10)
5. A very young plant growing from a seed (8)
6. A pretend figure to scare birds away from crops (9)
7. Hanging flower of willow, hazel, etc. (6)
8. Large open-air fire (7)
9. Plant these to grow flowers and plants (5)
10. Black, bushy-tailed, smelly weasel-like animal (5)

B	L	A	C	K	B	E	R	R	Y	N	L
M	P	K	A	O	L	D	W	N	F	B	P
E	I	N	T	E	K	L	Q	K	D	U	B
E	E	K	K	B	N	V	G	J	M	L	B
B	R	F	I	D	U	N	N	M	I	B	L
E	I	H	N	B	K	W	I	E	O	S	N
L	F	N	I	R	S	P	L	I	N	K	K
B	N	M	K	E	G	U	D	O	F	Q	P
M	O	L	W	O	R	C	E	R	A	C	S
U	B	O	L	K	F	H	E	S	K	N	K
B	W	N	F	T	T	E	S	B	D	M	F
C	A	R	P	P	Q	N	E	L	W	I	V

55. Desserts

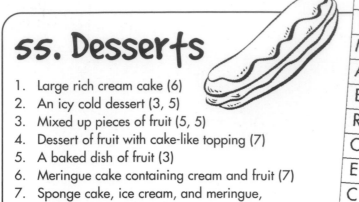

1. Large rich cream cake (6)
2. An icy cold dessert (3, 5)
3. Mixed up pieces of fruit (5, 5)
4. Dessert of fruit with cake-like topping (7)
5. A baked dish of fruit (3)
6. Meringue cake containing cream and fruit (7)
7. Sponge cake, ice cream, and meringue, Baked _____ (6)
8. Pastry with a cream filling and chocolate on top (6)
9. Pie or pastry flan with a sweet filling (4)
10. Baked sweet bread-like food (4)

D	O	K	V	U	E	H	S	W	G	K	C
B	A	C	Q	P	A	V	L	O	V	A	Y
M	N	L	Y	T	B	R	D	G	N	H	S
A	R	K	A	D	F	E	F	R	U	B	O
E	S	H	W	S	V	P	I	E	I	R	T
R	O	E	V	K	T	R	W	T	Y	A	V
C	Q	G	B	Y	N	I	C	H	O	K	E
E	C	L	A	I	R	G	U	B	R	S	K
C	K	C	O	B	B	L	E	R	C	A	T
I	S	O	C	R	U	S	E	V	F	L	R
V	H	W	U	A	E	T	A	G	K	A	A
G	B	E	K	A	C	O	K	B	U	S	T

56. Hobbies

1. Sport with touchdowns (8)
2. People like to play games on this (8)
3. Ballet, modern, tap, and more (7)
4. Planting and digging in the garden (9)
5. A love for books and magazines (7)
6. Walking is a form of _____ (8)
7. Hitting a ball over a net with rackets (6)
8. Passing a threaded needle through fabric (6)
9. Listening to this relaxes people (5)
10. Forming yarn into fabric of interlocking loops (8)

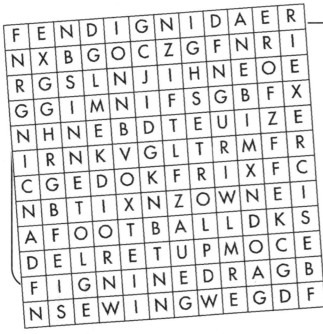

F	E	N	D	I	G	N	I	D	A	E	R
N	X	B	G	O	C	Z	G	F	N	R	I
R	G	S	L	N	J	I	H	N	E	O	E
G	G	I	M	N	I	F	S	G	B	F	X
N	H	N	E	B	D	T	E	U	I	Z	E
I	R	N	K	V	G	L	T	R	M	F	R
C	G	E	D	O	K	F	R	I	X	F	C
N	B	T	I	X	N	Z	O	W	N	E	I
A	F	O	O	T	B	A	L	L	D	K	S
D	E	L	R	E	T	U	P	M	O	C	E
F	I	G	N	I	N	E	D	R	A	G	B
N	S	E	W	I	N	G	W	E	G	D	F

57. Girls' Names

1. Short for Victoria (5)
2. The cowgirl from *Toy Story* (6)
3. The first woman in space (9)
4. Short for Rosemary (5)
5. Popeye's girlfriend _____ Oyl (5)
6. A famous orphan with orange curls (5)
7. Princess who was married to Prince Charles (5)
8. An American pop star with one name (7)
9. A nun who helped poor people in Calcutta (6)
10. The same name as a coin (5)

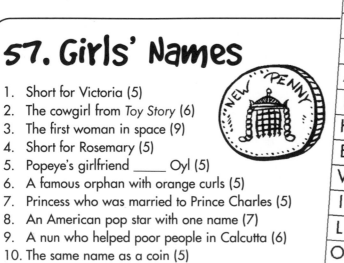

K	P	E	N	N	Y	L	I	O	R	S	T
U	K	T	A	S	E	R	E	T	H	H	J
O	I	J	K	H	F	T	E	I	S	O	R
A	N	N	I	E	J	D	U	W	X	K	S
F	R	L	W	B	S	P	C	X	R	D	P
H	I	A	N	I	T	N	E	L	A	V	I
E	N	N	K	T	J	D	I	T	B	S	V
V	D	A	U	O	F	E	F	J	K	F	I
I	S	I	J	H	L	K	S	G	U	H	C
L	X	D	W	F	R	P	D	S	H	W	K
O	T	P	B	U	K	R	C	X	I	K	Y
J	A	N	N	O	D	A	M	T	O	E	L

58. The Letter "M"

1. You need this when you're ill (8)
2. A two-wheeled motor vehicle (9)
3. Pour this on your cereal (4)
4. Vegetarians don't eat this (4)
5. Use this to find your way (3)
6. Cut the lawn (3)
7. The capital of Russia (6)
8. A planet in the solar system (4)
9. Everest is the world's highest (8)
10. Infectious disease causing red spots on the body (7)

E	S	T	M	N	I	A	T	N	U	O	M
C	W	R	I	X	F	T	W	S	N	C	K
L	M	E	D	I	C	I	N	E	E	M	I
N	B	U	S	Z	M	O	S	C	O	W	U
M	C	S	K	E	S	V	B	T	R	F	M
V	W	T	X	I	E	H	G	P	A	M	N
U	O	F	T	K	L	M	E	C	L	D	T
K	M	R	A	W	S	N	M	S	X	K	S
I	Z	B	E	C	A	U	T	K	L	B	R
M	M	E	M	J	E	I	R	I	E	R	A
R	U	X	S	T	M	F	M	X	F	Z	M
L	E	K	I	B	R	O	T	O	M	C	E

59. Flowers

1. Deep purple flower (6)
2. A cup-shaped flower (5)
3. A yellow flower that blooms early in spring (8)
4. Colorful flower that lives in warm areas (6)
5. Weed with yellow flowers that turn into seeds (9)
6. Flower that can be white, pink, or red (9)
7. Beautiful blue flower with long thin flat leaves (4)
8. Fertilizing powder from flowers (6)
9. A spring-flowering plant growing from a corm (6)
10. Plant with fragrant bell-shaped flowers (8)

N	O	I	L	E	D	N	A	D	C	O	U
F	Y	J	I	R	D	G	R	F	W	C	Y
R	H	Y	A	C	I	N	T	H	P	A	E
I	D	I	H	C	R	O	L	C	S	R	D
P	B	F	Y	M	B	J	I	M	U	N	F
I	O	S	I	R	I	K	D	G	Y	A	O
L	W	C	U	F	T	S	O	E	R	T	C
U	R	D	G	E	U	R	F	Y	M	I	J
T	J	F	L	C	I	P	F	C	I	O	D
R	S	O	O	D	B	O	A	K	F	N	R
K	I	R	C	R	R	U	D	W	R	J	S
V	C	D	Y	M	P	O	L	L	E	N	I

60. Birds

1. Bird of the crow family (3)
2. A nighttime bird of prey (3)
3. A sea bird (7)
4. A very small bird (4)
5. Small songbird that searches for insects (8)
6. One of the fastest flying birds (6)
7. Lays the biggest birds' eggs (7)
8. Small migratory bird with a forked tail (7)
9. A bird of prey that eats the flesh of dead animals (7)
10. Large water bird with a long slender neck (4)

H	I	N	E	R	W	A	C	N	O	C	Y
S	L	Y	V	J	B	E	F	W	R	B	G
W	E	O	G	W	D	I	L	Q	S	X	C
A	C	N	S	E	C	Y	V	J	H	F	E
L	V	I	H	T	F	S	A	E	L	A	R
L	U	L	T	N	R	D	B	J	Y	L	E
O	L	A	J	X	G	I	W	F	V	C	A
W	T	Q	H	R	T	Y	C	B	I	O	C
B	U	N	A	W	S	L	D	H	E	N	N
F	R	E	I	V	E	A	J	N	D	L	I
A	E	N	C	L	L	U	G	A	E	S	B
T	I	T	M	O	U	S	E	S	E	Q	Y

61. Fairies

1. Fairies sit on these (10)
2. Fairies use these to fly (5)
3. Fairies use their wands to create this (5)
4. They sing these (5)
5. Area of trees where fairies are found (5)
6. They make up these to make magic (6)
7. Fairies can rarely be seen by who? (6)
8. Something fairies do in the air that people can't (3)
9. It's supposedly unlucky to step in this (4)
10. The leader of the fairies (5)

M	R	I	N	G	B	V	D	O	K	F	I
H	A	Z	I	H	U	M	A	N	S	N	L
P	S	L	O	O	T	S	D	A	O	T	G
F	V	W	K	U	H	M	J	W	A	H	B
X	S	N	D	H	F	K	X	J	G	V	S
N	G	B	J	L	P	A	F	C	G	H	D
E	N	O	Y	I	Y	F	I	W	N	M	O
E	I	L	G	M	J	G	H	K	D	J	O
U	W	A	U	T	A	V	K	B	O	P	W
Q	P	H	N	M	J	N	A	Z	I	F	L
I	X	D	K	K	G	S	G	N	O	S	N
G	W	R	H	Y	M	E	S	B	M	U	O

P	R	O	B	E	N	J	M	H	B	I	A
F	A	C	D	K	P	A	I	N	A	H	T
W	B	S	H	R	U	Q	S	D	S	E	M
N	V	Y	E	I	J	I	S	W	T	T	O
Y	U	R	A	N	U	S	I	F	R	I	S
X	D	C	F	R	J	K	O	K	O	R	P
A	P	J	I	E	F	R	N	S	N	O	H
L	M	E	R	C	U	R	Y	P	O	E	E
A	F	R	A	H	W	N	C	J	M	T	R
G	N	O	R	T	S	M	R	A	Y	E	E
N	B	I	N	O	I	R	O	D	F	M	N
A	J	K	S	A	T	U	R	N	G	I	L

62. Space

1. A system of stars (6)
2. The ringed planet (6)
3. Planet nearest the Sun (7)
4. The name of a voyage to space (7)
5. Unmanned craft that explores space (5)
6. The study of stars and planets (9)
7. A planet in the solar system (6)
8. A meteor fallen to Earth (9)
9. A constellation of stars beginning with "O" (5)
10. Mixture of gases surrounding a planet (10)

63. The Park

1. You can swing on these (6)
2. What you do in the playground (4)
3. Make sandcastles from this (4)
4. Run about on this soft surface (5)
5. Merry-go-_____ (5)
6. Water where ducks swim (4)
7. Go down this fast! (5)
8. Go to the water to feed these birds with bread (5)
9. A meal you can have outside (6)
10. Things such as football and tag (5)

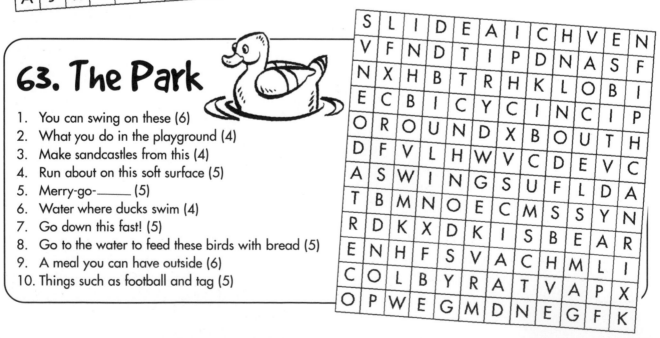

S	L	I	D	E	A	I	C	H	V	E	N
V	F	N	D	T	I	P	D	N	A	S	F
N	X	H	B	T	R	H	K	L	O	B	I
E	C	B	I	C	Y	C	I	N	C	I	P
O	R	O	U	N	D	X	B	O	U	T	H
D	F	V	L	H	W	V	C	D	E	V	C
A	S	W	I	N	G	S	U	F	L	D	A
T	B	M	N	O	E	C	M	S	S	Y	N
R	D	K	X	D	K	I	S	B	E	A	R
E	N	H	F	S	V	A	C	H	M	L	I
C	O	L	B	Y	R	A	T	V	A	P	X
O	P	W	E	G	M	D	N	E	G	F	K

64. Landmarks

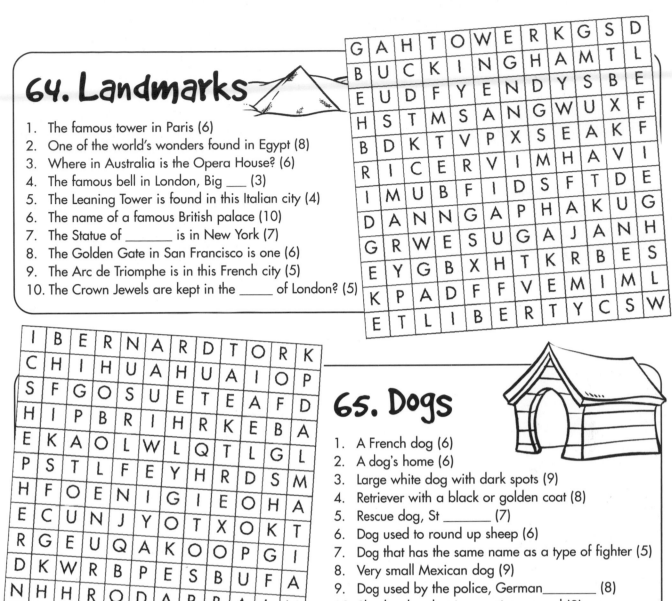

1. The famous tower in Paris (6)
2. One of the world's wonders found in Egypt (8)
3. Where in Australia is the Opera House? (6)
4. The famous bell in London, Big ___ (3)
5. The Leaning Tower is found in this Italian city (4)
6. The name of a famous British palace (10)
7. The Statue of _____ is in New York (7)
8. The Golden Gate in San Francisco is one (6)
9. The Arc de Triomphe is in this French city (5)
10. The Crown Jewels are kept in the _____ of London? (5)

Grid 64:

G	A	H	T	O	W	E	R	K	G	S	D
B	U	C	K	I	N	G	H	A	M	T	L
E	U	D	F	Y	E	N	D	Y	S	B	E
H	S	T	M	S	A	N	G	W	U	X	F
B	D	K	T	V	P	X	S	E	A	K	F
R	I	C	E	R	V	I	M	H	A	V	I
I	M	U	B	F	I	D	S	F	T	D	E
D	A	N	N	G	A	P	H	A	K	U	G
G	R	W	E	S	U	G	A	J	A	N	H
E	Y	G	B	X	H	T	K	R	B	E	S
K	P	A	D	F	F	V	E	M	I	M	L
E	T	L	I	B	E	R	T	Y	C	S	W

Grid 65 (Dogs):

I	B	E	R	N	A	R	D	T	O	R	K
C	H	I	H	U	A	H	U	A	I	O	P
S	F	G	O	S	U	E	T	E	A	F	D
H	I	P	B	R	I	H	R	K	E	B	A
E	K	A	O	L	W	L	Q	T	L	G	L
P	S	T	L	F	E	Y	H	R	D	S	M
H	F	O	E	N	I	G	I	E	O	H	A
E	C	U	N	J	Y	O	T	X	O	K	T
R	G	E	U	Q	A	K	O	O	P	G	I
D	K	W	R	B	P	E	S	B	U	F	A
N	H	H	R	O	D	A	R	B	A	L	N
D	N	U	O	H	Y	E	R	G	I	T	K

65. Dogs

1. A French dog (6)
2. A dog's home (6)
3. Large white dog with dark spots (9)
4. Retriever with a black or golden coat (8)
5. Rescue dog, St _____ (7)
6. Dog used to round up sheep (6)
7. Dog that has the same name as a type of fighter (5)
8. Very small Mexican dog (9)
9. Dog used by the police, German_____ (8)
10. Slender dog that is sometimes raced (9)

66. Spies

1. A loud bang (9)
2. A metal weapon spies use (3)
3. Someone who is not a friend (5)
4. This fast vehicle is used to escape (3)
5. Small mechanical device or tool (6)
6. Wear this so people won't know who you are (8)
7. Use these to see things far away (10)
8. A fictional spy with the number 007 (4)
9. Use this to photograph secret documents (6)
10. Someone who provides important information (8)

Grid 66:

E	U	F	O	E	G	R	S	R	A	C	T
N	B	D	K	B	W	N	X	V	K	H	J
E	I	Z	S	A	R	E	M	A	C	S	R
M	N	S	H	T	J	T	R	B	D	B	E
Y	O	F	H	L	K	D	G	N	F	Z	M
R	C	D	B	K	E	E	W	S	U	W	R
G	U	B	O	J	U	R	R	T	X	G	O
O	L	F	N	N	T	G	S	D	C	O	F
S	A	E	D	I	S	G	U	I	S	E	N
D	R	X	V	W	O	F	Z	K	B	U	I
K	S	G	A	D	G	E	T	T	E	G	N
J	H	N	O	I	S	O	L	P	X	E	D

67. Hairstyles

1. An elegant hair twist (5)
2. Two ponytails on either side of your head (7)
3. Use this to hold your hair back (4)
4. Hair tied back with a band is called a _____ (8)
5. A plait that starts right at the top of your head (6, 5)
6. Use this device to make your hair wavy (7)
7. These make your hair curly (7)
8. These make your hair look longer (10)
9. These are a straightening tool (5)
10. This is a haircut and a boy's name (3)

T	K	G	F	J	L	H	D	F	X	E	R
I	E	R	N	K	T	A	E	L	P	V	C
A	X	F	C	R	I	M	P	E	R	I	F
L	T	L	E	D	G	N	L	B	O	B	G
P	E	I	H	K	F	Z	W	T	R	U	K
H	N	A	L	S	E	H	C	N	U	B	V
C	S	T	J	D	I	D	G	X	E	X	Z
N	I	Y	M	S	S	R	E	L	R	U	C
E	O	N	H	N	V	K	E	H	P	J	I
R	N	O	X	O	L	R	F	I	L	F	D
F	S	P	F	R	D	N	L	W	G	D	S
E	N	H	L	I	C	C	V	Z	M	R	J

68. Sports Equipment

1. Wear these on your head to hold your hair back (5)
2. A round object you throw, catch, kick or hit (4)
3. Wear these on your feet when running around (8)
4. Jump over these in this athletics event (7)
5. Use this to hit a shuttlecock with (6)
6. Do judo or gymnastics on this (3)
7. Put sports equipment in this (3)
8. Wear these to kick a football (5)
9. These protect body parts (4)
10. Use this to hit a baseball (3)

M	C	B	A	F	H	N	D	W	B	L	G
A	Z	U	R	T	E	K	C	A	R	S	X
T	S	B	Q	C	Y	I	P	S	T	V	J
R	V	T	P	A	D	S	V	O	H	A	S
A	G	F	N	C	F	R	O	I	Y	C	N
H	B	D	S	L	V	B	D	V	G	F	E
S	R	A	W	X	U	S	B	T	G	P	A
D	I	Y	T	C	V	A	A	R	A	J	K
N	J	P	Q	B	L	C	I	S	B	R	E
A	J	G	T	L	R	H	F	Z	D	L	R
B	G	S	E	L	D	R	U	H	U	Q	S
X	V	A	C	N	N	G	W	R	V	B	Y

69. The Beach

1. Use this to dry yourself after a swim (5)
2. Women wear these to swim in (9)
3. Pictures of the beach you can send to people (9)
4. Men wear these to swim in (6)
5. You can see small sea creatures in this puddle (8)
6. Wooden construction that goes out over the sea (4)
7. Some beaches have these instead of sand (6)
8. Find pretty variations of these on the beach (6)
9. Flocks of these birds circle the beach (8)
10. Wear these to protect your eyes from the sun (10)

M	S	H	L	R	K	T	O	W	E	L	P
S	L	D	U	C	W	J	H	V	U	I	S
K	L	T	O	F	G	G	X	Y	E	J	H
N	U	R	M	J	R	D	G	R	J	H	G
U	G	I	Z	S	L	L	E	H	S	K	L
R	A	S	E	S	S	A	L	G	N	U	S
T	E	R	G	H	D	F	D	G	X	U	S
J	S	K	M	T	D	H	G	I	B	D	E
U	P	O	S	T	C	A	R	D	S	W	N
B	S	I	V	W	X	L	G	Z	J	D	O
R	D	L	O	O	P	K	C	O	R	M	T
F	S	W	I	M	S	U	I	T	S	H	S

70. Party Time

1. To go with food (6)
2. Give this with a present (4)
3. Decorations for the party (9)
4. Every party needs these! (6)
5. Party girl's pretty clothing (5)
6. Some people hire this bouncy treat (6)
7. Greetings that you hang up at a party (6)
8. A party for two people planning to get married (10)
9. A party to celebrate the date of an event (11)
10. People take these off when they arrive (5)

R	P	C	A	S	T	L	E	D	R	S	X
A	C	O	O	R	C	H	N	M	A	K	N
N	I	S	A	E	C	O	G	M	P	N	L
N	E	T	E	M	R	T	A	D	G	I	H
I	L	P	R	A	G	G	G	R	E	R	D
V	P	F	B	E	O	F	E	T	P	D	I
E	O	J	B	R	N	E	M	E	O	D	H
R	E	T	W	T	I	G	E	L	E	R	I
S	P	T	E	S	D	E	N	V	I	A	D
A	C	T	R	E	F	I	T	Z	Z	C	E
R	E	D	R	E	S	S	S	T	A	O	C
Y	D	D	W	O	R	E	N	N	A	B	R

71. Pets

K	J	P	A	R	R	O	T	U	Y	T	R
G	E	W	E	S	I	O	T	R	O	T	B
U	I	B	R	O	G	D	S	C	W	K	J
I	E	L	K	I	Y	F	I	S	H	H	Y
N	E	B	U	F	D	X	E	O	C	I	V
E	K	J	Y	J	L	I	B	R	E	G	R
A	A	O	T	K	C	D	S	L	F	S	E
P	N	R	G	B	S	E	C	V	D	K	T
I	S	D	G	W	C	A	U	H	J	G	S
G	U	E	O	M	T	J	I	Y	R	T	M
Y	J	D	D	N	F	X	J	O	B	E	A
S	I	R	A	B	B	I	T	D	C	W	H

1. Talking bird (6)
2. Rodent kept for a pet (6, 3)
3. Animal called a kitten when young (3)
4. Slow-moving reptile with a hard shell (8)
5. Rearrange the letters 'bilger' for this pet (6)
6. Four-legged domesticated animal (3)
7. A creature that lives in a water tank or bowl (4)
8. Burrowing animal with long ears (6)
9. Rodent pet that sometimes go round on a wheel (7)
10. This pet can be dangerous to keep (5)

72. The Letter "L"

1. Fabric (4)
2. Limbs you use to walk with (4)
3. Candy on the end of a stick (8)
4. Shellfish with large claws (7)
5. Oval yellow fruit (5)
6. A tree with heart-shaped leaves and also a fruit (4)
7. Plant related to the onion, used to make soup (4)
8. Rope with a noose for catching cattle (5)
9. Substance turned red by acids and blue by alkalis (6)
10. Takes people to different floors in a big building (4)

L	E	L	O	L	L	I	P	O	P	R	V
I	X	R	B	A	D	L	X	L	L	Y	W
M	C	L	X	N	O	Y	J	F	I	S	R
E	R	H	V	B	G	L	H	C	F	D	L
S	E	O	S	K	S	J	R	H	T	R	N
B	D	T	W	E	X	K	M	N	K	E	S
Y	E	N	C	F	E	T	A	O	H	F	G
R	G	J	H	E	R	L	B	M	H	G	E
E	C	A	L	F	S	D	V	E	O	T	L
V	R	R	S	U	M	T	I	L	D	W	H
D	L	X	O	S	S	A	L	Y	S	L	M
K	F	T	G	L	H	E	J	B	C	N	A

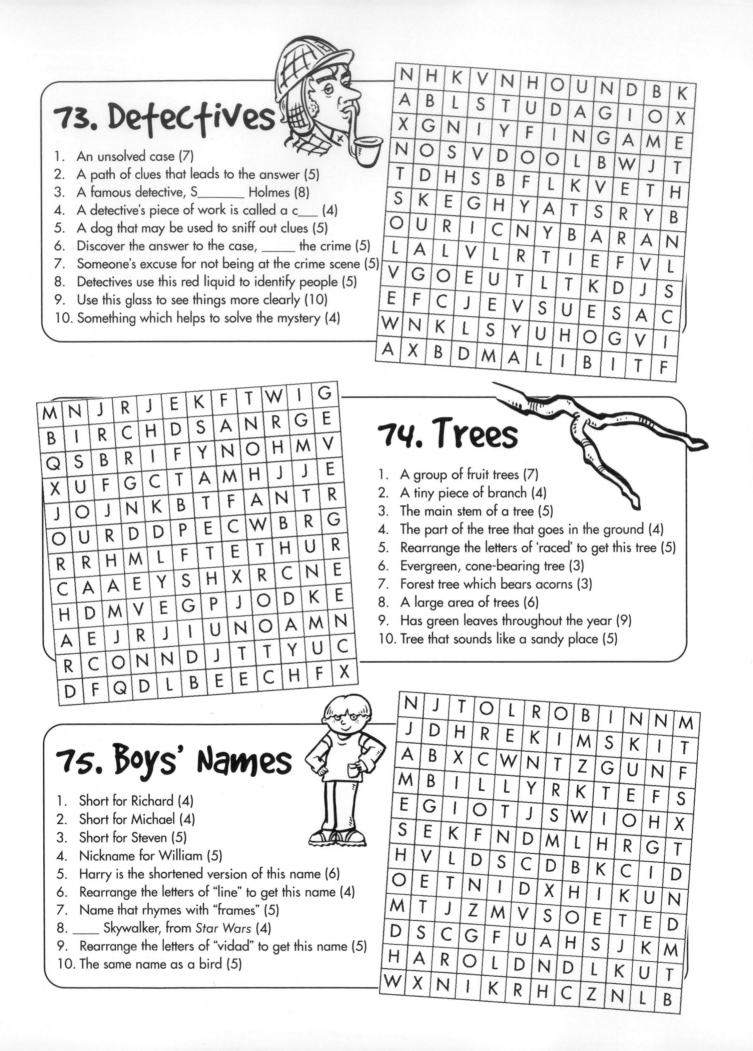

73. Detectives

1. An unsolved case (7)
2. A path of clues that leads to the answer (5)
3. A famous detective, S_____ Holmes (8)
4. A detective's piece of work is called a c___ (4)
5. A dog that may be used to sniff out clues (5)
6. Discover the answer to the case, _____ the crime (5)
7. Someone's excuse for not being at the crime scene (5)
8. Detectives use this red liquid to identify people (5)
9. Use this glass to see things more clearly (10)
10. Something which helps to solve the mystery (4)

N	H	K	V	N	H	O	U	N	D	B	K
A	B	L	S	T	U	D	A	G	I	O	X
X	G	N	I	Y	F	I	N	G	A	M	E
N	O	S	V	D	O	O	L	B	W	J	T
T	D	H	S	B	F	L	K	V	E	T	H
S	K	E	G	H	Y	A	T	S	R	Y	B
O	U	R	I	C	N	Y	B	A	R	A	N
L	A	L	V	L	R	T	I	E	F	V	L
V	G	O	E	U	T	L	T	K	D	J	S
E	F	C	J	E	V	S	U	E	S	A	C
W	N	K	L	S	Y	U	H	O	G	V	I
A	X	B	D	M	A	L	I	B	I	T	F

74. Trees

1. A group of fruit trees (7)
2. A tiny piece of branch (4)
3. The main stem of a tree (5)
4. The part of the tree that goes in the ground (4)
5. Rearrange the letters of 'raced' to get this tree (5)
6. Evergreen, cone-bearing tree (3)
7. Forest tree which bears acorns (3)
8. A large area of trees (6)
9. Has green leaves throughout the year (9)
10. Tree that sounds like a sandy place (5)

M	N	J	R	J	E	K	F	T	W	I	G
B	I	R	C	H	D	S	A	N	R	G	E
Q	S	B	R	I	F	Y	N	O	H	M	V
X	U	F	G	C	T	A	M	H	J	J	E
J	O	J	N	K	B	T	F	A	N	T	R
O	U	R	D	D	P	E	C	W	B	R	G
R	R	H	M	L	F	T	E	T	H	U	R
C	A	A	E	Y	S	H	X	R	C	N	E
H	D	M	V	E	G	P	J	O	D	K	E
A	E	J	R	J	I	U	N	O	A	M	N
R	C	O	N	N	D	J	T	T	Y	U	C
D	F	Q	D	L	B	E	E	C	H	F	X

75. Boys' Names

1. Short for Richard (4)
2. Short for Michael (4)
3. Short for Steven (5)
4. Nickname for William (5)
5. Harry is the shortened version of this name (6)
6. Rearrange the letters of "line" to get this name (4)
7. Name that rhymes with "frames" (5)
8. ____ Skywalker, from *Star Wars* (4)
9. Rearrange the letters of "vidad" to get this name (5)
10. The same name as a bird (5)

N	J	T	O	L	R	O	B	I	N	N	M
J	D	H	R	E	K	I	M	S	K	I	T
A	B	X	C	W	N	T	Z	G	U	N	F
M	B	I	L	L	Y	R	K	T	E	F	S
E	G	I	O	T	J	S	W	I	O	H	X
S	E	K	F	N	D	M	L	H	R	G	T
H	V	L	D	S	C	D	B	K	C	I	D
O	E	T	N	I	D	X	H	I	K	U	N
M	T	J	Z	M	V	S	O	E	T	E	D
D	S	C	G	F	U	A	H	S	J	K	M
H	A	R	O	L	D	N	D	L	K	U	T
W	X	N	I	K	R	H	C	Z	N	L	B

76. Musical Instruments

1. Stringed musical instrument you strum (6)
2. Percussion instrument you hit with sticks (4)
3. Has four strings and is played with a bow (6)
4. Woodwind instrument with finger-holes and keys (8)
5. Metal wind instrument with a flared tube (7)
6. Woodwind instrument of treble pitch (4)
7. Brass instrument like a small trumpet (5)
8. Triangular steel rod played in percussion (8)
9. Can be baby or grand (5)
10. Instrument with a trumpet-shaped end, French _____ (4)

```
J K R E T R I A N G L E
S T R U M P E T I U M N
W H B V A X J T E G H I
Q M K E P B D E Q U S L
R V O N E U R N H I F H
K B I S H G R I K T V R
O L U M C L B R P A B X
E A J U K E V A G R W I
W H G R V K S L K M J A
I B R D H Q H C E I N Q
P I A N O R X U N R O H
N V N I L O I V A L K P
```

77. Pirates

1. They sail on this (4)
2. Famous pirate called Long John _____ (6)
3. The thing that all pirates search for (8)
4. A pirate's _____ is called the Jolly Roger (4)
5. The _____ and crossbones is a pirate's symbol (5)
6. Pirates look for silver and what? (4)
7. Captain _____, the pirate from Peter Pan (4)
8. A pirate might have this bird on his shoulder (6)
9. They sometimes have this wooden limb (3)
10. A pirate might wear one of these over their eye (8)

```
O P A R R O T I B S K L
L C B E R U S A E R T V
G E L B R E X W H Q J O
S K R I H O O K A I N F
G D H K V O U D G T E B
F L H C E F L H G A L F
B O S Q T J K B D T I D
R G W I E A B I V S U L
O B V T L R P H C X O L
G X I L K V F E R L E U
E P I H S G E V Y Q W K
S U H C K D U R S E J S
```

78. Sports

1. A swimming stroke (5)
2. Also known as ping pong (5, 5)
3. Trying to punch a ball over a net (10)
4. Also known as gridiron (8)
5. Somersaults, flips, and splits (10)
6. Propelling a boat using oars (6)
7. Hitting a ball with clubs into holes (4)
8. Bouncing a ball and aiming for a hoop (10)
9. Sports, especially running, jumping, and throwing (9)
10. Game for two teams with balls and bats (8)

```
G B K T V S I M P H L Q
Y A E K C I R C L L N S
M S B L W F N L A J K A
N E H G L S A B D R S T
A B I O D B Y S W K L H
S A G T T E G U B S W L
T L V O L J M H T P A E
I L O L B N L N I D R T
C F O G G N I W O R C I
S V W H U S Q K M V H C
I L L A B T E K S A B S
T A B L E T E N N I S W
```

79. The Sky

1. Crescent, full, half or quarter (4)
2. They can black out the Sun (6)
3. These people-carrying vehicles travel the sky (6)
4. Shining objects in the sky (5)
5. Bright star which Earth travels around (3)
6. Feathered animals that fly in the sky (5)
7. These hot-air items float in the sky (8)
8. You look through this to see stars (9)
9. Aircraft with horizontal revolving blades (10)
10. Pretty chemical explosions that explode in the sky (9)

H	E	L	I	C	O	P	T	E	R	D	V
I	O	S	N	O	O	L	L	A	B	O	J
J	B	N	M	S	U	N	E	W	N	Z	Q
H	K	R	T	Y	X	C	N	V	B	V	R
E	V	A	D	B	J	U	I	H	C	B	Z
O	R	I	T	B	R	U	G	I	L	C	I
S	Y	N	B	I	R	D	S	H	O	T	E
K	J	M	C	U	Y	O	D	K	U	N	M
B	Q	Z	W	H	E	X	Y	R	D	B	O
D	S	E	N	A	L	P	I	V	S	M	O
F	I	R	E	W	O	R	K	S	N	J	N
N	E	P	O	C	S	E	L	E	T	O	Q

80. Shops

K	J	M	A	N	A	G	E	R	H	L	N
S	A	P	C	A	R	T	O	R	T	V	B
E	N	L	D	F	H	V	T	F	Z	G	F
C	F	H	D	I	R	K	D	L	A	D	K
U	E	G	B	J	S	X	B	N	L	A	T
R	L	P	G	V	X	P	J	N	S	I	X
I	S	F	L	A	S	X	L	M	F	Z	T
T	I	K	T	R	V	D	B	A	G	J	R
Y	A	P	R	I	C	E	S	B	Y	H	P
T	O	L	G	N	I	K	R	A	P	V	K
A	G	F	A	M	R	O	F	I	N	U	N
V	T	A	N	N	O	Y	H	L	P	T	B

1. Where the car is parked (7,3)
2. Push your shopping in this (4)
3. Where you pay (4)
4. Staff have to wear this (7)
5. How much you have to pay (5)
6. These guards protect the shop (8)
7. Announcements are called out over the _____ (6)
8. Passage between rows of products (5)
9. Goods in the window are on d_____ (7)
10. Talk to this person if you have a complaint (7)

81. In the Backyard

1. Matter used as fertilizer (7)
2. Small sharp points on a plant (6)
3. Wild plant with green blades (5)
4. Poles holding a net for soccer (9)
5. Small garden tool for digging (6)
6. These protect your hands while gardening (6)
7. Woody plant smaller than a tree (5)
8. Shrub with fragrant purple flowers (8)
9. A watery place for feathered friends (8)
10. Large cutting instrument shaped like scissors (6)

G	N	Y	H	M	P	B	U	R	H	S	K
O	L	T	R	O	W	E	L	P	C	L	U
A	T	E	G	N	B	T	S	K	E	B	N
L	S	M	C	K	R	N	U	R	C	S	K
P	E	Y	L	U	R	J	T	H	M	S	U
O	V	P	C	O	N	S	K	G	N	A	C
S	O	H	H	G	O	T	B	H	M	R	M
T	L	T	E	P	K	C	H	R	P	G	L
S	G	H	M	B	D	C	F	K	G	Y	H
C	M	O	N	S	R	A	E	H	S	C	T
Y	C	P	L	R	E	D	N	E	V	A	L
G	K	B	I	R	D	B	A	T	H	U	E

82. Food

1. Paste of meat (4)
2. Bird that's eaten as meat (7)
3. Finger-shaped yellow fruit (6)
4. Sauce made with milk and eggs or powder (7)
5. Warm liquid snack (4)
6. Plant with edible, crisp, juicy stems (6)
7. Light pastry for making cakes (5)
8. Small, soft, red, round fruit with a stone (6)
9. Baked dough topped with tomatoes and cheese (5)
10. Chinese dish of fried noodles and meat strips (4, 4)

M	G	C	H	E	R	R	Y	L	E	M	X
P	I	R	S	O	U	P	V	U	W	B	P
W	C	K	Z	E	Q	H	D	E	C	I	X
X	E	Y	M	J	N	F	S	W	Z	S	P
U	L	D	N	G	L	I	D	Z	S	G	C
O	E	R	I	B	K	D	A	R	M	Z	K
H	R	A	E	N	E	K	C	I	H	C	U
C	Y	T	M	V	G	X	T	G	N	D	R
E	D	S	W	I	P	A	T	E	M	L	I
G	M	U	O	U	K	E	G	Q	B	Y	P
P	L	C	H	B	A	N	A	N	A	V	T
Q	R	Z	C	D	W	F	M	E	R	X	D

83. The Farm

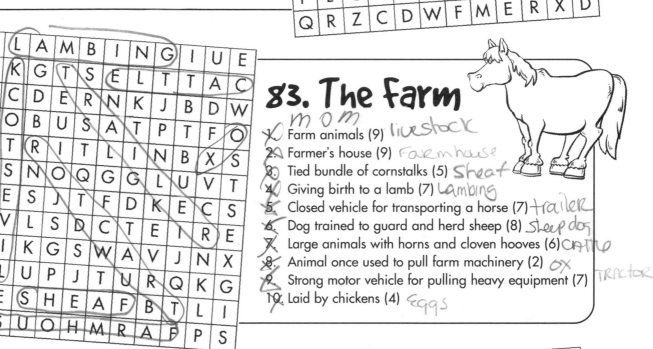

mom

1. Farm animals (9) livestock
2. Farmer's house (9) Farmhouse
3. Tied bundle of cornstalks (5) Sheaf
4. Giving birth to a lamb (7) Lambing
5. Closed vehicle for transporting a horse (7) trailer
6. Dog trained to guard and herd sheep (8) Sheep dog
7. Large animals with horns and cloven hooves (6) CATTLE
8. Animal once used to pull farm machinery (2) OX
9. Strong motor vehicle for pulling heavy equipment (7) TRACTOR
10. Laid by chickens (4) Eggs

U	T	L	A	M	B	I	N	G	I	U	E
S	P	K	G	T	S	E	L	T	T	A	C
H	L	C	D	E	R	N	K	J	B	D	W
E	W	O	B	U	S	A	T	P	T	F	O
E	A	T	R	I	T	L	I	N	B	X	S
P	E	S	N	O	Q	G	G	L	U	V	T
D	T	E	S	J	T	F	D	K	E	C	S
O	S	V	L	S	D	C	T	E	I	R	E
G	G	I	K	G	S	W	A	V	J	N	X
G	G	L	U	P	J	T	U	R	Q	K	G
D	E	E	S	H	E	A	F	B	T	L	I
I	E	S	U	O	H	M	R	A	F	P	S

84. The Letter "B"

1. Narrow-necked container (6)
2. Very young child or animal (4)
3. A green vegetable (8)
4. Way of behaving (9)
5. Person who boxes for sport (5)
6. Cloth used to cover someone's eyes (9)
7. Have temporary use of something (6)
8. Long-handled brush for sweeping floors (5)
9. Giant tropical grass that pandas eat (6)
10. Guitar-like instrument with a round body (5)

B	B	H	J	M	O	J	N	A	B	N	V
U	B	O	X	E	R	B	A	I	R	S	T
T	V	E	W	O	R	R	O	B	U	D	C
I	I	D	L	O	F	D	N	I	L	B	J
L	E	U	N	J	S	B	V	V	U	M	H
O	L	S	H	U	R	T	E	M	B	O	B
C	T	B	A	M	B	O	O	I	A	O	N
C	T	A	C	D	Y	V	I	J	T	R	D
O	O	V	B	M	T	B	H	N	R	B	E
R	B	S	R	K	N	C	A	A	M	S	B
B	U	H	E	J	C	T	U	B	K	M	V
T	I	R	U	O	I	V	A	H	E	B	N

85. Jobs

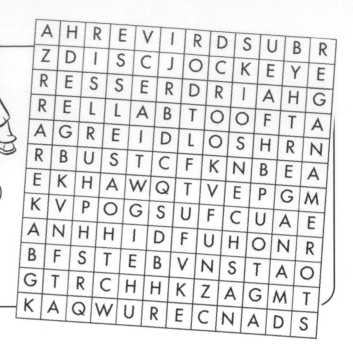

1. Person who drives a bus (3, 6)
2. Someone who runs a store (12)
3. Person who dances for a living (6)
4. Person who bakes and sells bread (5)
5. Introduces music at a party or on the radio (4, 6)
6. Someone who fights for the army (7)
7. Someone who styles and cuts hair (11)
8. Person who produces works of art (6)
9. Person in charge of a business (7)
10. Someone who plays professional football (10)

A	H	R	E	V	I	R	D	S	U	B	R
Z	D	I	S	C	J	O	C	K	E	Y	E
R	E	S	S	E	R	D	R	I	A	H	G
R	E	L	L	A	B	T	O	O	F	T	A
A	G	R	E	I	D	L	O	S	H	R	N
R	B	U	S	T	C	F	K	N	B	E	A
E	K	H	A	W	Q	T	V	E	P	G	M
K	V	P	O	G	S	U	F	C	U	A	E
A	N	H	H	I	D	F	U	H	O	N	R
B	F	S	T	E	B	V	N	S	T	A	O
G	T	R	C	H	H	K	Z	A	G	M	T
K	A	Q	W	U	R	E	C	N	A	D	S

A	B	I	S	W	I	N	T	E	R	T	J
L	U	C	J	F	V	X	E	P	K	C	Q
Z	O	T	H	O	D	A	Y	W	H	A	E
N	F	V	V	B	I	U	C	S	R	N	U
O	R	S	E	A	F	E	O	T	E	V	T
T	I	K	E	C	K	V	J	M	S	I	C
H	B	V	W	A	D	R	Y	J	A	G	R
I	P	J	T	D	T	F	M	U	B	F	E
N	X	S	Q	X	C	B	I	K	I	P	V
G	K	C	A	L	B	O	Z	N	S	E	E
F	I	E	T	U	R	A	D	C	J	A	N
K	A	T	H	G	I	L	W	B	V	S	X

86. Opposites

1. Opposite of summer (6)
2. Opposite of give (4)
3. Opposite of hate (4)
4. Opposite of friend (5)
5. Opposite of white (5)
6. Opposite of lose (4)
7. Opposite of dark (5)
8. Opposite of night (3)
9. Opposite of everything (7)
10. Opposite of forever (5)

87. House

1. Room where you sleep (7)
2. Room where you wash (8)
3. A place to park your car (6)
4. Houses are built with these (6)
5. Upper covering of a building (4)
6. People who live next to, or close to you (10)
7. Streets should have this beacon (5)
8. Where food can be heated (4)
9. Room where cooking is done (7)
10. Covers the floors of a house (6)

C	U	I	O	T	H	G	I	L	D	F	H
K	S	L	M	V	K	P	R	I	Z	B	C
F	R	Q	H	B	I	F	O	O	R	T	X
E	U	D	T	A	T	L	K	M	V	U	O
E	O	O	Z	T	C	C	A	R	P	E	T
T	B	V	F	H	H	H	L	F	C	H	B
E	H	E	I	R	E	F	I	M	E	S	E
G	G	N	K	O	N	G	D	V	K	P	D
A	I	K	U	O	S	H	N	C	M	V	R
R	E	E	P	M	F	Z	I	M	Q	O	O
A	N	R	R	C	B	R	X	U	K	C	O
G	X	D	M	V	B	P	L	I	H	C	M

88. Chores

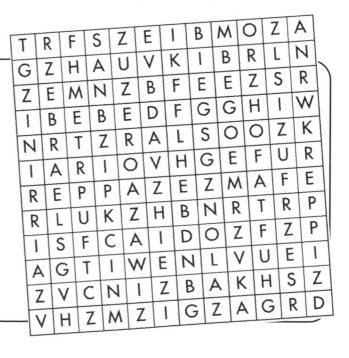

1. Removing dust (7)
2. Cutting the grass (6)
3. Cleaning carpets (9)
4. Making clothes clean (7)
5. Getting the wrinkles out of clothes (7)
6. Looking after other people's children (11)
7. Brushing away dirt (8)
8. Making everything clean (8)
9. Getting dishes really clean (8)
10. Making objects sparkle (9)

B	A	B	Y	S	I	T	T	I	N	G	G
A	T	S	G	N	I	T	S	U	D	B	G
G	G	C	M	G	N	I	P	E	E	W	S
N	N	O	C	P	B	J	G	R	M	G	T
I	I	U	R	T	A	H	N	B	W	N	B
H	N	R	W	S	D	M	I	C	A	I	D
S	O	I	G	C	V	P	W	R	T	N	J
I	R	N	H	V	X	F	O	T	G	A	C
L	I	G	D	A	B	N	M	H	S	E	M
O	D	W	A	S	H	I	N	G	H	L	P
P	G	T	C	M	B	J	R	T	D	C	W
A	R	P	G	N	I	M	U	U	C	A	V

89. Drinks

M	G	L	E	K	A	H	S	K	L	I	M
B	C	H	A	M	P	A	G	N	E	N	G
L	E	M	O	N	J	O	K	P	B	G	R
K	N	O	C	O	C	K	T	A	I	L	A
L	E	N	S	L	T	V	M	E	Z	H	P
E	T	I	E	I	H	T	O	O	M	S	E
M	L	C	R	B	W	H	G	T	N	H	F
O	B	U	P	O	U	J	N	M	V	B	R
N	J	E	G	V	S	B	K	Z	E	M	U
A	M	M	E	N	R	L	T	E	F	L	I
D	N	I	W	P	I	H	R	K	G	T	T
E	O	L	V	M	T	S	O	E	C	I	D

1. Flavored milk (9)
2. Carbonated lemon drink (8)
3. Lemon and ____ (4)
4. Drink this hot or cold (4)
5. A favorite at parties (8)
6. Alcoholic drink made from malt and hops (4)
7. Adults drink this on special occasions (9)
8. Add this to your drink to make it really cold (3)
9. Add this to a glass of water to add extra flavor (5)
10. Juice sometimes drunk at breakfast (10)

90. The Letter "Z"

1. African animal with black and white stripes (5)
2. Place where you can see animals (3)
3. Remote control for television (6)
4. Line turning left and right alternately (6)
5. Spell the word of the letter it begins with (3)
6. Number before one (4)
7. A monster (6)
8. Astrological signs (6)
9. Fastener (6)
10. Blue-white metal (4)

T	R	F	S	Z	E	I	B	M	O	Z	A
G	Z	H	A	U	V	K	I	B	R	L	N
Z	E	M	N	Z	B	F	E	E	Z	S	R
I	B	E	B	E	D	F	G	G	H	I	W
N	R	T	Z	R	A	L	S	O	O	Z	K
I	A	R	I	O	V	H	G	E	F	U	R
R	E	P	P	A	Z	E	Z	M	A	F	E
R	L	U	K	Z	H	B	N	R	T	R	P
I	S	F	C	A	I	D	O	Z	F	Z	P
A	G	T	I	W	E	N	L	V	U	E	I
Z	V	C	N	I	Z	B	A	K	H	S	Z
V	H	Z	M	Z	I	G	Z	A	G	R	D

91. Shapes

1. Round shape (6)
2. Shape with four equal sides (6)
3. Square but with two sides longer (6)
4. Five sides (8)
5. Five points, object in the sky (4)
6. Shape with three equal sides (8)
7. Shape with eight sides (7)
8. A stretched circle (4)
9. Shape with ten sides (7)
10. Shape of a dice or sugar lump (4)

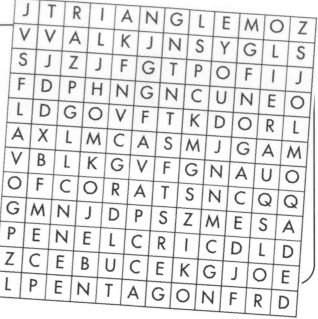

J	T	R	I	A	N	G	L	E	M	O	Z
V	V	A	L	K	J	N	S	Y	G	L	S
S	J	Z	Z	F	G	T	P	O	F	I	J
F	D	P	H	N	G	N	C	U	N	E	O
L	D	G	O	V	F	T	K	D	O	R	L
A	X	L	M	C	A	S	M	J	G	A	M
V	B	L	K	G	V	F	G	N	A	U	O
O	F	C	O	R	A	T	S	N	C	Q	Q
G	M	N	J	D	P	S	Z	M	E	S	A
P	E	N	E	L	C	R	I	C	D	L	D
Z	C	E	B	U	C	E	K	G	J	O	E
L	P	E	N	T	A	G	O	N	F	R	D

92. Weather

F	J	K	O	V	E	R	C	A	S	T	O
A	L	B	A	R	W	V	H	X	S	C	J
L	E	T	D	M	S	N	O	W	T	Q	J
L	V	C	S	T	H	U	N	D	E	R	D
M	A	O	J	P	H	D	G	K	D	B	G
N	W	J	S	B	R	E	E	Z	Y	F	X
R	T	K	V	C	A	J	H	T	H	R	H
V	A	L	S	T	O	R	M	K	D	J	E
A	E	W	H	Q	F	H	H	S	O	L	M
N	H	X	D	N	I	W	J	H	A	P	D
E	C	S	A	J	B	M	N	G	Q	C	B
R	D	I	M	U	H	T	O	K	V	W	R

1. Often comes with lightning (7)
2. Season when leaves drop (4)
3. Violent shower with strong winds (5)
4. An intense period of heat (8)
5. Current of air that blows (4)
6. Muggy, very hot (5)
7. Light wind (6)
8. Covered with cloud (8)
9. Very strong wind (4)
10. Frozen rain (4)

93. Girls' Names

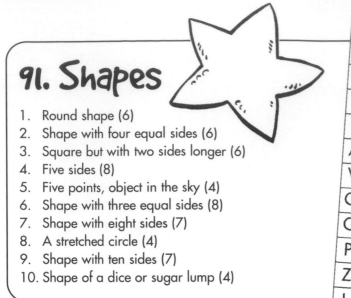

1. _____ Puddleduck (6)
2. Rhymes with Arthur (6)
3. Italian version of Marie (5)
4. She went up the hill with Jack (4)
5. Female version of Donald (5)
6. The same name as a blue flower (4)
7. Short version of Katherine (4)
8. First name of pop singer Aguilera (9)
9. Rearrange the letters in "Norahs" to get this name (6)
10. Name that can be shortened to Jo (6)

H	C	H	R	I	S	T	I	N	A	W	V
U	C	V	K	O	P	I	R	S	T	H	M
G	E	L	Q	J	Z	C	H	N	B	Y	T
T	I	L	H	J	K	A	A	D	C	V	L
A	L	M	T	G	R	N	S	U	K	W	T
H	L	B	H	O	N	W	S	I	R	I	Z
T	I	K	N	A	G	F	P	Q	J	R	E
R	J	K	O	T	H	A	M	I	M	E	J
A	R	J	L	C	V	I	C	K	Y	U	O
M	D	O	N	N	A	H	T	A	C	T	B
T	O	U	J	P	Q	M	A	R	I	A	C
K	A	T	E	A	R	K	H	W	G	M	J

94. Weddings

1. Female attending a bride (10)
2. The bride's is usually white (5)
3. Place where people marry (6)
4. The vacation after the wedding (9)
5. Traditionally, the wedding couple cut this (4)
6. A talk given at the party afterward (6)
7. The couple traditionally do this first (5)
8. Part of the church where the couple stand (5)
9. Net headdress the bride wears (4)
10. The man puts this on the bride's finger (4)

J	I	D	A	N	C	E	R	F	H	V	C
B	D	Q	K	E	D	R	E	S	S	I	B
C	I	F	S	J	W	J	M	U	E	B	T
R	A	V	N	O	O	M	Y	E	N	O	H
I	M	N	B	J	B	T	D	K	F	G	J
M	S	H	E	T	F	I	E	H	C	B	R
U	E	F	L	G	Y	Q	S	C	S	R	J
S	D	J	I	W	E	H	W	R	H	A	B
G	I	F	E	J	M	K	C	U	Z	T	W
N	R	B	V	S	U	M	A	H	B	L	V
I	B	H	C	J	B	I	N	C	F	A	R
R	K	Q	S	P	E	E	C	H	V	E	T

L	O	C	H	N	E	S	S	G	H	T	Z
F	W	P	T	R	O	L	L	O	F	P	M
L	A	M	O	D	O	P	S	I	U	U	L
N	L	H	N	G	F	W	U	H	M	D	F
A	U	K	E	T	E	L	Y	M	E	G	T
S	C	P	I	I	S	T	Y	N	K	R	N
U	A	D	L	A	L	L	I	Z	D	O	G
D	R	M	A	G	O	D	H	Y	J	F	H
E	D	F	Z	F	L	O	W	E	R	E	W
M	P	L	H	W	T	N	G	D	P	L	T
N	I	E	T	S	N	E	K	N	A	R	F
T	G	S	G	O	B	L	I	N	Z	S	O

95. Monsters

1. From another planet (5)
2. Mischievous ugly elf (6)
3. Famous vampire (7)
4. Woman with snakes for hair (6)
5. Monster wrapped in bandages (5)
6. Monster with a bolt through his neck (12)
7. Monster usually found under a bridge (5)
8. Huge famous monster from a film (8)
9. Scottish lake where Nessie lives (4, 4)
10. Person who at times turns into a wolf (8)

96. Nature

1. Black and white bird (6)
2. Group of birds or sheep (5)
3. Animal that catches mice (3)
4. Insect that annoys cattle (3)
5. A four-leaf one is lucky (6)
6. Stream that falls from a height (9)
7. Insect that produces a chirping sound (7)
8. Creature with long, soft body and no backbone (4)
9. Sweet substance made by bees (5)
10. They drop from trees in fall (6)

G	H	C	B	V	W	F	N	U	R	T	Z
J	C	A	C	A	T	C	D	H	I	G	S
R	H	D	W	A	T	E	R	F	A	L	L
D	M	A	G	P	I	E	D	J	M	G	D
F	G	N	L	E	A	V	E	S	A	L	S
C	L	O	V	E	R	D	T	S	H	W	Y
V	K	H	C	Y	U	B	J	G	O	F	E
R	C	F	Z	L	I	G	G	R	D	R	N
H	O	S	D	F	F	C	M	H	H	V	O
G	L	B	T	D	G	N	C	U	B	H
D	F	F	W	B	H	D	H	V	R	W	Z
N	I	J	E	G	T	E	K	C	I	R	C

97. The Letter "D"

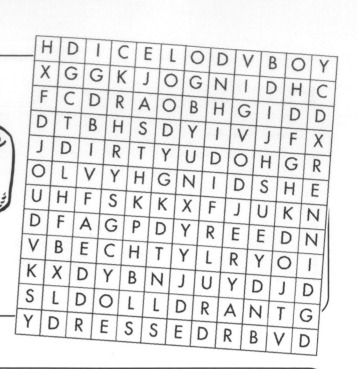

1. Unable to hear (4)
2. Girl's toy (4)
3. Do this with a spade (3)
4. Australian wild dog (5)
5. Not clean (5)
6. Main meal of the day (6)
7. Inflatable rubber boat (6)
8. Putting your clothes on, getting _____ (7)
9. Cube marked out on each side with 1–6 spots (4)
10. Animal with hooves and antlers (4)

H	D	I	C	E	L	O	D	V	B	O	Y
X	G	G	K	J	O	G	N	I	D	H	C
F	C	D	R	A	O	B	H	G	I	D	D
D	T	B	H	S	D	Y	I	V	J	F	X
J	D	I	R	T	Y	U	D	O	H	G	R
O	L	V	Y	H	G	N	I	D	S	H	E
U	H	F	S	K	K	X	F	J	U	K	N
D	F	A	G	P	D	Y	R	E	E	D	N
V	B	E	C	H	T	Y	L	R	Y	O	I
K	X	D	Y	B	N	J	U	Y	D	J	D
S	L	D	O	L	L	D	R	A	N	T	G
Y	D	R	E	S	S	E	D	R	B	V	D

98. Candy

1. Lemon _____ (5)
2. Menthol sweets (5)
3. Blow bubbles with this (9)
4. Comes in bars or squares (9)
5. Gummy _____ (5)
6. Soft candy made from sugar and butter (5)
7. Bean-shaped candies (5, 5)
8. Sweet black substance (8)
9. Really chewy candies (3, 8)
10. Saltwater _____ (5)

F	J	J	B	N	O	K	D	U	R	Z	C
J	E	E	Q	B	E	A	R	S	I	F	Q
A	L	V	Y	F	F	A	T	R	S	J	K
W	L	C	E	T	A	L	O	C	O	H	C
B	Y	O	T	U	E	E	D	F	Z	S	U
R	B	J	B	U	B	B	L	E	G	U	M
E	E	D	F	R	B	E	G	N	N	R	E
A	A	K	U	D	R	O	P	S	I	E	S
K	N	Z	A	Q	C	O	C	U	F	Y	B
E	S	Y	L	I	C	O	R	I	C	E	E
R	S	S	R	E	S	E	G	D	U	F	Q
S	B	M	I	N	T	S	N	U	V	K	O

99. Sports

1. Throwing a light spear (7)
2. Short for referee (3)
3. Referees blow this (7)
4. Top medal at the Olympics (4)
5. Seeing how far you can leap (4, 4)
6. Fighting and grappling as a sport (9)
7. Where soccer is played (5)
8. Game like hockey but played on horses (4)
9. Aiming an arrow at a bullseye (7)
10. Run as fast as you can (6)

J	A	R	C	H	E	R	Y	N	B	K	T
K	H	I	N	I	L	E	V	A	J	S	L
N	S	P	R	I	N	T	G	M	Z	F	H
R	Q	W	R	E	S	T	L	I	N	G	N
H	S	T	J	K	B	D	H	I	D	N	D
P	M	U	J	G	N	O	L	T	N	G	L
T	E	L	T	S	I	H	W	V	R	K	O
S	J	M	R	I	D	N	F	H	G	D	G
F	Z	N	H	Q	K	V	F	J	T	S	B
P	O	L	O	F	L	B	R	E	M	H	Z
R	B	N	T	F	T	B	S	F	R	I	H
V	H	C	T	I	P	R	H	D	Q	V	J

100. The Letter "F"

1. Person who manages a farm (6)
2. Musical instrument with mouth-hole at the side (5)
3. Where French people come from (6)
4. They're on the end of your hands (7)
5. "Old Glory" is one (4)
6. Opposite of stale (5)
7. It gives out heat (4)
8. 11 – 6 = ? (4)
9. Opposite of back (5)
10. Cunning animal (3)

W	V	U	O	X	K	D	B	L	A	H	E
F	F	A	R	M	E	R	A	B	J	W	F
I	J	F	G	J	Y	O	P	H	A	T	L
R	B	T	A	E	E	F	L	A	G	F	U
E	J	L	K	R	U	R	F	F	H	U	T
E	F	I	V	E	P	H	F	F	E	B	E
K	O	B	D	J	H	W	F	F	O	F	J
H	A	R	M	O	N	F	O	X	V	R	G
V	P	G	E	T	A	F	Y	B	G	A	D
F	R	O	N	T	L	O	X	P	J	N	K
E	F	R	E	S	H	A	B	J	U	C	H
F	I	N	G	E	R	S	K	G	T	E	Y

E	D	G	F	G	O	O	D	B	Y	E	S
N	G	O	B	L	E	T	M	F	T	Z	L
J	M	S	W	P	H	O	G	E	I	I	J
F	L	R	I	G	Q	G	R	E	U	F	P
Y	D	O	E	L	Z	H	F	J	R	Q	G
E	M	J	T	A	N	G	F	N	F	S	G
R	H	G	F	Q	D	F	S	S	E	O	R
G	I	L	W	O	R	G	H	D	P	L	O
M	E	N	P	D	H	J	G	H	A	P	W
G	R	U	M	B	L	E	I	M	R	Z	J
L	S	F	O	Z	G	K	J	E	G	N	Q
G	M	E	P	L	U	G	G	W	F	D	H

101. The Letter "G"

1. Large round yellow citrus fruit (10)
2. Opposite of boy (4)
3. Moan or complain (7)
4. Noise dogs make (5)
5. Drinking glass with a stem (6)
6. Color between black and white (4)
7. To get bigger (4)
8. Swallow quickly (4)
9. Small, biting fly (4)
10. Opposite of hello (7)

ANSWERS

1. Mother Nature

B	Q	R	S	S	Q	U	I	R	R	E	L	
T	H	E	D	G	E	H	O	G	U	T	S	
L	M	E	J	P	Z	R	O	L	V	Q	R	
Z	I	R	J	A	C	O	R	N	L	N	Z	
O	L	T	K	M	D	A	B	S	T	M	A	
E	N	P	Q	A	R	N	A	B	H	U	O	
A	L	A	D	Y	B	U	G	D	L	L	O	
R	A	L	E	A	V	E	S	P	K	A	W	
T	S	Y	L	W	A	T	S	M	R	F	D	
H	R	A	D	L	Q	P	R	V	O	J	I	
B	O	T	N	D	J	O	K	S	M	J	Q	
N	E	R	R	A	W	V	T	W	R	L	P	

2. Going Places

D	L	H	O	S	P	I	T	A	L	F	N	
T	U	O	G	E	T	T	H	A	O	I	A	
I	R	W	U	O	Z	O	O	T	O	R	C	
E	N	O	T	O	F	R	E	Y	P	E	U	
H	T	L	P	H	E	S	O	O	G	S	L	
L	A	E	M	R	C	O	U	J	N	T	O	
O	E	L	Y	I	L	D	U	I	A	N	
O	O	V	I	F	S	A	S	T	M	T	D	
H	L	Y	M	H	I	N	F	I	M	I	O	
C	O	F	F	I	C	E	N	C	I	O	N	
S	L	C	H	U	R	C	H	O	W	N	U	
P	A	L	A	C	E	C	T	I	S	N	E	

3. Getting Around

N	M	C	E	B	O	A	T	M	S	T	S	
V	O	D	A	F	D	R	O	R	H	U	E	
H	T	O	L	Y	I	K	C	E	P	E	T	
P	O	Z	G	D	S	R	S	T	N	Q	A	
B	R	N	A	A	E	L	S	A	F	L	K	
A	B	I	A	N	R	C	I	Z	G	S	S	
T	I	A	M	A	N	P	T	O	E	R	R	
G	K	R	Y	A	R	O	R	B	E	O	E	
W	E	T	N	I	A	C	U	H	K	T	I	
S	L	R	A	Z	N	A	C	Y	I	A	L	
U	E	A	M	E	S	R	K	E	B	P	O	
B	A	I	N	A	V	O	L	I	T	O	R	

4. Down on the Farm

S	R	A	B	B	I	T	U	N	T	Y	S	
L	I	N	A	T	C	O	E	S	R	O	H	
P	M	A	N	T	E	E	N	P	I	D	E	
E	F	R	E	R	H	E	O	D	N	T	B	
E	O	M	E	R	K	B	S	E	P	I	G	
H	V	A	F	C	I	R	H	O	T	R	H	
S	O	L	I	L	F	D	O	G	S	Z	G	
T	E	H	Z	D	E	H	D	E	E	F	W	
O	C	I	L	R	I	T	I	M	T	O	O	
D	M	Q	T	A	O	G	T	E	H	T	C	
I	I	G	T	O	N	M	A	N	N	O	I	
K	R	H	R	O	O	S	T	E	R	W	S	

5. Fantastic Food

L	A	E	R	E	C	A	Y	I	M	F	I	
U	Y	A	S	E	R	D	T	O	A	S	T	
T	O	R	W	Q	P	O	O	A	N	N	E	
O	L	L	B	H	E	K	D	J	T	P	H	
L	O	A	E	G	A	S	U	A	S	I	S	
L	O	S	I	T	M	C	Y	H	X	Z	I	
E	H	E	P	O	T	A	T	O	B	S	P	
J	P	I	N	E	A	P	P	L	E	H	A	
O	R	Y	W	F	G	L	U	Y	I	K	N	
T	C	A	K	E	G	U	S	O	U	T	S	
K	T	O	E	G	V	C	H	P	E	A	S	
L	A	T	E	R	U	A	P	L	S	E	A	

6. Cool Colors

L	W	R	R	Q	I	E	G	N	A	R	O
G	H	M	K	E	S	T	L	R	V	T	F
E	I	G	G	H	V	I	W	J	R	Z	G
P	T	I	K	U	S	I	I	Q	I	O	R
E	E	N	T	E	R	U	I	Q	N	S	E
L	I	D	E	R	P	H	R	S	G	E	E
W	G	O	L	D	T	E	U	M	G	D	N
O	E	L	S	V	I	C	K	C	A	L	B
L	R	E	W	P	D	K	H	F	P	Z	I
L	G	B	R	X	D	N	Y	L	A	N	N
E	W	U	E	R	D	I	N	B	S	L	S
Y	P	A	V	E	R	P	O	O	A	H	T

9. At the Circus

S	V	E	L	C	Y	C	I	N	U	L	D
T	R	Q	K	L	B	J	Z	G	N	I	R
R	M	S	A	W	D	U	S	T	T	V	L
O	L	P	Q	D	R	M	D	A	I	W	T
N	J	O	D	K	L	V	P	C	U	C	E
G	M	T	P	C	O	E	E	N	B	L	K
M	R	G	L	N	Z	C	Z	G	K	P	C
A	H	I	J	E	R	Q	L	J	N	R	I
N	S	B	P	E	F	I	R	A	W	O	T
B	C	A	A	D	C	B	D	Z	O	M	C
Z	R	M	T	V	R	X	L	K	L	S	T
T	I	E	S	R	O	H	W	J	C	R	O

7. In the Home

J	R	V	M	E	S	A	C	K	O	O	B
B	T	E	L	E	V	I	S	I	O	N	B
E	A	B	D	H	T	B	A	T	H	T	D
I	L	F	Y	X	C	W	G	A	Z	N	R
B	R	E	N	A	E	L	C	M	I	A	M
A	L	V	E	R	S	H	J	U	D	S	S
T	B	T	U	R	Q	C	T	U	L	H	K
A	C	N	J	O	K	U	P	C	K	C	E
R	A	A	O	T	E	O	V	A	L	A	T
C	T	S	I	U	R	C	T	V	B	N	T
S	Z	B	P	J	Z	D	K	P	S	T	I
S	F	I	L	M	D	E	B	R	V	Q	E

8. Toy Store

B	A	R	B	I	E	F	G	Q	D	B	R
S	R	O	Z	T	W	A	S	G	I	J	L
S	K	I	P	J	U	M	P	R	O	P	E
M	N	O	I	T	A	T	S	Y	A	L	P
H	E	R	A	E	B	Y	D	D	E	T	G
R	O	C	K	I	N	G	H	O	R	S	E
Z	Y	X	D	V	N	H	B	K	K	F	Z
Q	N	L	M	C	A	O	A	I	O	H	I
O	P	U	W	K	M	B	K	J	O	J	D
A	C	T	I	O	N	M	A	N	B	J	O
C	O	L	O	R	I	N	G	K	B	K	L
R	T	S	E	L	B	R	A	M	F	G	L

10. Girls' Names

Z	E	L	I	Z	A	B	E	T	H	X	O
X	M	E	I	L	N	D	Z	O	A	W	J
B	J	L	N	M	A	R	Y	B	C	T	S
M	D	T	E	R	A	G	R	A	M	R	P
K	V	R	C	I	B	Q	J	K	Z	O	Y
U	H	S	Y	E	N	T	I	R	B	V	E
K	A	O	U	S	R	O	J	P	I	H	C
L	R	M	K	O	C	M	A	E	P	R	A
D	A	B	S	T	Q	I	V	F	X	R	P
N	S	E	L	D	K	G	X	A	N	M	T
Z	I	V	N	W	O	B	W	B	Z	A	S
A	L	M	Z	R	J	E	N	N	Y	R	Z

11. At Work

B	C	N	S	T	W	R	I	T	E	R	S
F	L	O	R	I	S	T	R	U	N	A	R
S	D	O	C	T	O	R	S	U	U	R	E
R	Y	H	M	A	E	A	R	F	O	K	T
E	N	Y	C	R	I	S	L	T	B	Q	H
H	D	D	S	Z	E	O	C	O	W	V	G
C	R	K	I	S	L	A	P	L	T	B	I
A	T	N	E	D	I	S	E	R	P	E	F
E	Q	P	U	L	L	W	M	S	L	M	E
T	Z	L	W	R	E	K	M	F	K	I	R
F	X	S	R	E	M	R	A	F	Q	R	I
S	I	N	G	E	R	S	W	T	I	P	F

12. Wild Animals

N	Z	R	R	A	E	B	S	E	I	D	D
Z	Y	E	U	V	X	H	U	L	L	P	C
N	B	O	B	R	I	V	M	E	X	V	R
H	L	L	D	R	P	Y	A	P	K	G	O
A	L	I	S	Z	A	K	T	H	M	I	C
T	C	U	O	L	O	N	O	A	N	R	O
E	V	K	B	N	I	M	P	N	I	A	D
E	O	A	X	U	Z	E	O	T	U	F	I
H	S	R	G	U	N	K	P	N	G	F	L
C	U	N	A	P	I	N	R	N	E	E	R
O	E	L	C	V	R	C	I	T	E	D	R
P	M	O	N	K	E	Y	H	B	B	O	L

13. Holidays

C	Z	C	S	A	M	T	S	I	R	H	C
M	M	A	N	G	E	R	O	Y	X	S	R
G	R	H	B	T	C	A	R	O	L	S	E
N	U	R	I	D	U	A	C	U	M	F	H
I	D	Z	N	M	W	R	P	A	T	N	T
K	D	A	T	A	V	S	K	M	O	I	A
C	I	M	X	L	K	L	Z	E	K	H	F
O	N	P	M	E	F	K	M	S	Y	Z	A
T	G	O	E	I	B	Q	U	D	F	W	Q
S	C	R	P	O	A	X	Y	N	W	N	B
N	T	Y	U	L	E	L	O	G	A	Z	X
Q	S	T	N	E	S	E	R	P	L	H	H

14. Under the Sea

```
J Y X H U P W M J F F
D C V N S H A R K Y D X
Y F U E K X E F J P N P
D D O L P H I N U D E U
E Q H D S V L R C I Q E
E M K U C F E H D A H H
W S W R J L K F M M R
A L A C S S U X E R V O
E B X B V Y E C H E P H
S F O K D M Y K M E A
Y L E H S I F E A N Q E
O C T O P U S V H W J S
```

15. TV characters

```
N B O B F I X W T S A H
P A S H L T C H J U F I
L C U B O Y O K P S W D
E D Y M A M F T B E N L
I K M Y A I L A H I Y P
G Y B S H N K C Y B E I
G N X P A S M P F S N U
A S L M Y S J O A G R B
M C E K W G U T X U A S
L H A F B J P H N B B X
S C O O B Y D O O C Y H
U H E N R Y A N L A W G
```

16. Family Fun

```
B E C E I N U I F K E M
H R X A L C J I H Z O W
N E P H E W S X B M R P
I S C B A M D N A R G U
Z F O H I F G E M C E I
E A U J R D L A W N L O
I R S N E P A S H D H W
T M I R T I U D P K A U
N C N S S J H O N D K D
U O A M I H Z E I A Y X
A B L X S D N P F W R K
R B R O T H E R R U E G
```

17. Clothes

```
G S E O H S Q I L U D L
A K H V F Y R B G M R F
U M X R I E N R U O E A
I N A O P F U N V K S T
H C L M H Q D A S O S R
S R U G B E M R K N O I
Y Y E K R H E H H I M H
N U V W L S Y X B H Q S
F Q E I T R T A O C F T
M A V N A G T R I K S N
R B A L K N M U V E O G
Y P R I U S O C K S Y X
```

18. In the Backyard

```
W R I R E W O M N W A L
H Y J T A L P A T I O B
E F D K O T R B L G N D
E L E L N P E T Y C Z S
L O A C B Z R J I D Q D
B W G W N D H E U C U E
A E R Y I E E L W B J E
R R J T D Q F B K O L W
R K T A B K N G T I L K
O U P D W Y N A Q U Z F
W S R E S U O H Y A L P
J K G R E E N H O U S E
```

19. Space

```
Q G H G T E K C O R I V
B O M R L D Q Z B A H O
R M E A U W M G T S K L
D E T V V B O E N T O G
H T S I K L N X S R K E
M Z Y T G A R D G O S L
O B S Y L H M T K N W T
O I R P V T U H Y A X T
N U A T Q B T I L U O U
S K L D S R Z D Z D T H
Q G O H A X N V O N M S
Z R S E L S R A T S X D
```

20. The Body

```
F O T R A E H S T U A R
T C Z Q H K E O D A E H
E R L A T U L M Z K B N
E K N M U S C L E Q F V
F D F C S Q N V E S T P
S L R E O A M N A R E T
A T Y U S N O B C L E N
C E P Q C B T K B R N O
F Z U K R L F A T Z K H
S L I A N R E G N I F B
R P C L Q N O V R S H L
K N O T T U B Y L L E B
```

21. Opposites

```
Z F P D Y L W O L S P E
O R E S Q K S X H C H N
U X M E D H B L Y S A E
D N K K T R D O X N K T
N B T F U Z A R J T J G
W K E R F N F W I S F D
O L S L P K R U R Q L S
D X T D B O M G T O C M
Q F O C U E G A X K F A
G I H G E J P P I E S L
K Z H D N O F T K Z D L
M U D U O L R B H R S J
```

22. Magic

F	E	I	H	C	R	E	K	D	N	A	H
A	B	R	A	C	A	D	A	B	R	A	M
Q	H	N	F	D	H	S	E	S	W	Q	A
T	L	K	J	H	S	O	N	N	L	J	A
S	E	A	B	D	V	A	M	K	H	S	R
E	M	W	R	L	I	R	F	C	S	S	A
R	D	A	Q	C	E	H	D	I	V	X	B
P	C	K	I	T	N	N	S	N	Q	K	B
S	F	G	T	A	E	T	D	C	M	S	I
L	A	O	J	O	A	B	W	N	L	F	T
M	P	H	V	M	B	K	D	M	A	S	A
A	Q	M	T	R	I	C	K	S	J	W	Z

25. Drinks

J	O	T	C	H	O	C	O	L	A	T	E
G	O	R	D	I	A	L	H	K	D	S	X
Y	C	B	E	D	A	Z	R	E	E	B	D
C	A	R	B	O	N	A	T	E	D	M	B
K	H	E	E	F	F	O	C	V	H	J	D
J	D	M	C	N	N	S	K	W	I	N	E
S	X	T	B	B	T	Y	O	N	L	H	K
S	E	B	H	I	Z	R	A	V	C	F	C
A	L	K	V	Z	B	J	R	E	T	A	W
W	N	M	I	Y	W	D	B	V	S	X	S
O	Z	F	F	M	I	L	K	N	A	O	L
I	A	S	N	M	C	J	U	I	C	E	Z

23. The Beach

O	G	H	R	S	W	I	M	S	U	I	T
D	T	E	W	I	N	D	B	R	E	A	K
U	S	L	C	S	A	Y	W	Q	L	N	C
N	A	T	J	U	D	H	X	D	H	O	J
W	N	S	G	S	O	G	D	P	T	J
P	D	A	H	Y	C	T	R	K	G	J	X
L	W	C	D	Q	U	L	F	H	C	N	H
E	I	D	C	H	T	C	N	B	W	E	R
W	C	N	P	A	D	D	L	I	N	G	
O	H	A	H	S	I	F	R	A	T	S	C
T	E	S	D	G	H	S	O	P	U	Q	Y
Y	S	L	I	F	E	G	U	A	R	D	T

27. Party Time

B	Q	W	S	D	V	C	V	E	B	N	C
N	F	S	S	E	R	D	Y	C	N	A	F
P	R	E	S	E	N	T	F	D	Y	F	E
E	M	G	H	L	M	C	Y	K	H	G	F
L	K	U	C	D	F	D	S	P	W	Q	B
E	D	V	O	F	X	R	C	N	P	K	Y
C	F	O	M	Q	I	G	O	D	X	A	L
R	P	H	W	A	B	E	G	H	D	F	H
A	M	V	H	L	Y	S	U	D	G	F	K
P	D	C	N	F	M	U	S	I	C	M	G
S	N	O	I	T	A	T	I	V	N	I	A
C	I	C	E	C	R	E	A	M	Q	V	B

26. The Playground

G	L	Y	T	R	O	F	Y	S	E	E	K
K	E	L	N	I	J	D	S	I	O	Y	U
O	E	P	A	L	A	D	D	E	R	S	H
U	R	L	V	B	H	X	F	D	V	W	C
H	L	L	D	Z	T	D	F	K	U	G	T
B	K	I	A	A	S	Q	P	X	I	M	O
E	F	N	W	Y	R	G	O	J	N	R	C
L	D	Y	T	R	T	C	T	F	H	Y	S
L	S	H	T	A	G	I	S	X	D	F	P
I	J	I	K	V	F	I	M	T	K	F	O
G	N	I	P	P	I	K	S	E	A	N	H
P	F	N	X	Z	H	W	T	V	J	C	S

28. Holidays

T	E	N	T	G	B	F	D	S	W	E	Q
A	M	E	K	B	N	A	V	A	R	A	C
S	L	E	E	P	I	N	G	B	A	G	F
L	P	H	S	U	R	B	H	T	O	O	T
N	O	F	J	R	H	U	Q	H	D	E	D
W	S	S	U	N	N	Y	F	G	F	S	N
G	T	B	E	M	L	D	V	A	B	A	L
Q	C	D	F	A	E	E	N	Q	R	C	W
K	A	S	D	J	H	W	T	B	U	T	K
E	R	B	P	A	M	G	E	O	D	J	
N	D	L	F	R	M	S	H	Q	H	U	B
S	S	T	R	O	P	R	I	A	F	S	A

29. Farmyard Animals

M	J	L	N	D	F	V	H	B	C	N	X
L	N	K	T	I	K	Q	N	E	H	H	K
I	G	O	O	S	E	U	E	D	V	I	Y
A	C	E	D	U	C	K	M	D	G	K	E
M	X	J	H	X	C	H	I	C	L	T	K
A	T	C	N	X	H	B	Y	V	B	V	R
D	A	B	K	G	N	E	J	N	M	M	U
F	O	L	V	T	D	C	B	G	R	U	T
G	G	I	K	Q	M	J	H	Q	U	X	
V	X	E	B	U	A	F	X	D	T	L	P
B	U	L	L	F	N	K	K	I	C	J	
C	J	M	Q	G	E	T	A	C	V	F	B

24. Time

O	M	I	N	U	T	E	C	P	S	Y	T
A	D	M	U	E	V	W	F	R	N	X	F
B	S	H	C	T	A	W	G	E	M	O	B
S	D	N	O	C	E	S	D	H	W	B	G
D	O	T	N	S	N	D	R	T	E	A	P
R	P	X	Y	A	C	A	H	A	Y	L	X
U	W	E	F	D	E	N	N	F	S	A	G
O	G	V	D	Y	M	B	T	D	U	R	B
H	A	S	B	A	O	P	S	N	F	M	S
T	N	H	E	Y	C	D	U	A	V	D	Y
C	B	M	D	X	W	E	M	R	N	X	A
S	H	T	N	O	M	G	D	D	G	S	D

30. Bedtime

```
G J K B V C F D S W H S
Q E I T H G I N R T Y C
S K W Z C U I K L I M I
K W I Q V G M S C C F T
C B X S J G M C N X W Q
U T H R S A F W K A G J
T E D Y E M T H T C I S
K D V R C V B E Z V H T
G D D W U Q R U J B D O
F Y C H R X K C F S W R
S B Z F T W O L L I P Y
X T H G I L Y D H G V K
```

31. The Desert

```
B M N H U S A N D I D F
H I G K T Y U G N H C O
N R V B D L F C E U A T
U A C H B I F R D S X N
E G X E G Z T E I V G O
T E G E I A U S H T B I
O U F R K R L T N G Y P
Y E N T D D C E I D R R
O V I M B N F E M U F O
C U G L H T X G K A N C
B R T A E H Y V B G C S
K D E P D R E T A W I H
```

32. Flowers

```
J K N P A N S I E V H C
X D A D A I S Y R F O J
H R T N Y S N A P G L K
P C E B J F G D U C L X
R N F W Z F K G C N Y A
E E G E O M B D R V J Y
T V F N E L A M E N T L
A K H S S X F P T Q E L
L M O Z B D R N T N S L
J R D E P A T S U H G K
X A T E U Q U O B S J P
D N G M V Q N G F A E L
```

33. The Letter "W"

```
W V H F W A T E R F D S
A D C E D W R I T E W R
L R T E S X W Y N W H G
I K S J J R O Y R E I S
W N D F S H E R I A T W
G F T G C I P X D K E C
D X N A F S H R S G S V
Y I E V T N T S E I G S
W W H R A G X N A F H E
V K S M D S S Y C W T W
T F O G A W A T C H T F
S W A R D R O B E E A S
```

34. The Letter "S"

```
S D F G M H S L E E P J
I K S E L S P C O S R S
L E T I K U D I T J I T
Y S O R S O E A S S D S
E D K O S W R A K R R I
R W R Z O S N F G E L D
F R L C D A D E S P O N
Y H J S T S K N D P H E
G S R N U W A R A I C Y
I E U O J I L J S L G E
K S Z X L D T R K S F S
R U S Y G N O S R O S H
```

35. Spies

```
K O S U N G L A S S E S
L R E V O C R E D N U K
A E N O H P L L E C O M
R E D O C V J E A E R I
S O T L A K F L T S L O
J E W I P N L G B A A J
F R A O N E T E R C E S
K V R K R J J P W F N O
C D A B T S R I S E B K
A M M G R K L O E I P V
L U E J F A V A M R K J
B S I O W N M A T B G R
```

36. Birds

```
N R O B I N F C H S T U
D I K X E G O K C U C Y
W R A G G N I M A L F M
S N I M O P K E N B O A
H W F B N D T O R R A P
Y O T E G C I R C U V F
M R U A E N E B Y P M H
N R X G S O T I N U K E
B A A L W H F M G T I X
I P D E O K M A M D J F
N S Y T R C P F E U U C
M E F B C U N W X S H B
```

37. Creepy Crawlies

```
R I S T U I C K L P M V
N G R A S S H O P P E R
S F H E W Q R G B B I W
E M Y L F N O G A R D P
L C C R B L Z S K G L S
R R K E E B R E C T G A
W I T S U H I L F V K W
O C I P E C N T K M H Y
R K G I W R A E R B L R
M E V K I W I G E Q P N
U T H R F T P B S Z C K
N C O T I U Q S O M U E
```

38. Jewelry

```
K L N I A H C Y L L E B
D P E A R L S V X U E R
R J E C A L K C E N N S
S N W O B L R Q K D I Z
G A U J R W C L A S P R
N N B E A D L N W S L J
I K V J C Y B E H J A K
R L X D E I D E O R Q S
R E O W L L S B A R F D
L T K Q E Z U I D W B L
N E S R T O T J V J I O
L S G N I R R A E W X G
```

41. Wild Animals

```
L O E L L E Z A G M D S
D G R U Y W U T V B D N
M L H C K B A B O O N D
H W V I D X E K A N S R
U T L N M D M A Q J Y N
S S E A L P U S O G R O
K U S R Y H A C K W H O
Y R O V H Y E N A L D S
W L M A U T A Q Z D C A
C A K D L N Y W V E M B
R W X R A U G A J O E T
A T L E O P A R D S U N
```

39. Boys' Names

```
S D K O M A R K P V W Q
Y U G C L I V E B R D L
B H N D H U G W F N D N
V Q S P Z I X H G N S O
A R E L W K U I H V K T
N P L H D C O P B P D
D W R S L B J O Y R U H
R F A D L G G Q V I N M
E L H N I U H X B K L A
W Y C Z A P B O B D O D
Q D K G M F R P Z S W A
B V D R E T E P I N Y C
```

42. The Sea

```
O J K O C T O P U S O N
I E L V D X Z S D E W E
D S T P I R A N H A O X
U S J O G H I T K S D
V O J E E D O P J U F R
E H W L V F C L B G D A
R T L A T C E M J L B U
K H Z H S T A I B O C G
I G J W B R N G A E Z E
V L D X K H T W V D F
S L E M P L J J X L K
W G E F D I U Q S O H L
```

40. Countries

```
B N M S A M E R I C A C
D N A L R E Z T I W S M
K C E A I N F L C U S A
M Z I T A L Y B E G G U
F H L W K A H R E D K S
K O E S T I G R U N N T
A L C U C E M T A A S R
I L N B N A Z N M L B A
C A A M N F I C E G H L
L N R Y S H K L N N W
F D P E C A U H F E S A
W B Z S P A I N R I M E
```

43. Weather

```
I T E M P E R A T U R E
H G O N S T G K M I E B
V N B F R O S T R O N T
O I M Q Z V C G B V I H
K N E N A C I R R U H S
B T C I R E P O R T S O
O H B G O C H F R C N I
O G S T D N C S L I U K
T I V N M U V K N Q S M
S L R H Z O V B O N N
E O Q A I G V L T G W M
S N K R L K J H C H S Z
```

44. Creepy Crawlies

```
H A R V E S T M A N R C
N R H T Y R U B K N Y W
T E Q C E N T I P E D E
W T Z O D I K G J S H I
O A R C H G J S G D H U
O K L K B W L N H C T F
D S S R Y U S F E R G H
W D I O G Z S E H D H G
O N N A T K L D I U Q L
R O Y C B H I N L T B O
M P N H D P G T W U N J
K S R L S N A I L T Z A
```

45. Characters

```
J O B I V H A G R I D R
B E L L E A J E S O R W
Y C J Y D O O W D G A C
I S R H G V Y C K J E N
O H E W J N J M C Y A
X E T A N A R B O B T I
B R S C P H A K R H T
E A M R N R I M E D G S
D Y O C V E O B N C A
S V N I E T W A X L E
N J E H N E S C V J V E
S I M B A P B C O Y I S
```

46. Films

G	B	L	M	E	R	M	A	I	D	L	D
N	C	A	S	F	E	T	X	H	N	O	G
K	I	O	L	B	E	A	S	T	R	U	I	S
K	N	L	H	D	M	W	E	B	L	B	N
F	G	E	R	I	H	Y	T	K	D	M	A
K	D	R	I	W	H	F	S	G	I	T
L	E	E	T	B	I	K	C	O	X	F	T
U	C	D	O	R	G	R	I	N	C	H	A
H	L	N	E	H	N	F	E	M	R	D	M
S	H	R	G	P	M	A	R	T	H	L
T	F	C	X	D	O	C	T	I	B	N	A
E	T	O	Y	S	T	O	R	Y	L	S	D

47. Games

I	L	M	N	R	S	T	U	W	C	B	P
H	Y	R	A	N	O	I	T	C	I	P	E
O	P	E	R	A	T	I	O	N	T	D	T
P	W	Y	B	I	E	K	Y	G	M	L	W
A	S	L	U	S	C	F	G	D	I	B
R	C	O	N	L	R	J	S	Y	N	H	S
T	R	P	M	P	T	E	E	H	T	D
E	A	O	I	R	E	D	D	N	E	P	E
S	B	N	H	D	L	B	K	D	G	W
U	B	O	S	D	R	A	C	U	A	A	C
O	L	M	U	P	M	T	I	N	E	L	T
M	E	S	C	L	U	E	D	Y	R	L	H

48. Royalty

L	B	V	C	D	Y	N	W	E	X	Q	L
J	O	P	W	A	L	E	S	E	S	S	F
G	D	F	S	T	I	E	C	N	I	R	P
G	Y	N	S	E	R	V	A	N	T	S	E
A	G	C	E	D	O	Z	T	Y	N	J	E
S	U	V	T	Q	K	C	R	O	W	N	S
T	A	Y	L	H	J	F	D	S	E	V	N
I	L	R	R	Y	W	R	K	G	M	Z	N
E	F	D	N	P	I	N	O	V	T	I	L
Q	D	E	S	N	C	M	N	D	Y	E	U
L	T	H	F	E	Z	O	X	E	Q	W	Q
I	V	E	C	A	L	A	P	G	J	C	M

49. The Letter "P"

A	P	A	J	A	M	A	S	T	O	N	A
R	D	P	T	P	N	G	P	A	S	E	P
D	P	A	R	T	R	I	D	G	E	O	R
P	O	N	A	R	E	H	T	N	A	P	D
A	P	E	S	U	R	C	H	A	J	N	X
S	G	T	P	I	R	A	T	E	G	O
R	N	A	A	O	D	P	N	U	T	M	S
N	S	H	R	M	A	D	A	O	D	P	T
U	R	P	I	G	E	G	R	T	R	E	N
T	A	C	A	U	P	R	A	M	A	G	A
A	P	R	P	J	A	G	P	S	O	C	P
K	M	A	O	P	D	G	R	U	K	P	T

50. School

B	L	E	S	S	O	N	S	T	J	L	I
K	U	F	O	E	R	E	H	C	A	E	T
H	B	M	I	B	V	S	W	X	M	K	T
O	L	S	T	J	L	F	S	R	D	A	N
M	A	T	U	K	G	Q	O	A	G	O	X
E	C	R	S	U	F	F	D	M	I	U	Z
W	K	O	T	I	B	J	T	S	W	S
O	B	K	D	N	V	I	A	T	G	M	R
R	O	S	U	M	E	C	S	S	A	Q	E
K	A	M	K	U	A	X	O	X	L	B	L
S	R	Y	J	V	W	G	E	D	S	F	U
O	D	G	I	R	E	N	N	I	D	V	R

51. Food

D	E	S	S	E	R	T	L	B	U	A	G
W	R	E	A	T	H	R	W	B	M	S	R
Y	V	A	R	G	L	Y	E	L	O	H	A
A	E	H	A	Y	T	F	A	G	Y	O	P
S	U	N	D	A	Y	I	E	L	R	J	E
U	N	E	M	O	M	A	C	B	K	U	S
D	E	W	H	I	T	H	U	T	H	A	B
J	L	L	B	N	I	M	A	E	N	I	S
K	P	T	A	D	Y	F	K	D	E	I	W
E	P	S	S	I	N	S	E	L	O	B	M
I	A	P	N	G	E	N	O	C	A	B	D
Y	M	G	N	I	L	L	I	F	E	A	E

52. Christmas

K	D	U	V	I	S	E	L	B	U	A	B
W	R	E	A	T	H	F	G	X	E	A	W
L	E	P	F	N	A	M	W	O	N	S	K
S	E	J	K	N	K	H	C	E	I	K	U
H	D	A	L	H	C	I	E	L	S	I	E
F	N	E	I	C	O	A	L	M	F	J	N
K	U	V	Y	T	K	H	O	N	A	F
D	E	G	W	N	S	D	E	E	R	L	Y
P	R	X	A	F	L	F	K	V	U	A	G
J	W	S	T	I	N	S	E	L	W	E	C
F	P	A	N	G	E	L	A	S	I	J	X
V	M	I	S	T	L	E	T	O	E	L	D

53. Clothes

C	A	P	R	I	E	D	C	U	R	E	R
T	O	C	Y	S	A	G	V	T	A	V	T
C	V	S	W	F	J	L	P	B	I	C	R
N	A	E	Z	T	U	O	I	X	N	T	I
J	R	M	S	Y	W	V	K	J	C	A	H
T	V	D	F	T	I	E	H	D	O	O	S
I	R	A	S	G	D	S	O	C	A	C	R
U	B	Q	G	F	C	S	W	E	T	I	E
E	A	S	F	A	J	R	U	I	S	T	D
W	C	X	E	F	V	T	F	Z	H	T	N
D	M	K	I	L	T	B	A	S	F	E	U
B	I	K	I	N	I	O	T	H	D	P	A

54. Nature

```
B L A C K B E R R Y N L
M P K A O L D W N F B P
E I N T E K L Q K D U B
E K K B N V G J M I B L
B R F D U N N M I B L
E H N B K W I E O S N
L F N I R S P L I N K K
B N M K E G U D O F Q P
M O L W O R C E R A C S
U B O L K F H E S N K
B W N F T T E S B D M F
C A R P P P Q N E L W I V
```

55. Desserts

```
D O K V U E H S W G K C
B A C Q P A V L O V A Y
M N L Y T B R D G N H S
A R K A D F E F R U B O
E S H W S V P I E I R T
R O E V K T R W T Y A V
C Q G B Y N I C H O K E
E C L A I R G U B R S K
C K C O B B L E R C A T
I S O C R U S E V F L R
V H W U A E T A C K A A
G B E K A C O K B U S T
```

56. Hobbies

```
F E N D I G N I D A E R
N X B G O C Z G F N R I
R G S L N J J H N E O F
G G M N I F S G B F X
N H N E B D T E U I Z E
I R N K V G L T R M F R
C G E D O K F R I X F C
N B T I X N Z O W N E I
A F O O T B A L L D K S
D E L R E T U P M O C E
F I G N I N E D R A G B
N S E W I N G W E G D F
```

57. Girls' Names

```
K P E N N Y L I O R S T
U K T A S E R E T H H J
O I J K H F T E I S O R
A N N I E J D U W X K S
F R L W B S P C X R D P
H I A N I T N E L A V I
E N N K T J D I T B S V
Y D A U O F E F J K F
S I J H L K S G U H C
L X D W F R P D S H W K
O T P B U K R C X I K Y
J A N N O D A M T O E L
```

58. The Letter "M"

```
E S T M N I A T N U O M
C W R I X F T W S N C K
L M E D I C I N E E M I
N B U S Z M O S C O W U
M C S K E S V B T R F M
V W T X I E H G P A M N
U O F T K L M E C L D T
K M R A W S N M S X K S
I Z B E C A U T K L B R
M M E M J E I R I E R A
R U X S T M F M X F Z M
L E K I B R O T O M C E
```

59. Flowers

```
N O I L E D N A D C O U
F Y J I R D G R F W C Y
R H Y A C I N T H P A E
I D I H C R O L C S R D
P B F Y M B J I M U N F
I O S I R I K D G Y A O
L W C U F T S O E R T C
U R D G E U R F W M J
T J F L C I P F C I O D
R S O O D B O A K F N R
K I R C R R U D W R J S
V C D Y M P O L L E N I
```

60. Birds

```
H I N E R W A C N O C Y
S L Y V J B E F W R B G
W E Q G W D I L Q S X C
A C N S E C Y V J H F E
L V I H T F S A E L A R
L U L T N R D B Y Y L E
O L A J X G I W F V C A
W T Q H R T Y C B I O C
B U N A W S L D H E N N
F R E I V E A J N D L I
A E N C L L U G A E S B
T I T M O U S E S E Q Y
```

61. Fairies

```
M R I N G B V D O K F I
H A Z I H U M A N S N L
P S L O O T S D A O T G
F V W K U H M J W A H P
X S N D H E K X J G V S
N G B J L P A F C G H D
E N O Y I Y F I W N M O
E L G M J G H D K D J O
U W A U T A V K B O P W
Q P H N M J N A Z I F L
I X D K K G S G N O S N
G W R H Y M E S B M U O
```

62. Space

```
P R O B E N J M H B I A
F A C D K P A I N A H T
W B S H R U Q S D S E M
N V Y E I J I S W T T O
Y U R A N U S I F R I S
X D C F R J K O K O R P
A P J I E F R N S N O H
I M E R C U R Y P O E E
A F R A H W N C J M T E
G N O R T S M R A Y E E
N B I N O I R O D F M N
A J K S A T U R N G I L
```

63. The Park

```
S L I D E A I C H V E N
V F N D T I P D N A S F
N X H B T R H K L O B I
E C B I C Y C I N C I P
O R O U N D X B O U T H
D F V L H W V C D E V C
A S W I N G S U F L D A
T B M N O E C M S S Y N
R D K X D K I S B E A R
E N H F S V A C H M L I
C O L B Y R A T V A P X
O P W E G M D N E G F K
```

64. Landmarks

```
G A H T O W E R K G S D
B U C K I N G H A M T L
E U D F Y E N D Y S B E
H S T M S A N G W U X F
B D K T V R X S E A K F
R I C E R V I M H A V I
I M U B F I D S F T D E
D A N N G A R H A K U G
G R W E S U G A J A N H
E Y G B X H T K R B E S
K P A D F F V E M I M L
E T L I B E R T Y C S W
```

65. Dogs

```
I B E R N A R D T O R K
C H I H U A H U A I O P
S F G O S U E T E A F D
H I P B R I H R K E B A
E K A O L W L Q T L G L
P S T L F E Y H R D S M
H F O E N I G I E O H A
E C U N J Y O T X O K T
R G E U Q A K O O P G
D K W R B P E S B U F A
N H H R O D A R B A L N
D N U O H Y E R G I T K
```

66. Spies

```
E U F O E G R S R A C T
N B D K B W N X V K H J
E I Z S A R E M A C S R
M N S H T J T R B D B E
Y O F H L K D G N F Z M
R C D B K E E W S U W R
G U B O J U R R T X G O
O L F N N T G S D C O F
S A E D I S G U I S E N
D R X V W O F Z K B U F
K S G A D G E T T E G N
J H N O I S O L P X E D
```

67. Hairstyles

```
T K G F J L H D F X E R
E R N K T A E L P V C
A X F G R I M P E R I F
L T L E D G N L B O B G
P E H K F Z W T R U K
H N A L S E H C N U B V
C S T J D I D G X E X Z
N I Y M S S R E L R U C
E O N H N V K E H P J I
R N O X O L R F L F D
F S P F R D N L W G D S
E N H L I C C V Z M R J
```

68. Sports Equipment

```
M C B A F H N D W B L G
A Z U R T E K C A R S X
T S B Q C Y I P S T V J
R V T P A D S V O H A S
A G F N C F R O I Y C N
H B D S L V B D V G F E
S R A W X U S B T G P A
D I Y T C V A A R A J K
N J P Q B L C I S B R E
A J G T L R H F Z D L R
B G S E L D R U H U Q S
X V A C N N G W R V B Y
```

69. The Beach

```
M S H L R K T O W E L P
S L D U C W J H V U I S
K L T O F G G X Y E J H
N U R M J R D G R J H G
U G I Z S L L E H S K L
R A S E S S A L G N U S
T E R G H D F D G X U S
J S K M T D H G I B D E
U P O S T C A R D S W N
B S I V W X L G Z J D O
R D L O O P K C O R M T
F S W I M S U I T S H S
```

70. Party Time

```
R P C A S T L E D R S X
A C O O R C H N M A K N
N I S A E C O G M P N L
N E T E M R T A D G E H
I L P R A G G G R E R D
V P F B E O F E T P D I
E O J B R N E M E O D H
R E T W I G E L E R I I
S P T E S D E N V I A D
A C T R E F I T Z Z C E
R E D R E S S S T A O C
Y D D W O R E N N A B R
```

71. Pets

```
K J P A R R O T U Y T R
G E W E S I O T R O T B
U I B R O G D S C W K J
I E L K I Y F I S H H Y
N E B U F D X E O C I V
E K J Y J L I B R E G R
A A O T K C D S L F S E
P N R G B S E C V D K T
I S D G W C A U H J G S
G U E O M T J P I Y R T M
Y J D D N F X J O B E A
S I R A B B I T D C W H
```

72. The Letter "L"

```
L E L O L L I P O P R V
X R B A D L X L L Y W
M C L X N O Y J F S R
E R H V B G L H C F D L
S E O S K S J R H T R N
B D T W E X K M N K E S
Y E N C F E T A O H F G
R G J H E R L B M H G E
E C A L F S D V E O T L
V R R S U M T I L D W H
D L X O S S A L Y S L M
K F T G L H E J B C N A
```

73. Detectives

```
N H K V N H O U N D B K
A B L S T U D A G I O X
X G N I Y F I N G A M E
N O S V D O O L B W J T
T D H S B F L K V E T H
S K E G H Y A T S R Y
O U R I C N Y B A R A N
L A L V L R T I E F V L
V G O E U T L T K D J S
E F C J E V S U E S A C
W N K L S Y U H O G V I
A X B D M A L I B I T F
```

74. Trees

```
M N J R J E K F T W I G
B I R C H D S A N R G E
Q S B R I F Y N O H M V
X U F G C T A M H J J E
J O J N K B T F A N T R
Q U R D D P E C W B R G
R R H M L F T E T H U R
C A A E Y S H X R C N E
H D M E G P J O D K E
A E J R J I U N O A M N
R C O N N D J T T Y U C
D F Q D L B E E C H F X
```

75. Boys' Names

```
N J T O L R O B I N N M
I D H R E K I M S K I T
A B X C W N T Z G U N F
M B I L L Y R K T E F S
E G I O T J S W I O H X
S E K F N D M L H R G T
H V L D S C D B K C I D
O E T N I D X H I K U N
M T J Z M V S O E T E D
D S C G F U A H S J K M
H A R O L D N D L K U T
W X N I K R H C Z N L B
```

76. Musical Instruments

```
J K R E T R I A N G L E
S T R U M P E T I U M N
W H B V A X J T E G H I
Q M K E P B D E Q U S L
R V O N E U R N H I F H
K B I S H G R I K T V R
O L U M C L B R P A B X
E A J U K E V A G R W I
W H G R V K S L K M J A
I B R D H Q H C E I N Q
P I A N O R X U N R O H
N V N I L O I V A L K P
```

77. Pirates

```
O P A R R O T I B S K L
L C B E R U S A E R T V
G E L B R E X W H Q J O
S K R I H O O K A I N F
G D H K V O U D G T E B
F L H C E F L H G A L F
B O S Q T J K B D T I D
R G W I E A B I V S U L
O B V T E R R H C X O L
G X I L K Y F E R L E U
E P I H S G E V Y Q W K
S U H C K D U R S E J S
```

78. Sports

G	B	K	T	V	S	I	M	P	H	L	Q
Y	A	E	K	C	I	R	C	L	L	N	S
M	S	B	L	W	F	N	L	A	J	K	A
N	E	H	G	L	S	A	B	D	R	S	T
A	B	I	O	D	B	Y	S	W	K	L	H
S	A	G	T	T	E	G	U	B	S	W	L
T	L	V	O	L	J	M	H	T	P	A	E
L	O	L	B	N	L	N	I	D	R	T	T
C	F	O	G	G	N	I	W	O	R	C	R
S	V	W	H	U	S	Q	K	M	V	H	C
I	L	L	A	B	T	E	K	S	A	B	S
T	A	B	L	E	T	E	N	N	I	S	W

79. The Sky

H	E	L	I	C	O	P	T	E	R	D	V
I	O	S	N	O	O	L	L	A	B	O	J
J	B	N	M	S	U	N	E	W	N	Z	Q
H	K	R	T	Y	X	C	N	V	B	V	R
E	V	A	D	B	J	U	I	H	C	B	Z
O	R	I	T	B	R	U	G	I	L	C	I
S	Y	N	B	I	R	D	S	H	O	T	E
K	J	M	C	U	Y	O	D	K	U	N	M
B	Q	Z	W	H	E	X	Y	R	D	B	O
D	S	E	N	A	L	P	I	V	S	M	O
F	I	R	E	W	O	R	K	S	N	J	N
N	E	P	O	C	S	E	L	E	T	O	Q

80. Shops

K	J	M	A	N	A	G	E	R	H	L	N
S	A	P	C	A	R	T	O	R	T	V	B
E	N	L	D	F	H	V	T	F	Z	G	F
C	F	H	D	I	R	K	D	L	A	D	K
U	E	G	B	J	S	X	B	N	L	A	T
R	I	L	P	G	V	X	R	J	N	S	X
I	S	F	L	A	S	X	L	M	F	Z	T
T	A	K	T	R	V	D	B	A	G	J	R
Y	A	P	R	I	C	E	S	B	Y	H	P
T	O	L	G	N	I	K	R	A	P	V	K
A	G	F	A	M	R	O	F	I	N	U	N
V	T	A	N	N	O	Y	H	L	P	T	B

81. In the Backyard

G	N	Y	H	M	P	B	U	R	H	S	K
O	L	T	R	O	W	E	L	P	C	L	U
A	T	E	G	N	B	T	S	K	E	B	N
L	S	M	C	K	R	N	U	R	C	S	K
P	E	Y	L	U	R	J	T	H	M	S	U
O	V	P	C	O	N	S	K	G	N	A	C
S	O	H	H	G	O	T	B	H	M	R	M
T	L	T	E	P	K	C	H	R	P	G	L
S	G	H	M	B	D	C	F	K	G	Y	H
C	M	O	N	S	R	A	E	H	S	C	T
Y	C	P	L	R	E	D	N	E	V	A	L
G	K	B	I	R	D	B	A	T	H	U	E

82. Food

M	G	C	H	E	R	R	Y	L	E	M	X
P	I	R	S	O	U	P	V	U	W	B	P
W	C	K	Z	E	Q	H	D	E	C	I	X
X	E	Y	M	J	N	F	S	W	Z	S	P
U	L	D	N	G	L	I	D	Z	S	G	C
O	E	R	I	B	K	D	A	R	M	Z	K
H	R	A	E	N	E	K	C	I	H	C	U
C	Y	T	M	V	G	X	T	G	N	D	R
E	D	S	W	I	P	A	T	E	M	L	I
G	M	U	O	U	K	E	G	Q	B	Y	P
P	L	C	H	B	A	N	A	N	A	V	T
Q	R	Z	C	D	W	F	M	E	R	X	D

83. The Farm

U	T	L	A	M	B	I	N	G	I	U	E
S	P	K	G	T	S	E	L	T	T	A	C
H	L	C	D	E	R	N	K	J	B	D	W
E	W	O	B	U	S	A	T	P	T	F	O
E	A	T	R	I	T	L	I	N	B	X	S
P	E	S	N	Q	Q	G	G	L	U	V	T
D	T	E	S	J	T	F	D	K	E	C	S
O	S	V	L	S	D	C	T	E	I	R	E
G	G	G	K	G	S	W	A	V	J	N	X
G	G	L	U	P	J	T	U	R	Q	K	G
D	E	E	S	H	E	A	F	B	T	L	I
I	E	S	U	O	H	M	R	A	F	P	S

84. The Letter "B"

B	B	H	J	M	O	J	N	A	B	N	V
U	B	O	X	E	R	B	A	I	R	S	T
T	V	E	W	O	R	R	O	B	U	D	C
I	I	D	L	O	F	D	N	I	L	B	J
I	E	U	N	J	S	B	V	V	U	M	H
O	L	S	H	U	R	T	E	M	B	O	B
C	T	B	A	M	B	O	O	I	A	O	N
C	O	A	C	D	V	I	J	T	R	D	
O	O	V	B	M	T	B	H	N	R	B	E
R	B	S	R	K	N	C	A	A	M	S	B
B	U	H	E	J	C	T	U	B	K	M	V
T	I	R	U	O	I	V	A	H	E	B	N

85. Jobs

A	H	R	E	V	I	R	D	S	U	B	R
Z	D	I	S	C	J	O	C	K	E	Y	E
R	E	S	S	E	R	D	R	I	A	H	G
R	E	L	L	A	B	T	O	O	F	T	A
A	G	R	E	I	D	L	O	S	H	R	N
R	B	U	S	T	C	F	K	N	B	E	E
E	K	H	A	W	Q	T	V	E	P	G	M
K	V	P	O	G	S	U	F	C	U	A	E
A	N	H	H	I	D	F	U	H	O	N	R
B	F	S	T	E	B	V	N	S	T	A	O
G	T	R	C	H	H	K	Z	A	G	M	T
K	A	Q	W	U	R	E	C	N	A	D	S

86. Opposites

```
A B I S W I N T E R T J
L U C J F V X E P K C Q
Z O T H O D A Y W H A E
N F V V B I U C S R N U
O R S E A F E O T E V T
I I K E C K V J M S I C
H B V W A D R Y J A G R
  P J T D T F M U B E
N X S Q X C B I K I P E
G K C A L B O Z N S E E
F I E T U R A B C J A N
K A T H G I L W B V S X
```

87. House

```
C U I O T H G I L D F H
K S L M V K P R I Z B C
F R Q H B I F O O R T X
E U D T A T L K M V U O
E O Q Z T C C A R P E T
T B Y F H H H L F C H B
E H E I R E F I M E S E
G G N K O N G D V K P D
A K U O S H N C M V R
R E E P M F Z I M Q O C
A N R R C B R X U K C O
G X D M V B P L I H C M
```

88. Chores

```
B A B Y S I T T I N G G
A T S G N I T S U D B G
G G C M G N I P E E W S
N N O C P B J G R M G T
I I U R T A H N B W N B
H N R W S D M I C A I D
S O I G C V P W R T N J
I R N H V X F O T G A C
L L G D A B N M H S E M
O D W A S H I N G H L P
G T C M B J R T D C W D
A R P G N I M U U C A V
```

89. Drinks

```
M G L E K A H S K L I M
B C H A M P A G N E N G
L E M O N J O K P B G R
K N O C O C K T A I L A
L E N S L T V M E Z H P
E T I E I H T O O M S E
M L C R B W H G T N H F
O B U P O U J N M V B R
N J E G V S B K Z E M U
A M M E N R L T E F L
D N   W P T H R K G T T
E O L V M T S O E C H D
```

90. The Letter "Z"

```
T R F S Z E I B M O Z A
G Z H A U V K I B R L N
Z E M N Z B F E E Z S R
I B E B E D F G G H I W
N R T Z R A L S O O Z K
I A R I O V H G E F U R
R E P P A Z E Z M A F E
R L U K Z H B N R T R P
I S F G A I D O Z F Z F
A G T I W E N L V U E I
Z V C N I Z B A K H S Z
V H Z M Z I G Z A G R D
```

91. Shapes

```
J T R I A N G L E M O Z
V V A L K J N S Y G L S
S J Z J F G T P O F I J
F D P H N G N C U N E O
L D G O V F T K D O R L
A X L M C A S M J G A M
V B L K G V F G N A U O
O F C O R A T S N C Q Q
G M N J D P S Z M E S A
P E N E L C R I C D L D
Z C E B U C E K G J O E
L P E N T A G O N F R D
```

92. Weather

```
F J K O V E R C A S T O
A I B A R W V H X S C J
L E T D M S N O W T Q J
L V C S T H U N D E R D
M A O J P H D G K D B G
N W J S B R E E Z Y F X
R T K V C A J H T H R H
V A L S T O R M K D J E
A E W H Q F H H S O L M
N H X D N I W J H A P D
E C S A J B M N G Q C B
R D I M U H T O K V W R
```

93. Girls' Names

```
H C H R I S T I N A W V
U C V K O P I R S T H M
G E L Q J Z C H N B Y T
T I L H J K A A D C V L
A L M T G R N S U K W T
H L B H O N W S I R I Z
T K N A G F P Q J R E
R J K O T H A M I M E J
A R J L C V I C K Y U O
M D O N N A H T A C T B
T O U J P Q M A R I A C
K A T E A R K H W G M J
```

94. Weddings

```
J I D A N C E R F H V C
B D Q K E D R E S S I B
C F S J W J M U E B T
R A V N O O M Y E N O H
I M N B J B D K F G J
M S H E T F I E H C B R
U E F L G Y Q S C S R J
S D J W E H W R H A B
G F E J M K C U Z T W
N R B V S U M A H B L
B H C J B I N C F A R
R K Q S P E E C H V E T
```

95. Monsters

```
L O C H N E S S G H T Z
F W P T R O L L O F P M
L A M O D O P S I U U L
N L H N G F W U H M D F
A U K E T E L Y M E G T
S C P I S T Y N K R N
U A D L A L L I Z D O G
D R M A G O D H Y J F H
E D F Z F L O W E R E W
M P L H W T N G D P L T
N I E T S N E K N A R F
T G S G O B L I N Z S O
```

96. Nature

```
G H C B V W F N U R T Z
J C A C A T C D H I G S
R H D W A T E R F A L L
D M A G P I E D J M G D
F G N L E A V E S A L S
C L O V E R D T S H W Y
V K H C Y U B J G O F E
R C F Z L I G G R D R N
H O S D F F C M H H V O
G B T D G N G C U B H
D F F W F H D H V R W Z
N I J E G T E K C I R C
```

97. The Letter "D"

```
H D I C E L O D V B O Y
X G G K J O G N I D H C
F C D R A O B H G I D D
D T B H S D Y I V J F X
J D I R T Y U D O H G R
O L V Y H G N I D S H E
U H F S K K X F J U K N
D F A G P D Y R E E D N
V B E C H T Y L R Y O
K X D Y B N J U Y D J D
S L D O L L D R A N T G
Y D R E S S E D R B V D
```

98. CANDY

```
F J J B N O K D U R Z C
J E E Q B E A R S I F Q
A L V Y F F A T R S J K
W L C E T A L O C O H C
B Y O T U E E D F Z S U
R B J B U B B L E G U M
E E D F R B E G N N R E
A A K U D R O P S I E S
K N Z A Q C O C U F Y B
E S Y L I C O R I C E E
R S S R E S E G D U F Q
S B M I N T S N U V K O
```

99. Sports

```
J A R C H E R Y N B K T
K H I N I L E V A J S L
N S P R I N T G M Z F H
R Q W R E S T L I N G N
H S T J K B D H I D N D
P M U J G N O L T N G L
T E L T S I H W V R K O
S J M R I D N F H G D G
F Z N H Q K V F J T S B
P O L O F L B R E M H Z
R B N T F T B S F R I H
V H C T I P R H D Q V J
```

100. The Letter "F"

```
W V U O X K D B L A H E
F F A R M E R A B J W F
I J F G J Y O P H A T L
R B T A E E F L A G F U
E J L K R U R F F H U T
E F I V E P H F F E B E
K O B D J H W F F O F J
H A R M O N F O X V R G
V P G E T A F Y B G A D
F R O N T L O X P J N K
E F R E S H A B J U C H
F I N G E R S K G T E Y
```

101. The Letter "G"

```
E D G F G O O D B Y E S
N G O B L E T M F T Z L
J M S W P H O G E I I J
F L R I G Q G R E U F P
Y D O E L Z H F J R Q G
E M J T A N G F N E S G
R H G F Q D F S S E O R
G I L W O R G H D P L O
M E N P D H J G H A P W
G R U M B L E I M R Z J
L S F O Z G K J E G N Q
G M E P L U G G W F D H
```